GROWING UP INTO REVOLUTION

For JANE in NEW YORK

An immaterial gift, since material ones are hard to send

GROWING UP INTO REVOLUTION

By

MARGARET COLE

Author of " Beatrice Webb," " Makers of the Labour Movement," etc.

LONGMANS, GREEN AND CO

LONDON · NEW YORK · TORONTO

LONGMANS, GREEN AND CO LTD
6 & 7 CLIFFORD STREET LONDON W 1

ALSO AT MELBOURNE AND CAPE TOWN

LONGMANS, GREEN AND CO INC
55 FIFTH AVENUE NEW YORK 3

LONGMANS, GREEN AND CO
215 VICTORIA STREET TORONTO 1

ORIENT LONGMANS LTD
BOMBAY CALCUTTA MADRAS

First Published - - - 1949

Printed in Great Britain at THE DARIEN PRESS LTD., *Edinburgh*

Preface

THESE reminiscences are called *Growing Up Into Revolution* because their intention is not merely to recount the events of one not particularly important life, but to present a picture, as seen through the lens of one mind and one set of experiences, of the revolution of our times. I started my conscious life in a world which seemed to me—and I believe to most other people—completely stable and solid, in which the only mischances were individual or family mischances. As I grew up this world began to crack and change, and soon the changes came so fast that " revolution " is now the only word for them, even though in our country that revolution has not taken the violent physical form which it took in the France of 1789 or the Russia of 1917. This revolution is as great as that which changed the Europe of medieval Church and Gild into the Europe of nineteenth-century industrialism ; it is accompanied by as much conflict, as much bigotry and violence, as much enthusiasm and single-minded devotion, as Europe saw during the century of religious wars—all in the life-time of those of us who were children under Victoria.

It is this change that I am trying to picture, as a swimmer being sucked down through the rocks and rapids of a swiftly-running river might from time to time lift his head above water and gain an instant's impression of the scenery through which he is being drawn ; what I have written, therefore, makes no claim to being a " history of our times "—only of what one developing intelligence made of them. My World War I, for example, was not the world war of David Lloyd George or even of the majority of wartime novels ; it was a different war, but a war very real to one group of people ; and the same could be said of other events described in the following pages, which might be seen quite differently through another pair of eyes. The book is partisan, of course, because it is personal ; but it is honest, so far as I can make it, and so far as I can check it from available records. For ever since at the age of twenty-one I discovered a four-year-old diary of mine, whose sententiousness made me blush so much that I instantly burned it, I have kept no journal of any kind ; these chapters are the work of memory alone.

HENDON
October, 1948

Contents

Part IV
NINETEEN-TWENTIES

Part V
TURN OF THE TIDE

Part VI
NINETEEN-THIRTIES

Part VII
WAR AND POST-WAR AGAIN

Illustrations

PART ONE

EARLY DAYS

Chapter One

When I read or think about the life of any human being there are always three questions to which I want to know the answers immediately. First, who and of what kind were his family? I want to know what sort of blood and what type of inherited experience went to his making; and I have often wished that it were, if not compulsory, at least customary for people outside the rather monotonous groupings found in Debrett, etc., to preserve their family pedigrees. Secondly, what was his social class or group, that is to say, with what kind of persons did he associate in his early years, and what were they doing? How did they earn —or not earn—their livings, and how did they spend their playtime? And thirdly, what was his physical home, if he had the same home for long enough for it to leave an impression on him? What sorts of hills and fields, or what sorts of streets and shops came up before his eyes as he was dreaming or dying, like that Virgilian hero who breathed his last "remembering sweet Argos"?

The modern Western world, which moves about so fast and so frequently, does not develop these basic place-memories, I think, to the same extent as did earlier generations. People stay for too little while in the place where they were born; even if they do stay for a few years the place is apt to change its physical shape out of all measure, so that it never becomes part of themselves, a thing which, ugly or beautiful—for I believe æsthetics have very little to do with it—is as inescapable as the shape of their noses. Plenty of my contemporaries have no homeland in the sense that the man from Argos had, and I doubt whether my own children, moved from a London suburb to Oxford and back again to another and more distant London suburb, could say instantly where they belonged—certainly they are not Londoners in the sense that Dickens was a Londoner, or the young Sidney Webb, who in the 'sixties of the last century lived in Leicester Square, and wrote of his London :—

"It was from the steps of St Martin's Church that, as a very little boy, I saw my first Lord Mayor's Show. I remember my mother telling me on that occasion—and it seems to have sunk in—that if I was a good boy I might myself one day be Lord Mayor ! In short, I grew up a patriotic Londoner, very early declaring that no place on earth (I knew nothing about any other place) would content me for habitation, other than the very middle of London that I knew." [1]

This is lover's language ; it contrasts curiously with the style which Lord Passfield employed in his important sociological works, and shows that, in so far as that most unsentimental man ever betrayed any touch of sentimentality, it was not attached to any person but to his city. Beatrice Webb, on the other hand, in her autobiography shows no trace of sentimental affection for any place whatever.

For myself, I was born in Cambridge and brought up there, on the edge of the Fen country, for nearly seventeen years. For fourteen of them, except for an occasional excursion that left no deep impression, I never went outside East Anglia, for our summer holidays were taken on the East Coast, in seaside towns and villages reached by trains which ran across the black flat land surrounding Ely ; and my physical home, the place where my ghost will walk, is Cambridge and the Fens. I have seen many parts of England and the world which are more beautiful in any accepted sense of the word. I do not argue with those who point to the Horseshoe Pass above Llangollen or the outline of the Malverns and say, " Have you anything like that in the east ? " —I merely think they are being irrelevant. I do not deny that the wind which blows unimpeded down Cambridge streets from the Urals or thereabouts can be most unpleasant, that on a wet day in winter the prospects one can see from Soham over miles of field, lode, and drove, hardly relieved by trees, are not inviting, or that the fourteen long miles of road from Cambridge to Godmanchester are featureless, unbroken (since nearly all the villages lie just off the road), and very dull going for a walker or even for a cyclist ; if pressed, I will admit that the greyish-yellow Cambridgeshire brick, of which the slum quarters of Cambridge and many nearby villages are mostly built, is one of the ugliest building materials ever used by man. I know all that the highlander or the downlander or the man from deep valleys can say against the flat lands ; nevertheless, as soon as I get on the raised highway, with the white posts marking its corners, that runs through Hereward's country, and from six miles away, through a gap in

[1] " Reminiscences," by S. and B. Webb, *St Martin's Review*, 1928.

the hedge, catch sight of the Octagon of Ely, fullest of light of all English cathedrals ; or stand on Fleam Dyke, the low earth rampart that runs for miles beyond Fulbourn and still grows wild flowers which you can pick nowhere else in the county ; or see the huge expanses of sky with fat Queen Victoria clouds processing solemnly through the blue, or the sun " drawing water " in long silvery shafts, something moves in me that is as old as my birth, and my senses recognise that I have come home. And I shall always think Cambridge in a late spring one of the most satisfying places in the world.

My ancestry was reasonably mixed. On my father's side we came from Yorkshire. There are records of Postgates—the name has been held to mean " keepers of the postern gate "—holding land in the sixteenth century, and in 1679 a Father Nicholas Postgate was executed under a statute of Elizabeth for baptizing a child during the Popish Plot scare. He wrote a hymn which is still in print, and on one occasion an enterprising relic-monger endeavoured to sell my father the reverend martyr's thumb ! The family must have gone down in the world, however, for my great-grandfather was a small builder in Scarborough, and his son, John Postgate, the only one of my forbears to reach the dignity of the *Dictionary of National Biography*, started life as a grocer's boy.

This John Postgate, my grandfather, was a good specimen of the selfless, difficult Victorian reformer. Long before the days of *Sybil* and the Chartists the grocer's boy was outraged by the trading practices of his masters, the sand in the sugar and the mouse-dirt in the tea, and made up his mind to fight them. When he was fourteen he left the grocery to be a surgeon's boy at half-a-crown a week and in his spare time worked to pass the medical examinations which, after ten years' hard labour, made him a member of the Royal College of Surgeons. Ten years after that, when he was settled as doctor (and afterwards professor) in Birmingham, he began a life's campaign against the adulteration of food—nine Bills, according to the D.N.B., were introduced into Parliament by the Members for Birmingham in response to his prodding. He was fought hard by all the " wicked grocers " in all their ranks, but he lived to see his work made effective by the 1875 Sale of Food and Drugs Act.

It was pretty much of a lone campaign. He " obtained no public recognition of any kind for his services " (D.N.B.). In Birmingham they remember him faintly, but not very well. I think he must have been a very difficult and cornery person to deal with ; his mind was on the one subject and he did not care whom he offended. Neither did he care—at any rate, not much—what happened to his family. He was, in fact, the kind of public agitator who should never have had a family; but, being a Victorian, he had seven children who were all kept very short in their youth in order that their father might meet the expenses of his unpaid public work, and he and my grandmother had perpetual disputes about money for the household. My grandfather died long before I was born; his portrait, clean-shaven, close-lipped, formidably Victorian, used to hang in our dining-room. My grandmother lived on until my sixth year, but she was either wholly or partly bedridden. I remember being taken to see her in her big bed, a grim old lady with a cap and a nose and by her side a parrot in a cage (with much the same kind of nose) which squawked out menacingly, "Maar-*gret*! Maar-*gret*!" when I came near. I was terrified of both the parrot and my grandmother; and in my recollection they are mingled with a grimy little "park" in the Small Heath part of Birmingham, and the black smoke of a horrible little steam tram that ran through it in those days. I thought Birmingham a horrid place; though it has become cleaner since then, and I have visited more comely parts of it than Small Heath, I am not sure but that I think so still.

That family had character and persistence, obviously, but no æsthetic sense whatever and none of the graces of living. Two of my aunts went melancholy mad before they died; and I think that my father, the eldest son,[1] was affected all his life by the harsh conditions of his youth; he had, for example, a panic fear of spending money, particularly in small amounts. If we put too much butter or jam on our bread, he pounced upon us and scraped it off, and we were always kept very short of pocket-money, even for those days—at fourteen I was allowed only a shilling a month, and my ten-year old brother sixpence. Partly as a result of this, we were less than strictly honest in the methods we took to eke out our incomes; when we were offered a penny a hundred for picking suckers off the strawberry-beds (which were in an annex garden well out of sight of the house) we discovered that if we let the suckers grow they would obligingly multiply, so that we could pick five or six with one pull. I cannot remember that we felt any pricks of conscience about doing this.

[1] A younger brother was drowned at Oxford; another, my uncle Langdale, became an Anglican cleric and had a living at Shillington in Bedfordshire. This uncle did himself very comfortably; he grew fat and amiable, and on the culmination of his black-covered paunch we used to watch, fascinated, a small gold cross swinging. He had a huge church very scantily filled, and his lady parishioners embroidered him slippers in purple.

My father, John Percival Postgate, for over a generation Lecturer at Trinity College, Cambridge, and then Professor of Latin at Liverpool, editor of the *Corpus Poetarum Latinorum* and of Tibullus and others of the (to my mind) least interesting of the Roman poets, was a crusader like his father before him, but a crusader in the linguistic field. He was the great protagonist of the modern pronunciation of Latin and of the teaching of Latin by " the direct method," *i.e.*, by making the children *talk* Latin as though it were any modern language. (He also wrote a grammar, *Postgate's Latin Grammar*, which was intended to supersede Kennedy's grammar in the public schools. It never did that, but it had sufficient success to earn me some vicarious unpopularity among those who had suffered from it at school.) His chief collaborator in the " direct method " campaign was W. H. D. Rouse, long headmaster of the Perse School at Cambridge, where all the boys were taught on the direct method.[1] Not being a boy, I never had experience of the direct method in class ; but I had plenty of it at home. I began Latin on my fifth birthday, by being sent into my mother's room to announce the event in the words " Hodie quinque annos nata sum " ; thereafter I had to learn to talk on common subjects in Latin, and on Sundays, when such of the children as could sit upright and feed tidily dined downstairs, I had to ask for my dinner in Latin under the threat of not getting any. I still remember the awful occasion on which, at the age of six or thereabouts, I asked for " the beef " instead of " some of the beef," and my father pushed the huge sirloin on its dish over in my direction and I dissolved into tears ; and I have been told of another time when, having forgotten the Latin for sausage, I was told that if I could say " half " I might have *half* a sausage—and squealed out " dimidium ! " through sobs. There was also a blackboard on which my father drew objects and persons and required me and my two younger brothers to discourse in Latin upon them—the youngest of us, much to his elders' annoyance, turned out to have much the best memory for the tiresome words we were supposed to know.

The direct method, however, never " took " with me ; all I retain of that early training is a few scraps of totally useless information, as that *sinapi* is the Latin for mustard, and that the Romans,

[1] Spike Hughes is one of the people who have paid unexpected tribute to the success of Rouse's teaching methods with his own boys ; he was an unattractive scrubby little man with no manners, but he loved turning ancient Latin and Greek into flexible tongues for modern speech. His book of nursery rhymes, in which the French " Malbrouck s'en va t'en guerre " turns up as " Themistocles apelthen, apelthen es machen," is very entertaining for those who have Latin or Greek enough to follow the jokes. But I think he has had no successor.

in order to plague English children, invented *two* words for aunt, one for the father's sister and one for the mother's. My father continued to teach me Latin—including verse-composition, at which I was always bad—even after I had gone to school. He was an exacting and irritable teacher, and what was perhaps more unfortunate, he did not succeed in giving me any idea that there was anything worth reading for its own sake in the horrible tongue —I am not sure that he saw much himself; his was always a linguistic, rather than a literary, scholarship. I hated Latin, all through my childhood, as bitterly as anyone can ever have hated it; and it was not until I had ceased to be his pupil that I found any beauty in it at all.

Looking back, I see my father as in some ways an unfortunate man, disappointed, in spite of the estimation in which he was held, of his highest academic aspirations—he wanted above all things to be Professor of Latin in his own University, but the post went to A. E. Housman—almost pathologically afraid of poverty, cursed with an irritable temper which he could not control, convinced, and more convinced as the years went on, that the world was marching to political damnation, and that the working-man, whom he firmly believed to be "in the loomp, baad," was coming more and more to control *his* destiny—in which, of course he was partly right—and burdened with a pack of six children whom he may have desired and loved in theory but certainly found exasperating, noisy, destructive and unfilial in practice. Not that this attitude was by any means without excuse; the first three of his children, myself, and my brothers Raymond and Esmond, were not, I think at all nice children in our early years.[1] We quarrelled and fought one another on the slightest provocation, much more than any children that I know do nowadays, and that not as puppies do but in real, if not constant, dislike of one another. I, so conventionally pretty a small child that my father used to delight to watch me cry my "crystal tears," was certainly a young bully to my juniors; Raymond, my mother's favourite, was one of the most obstinate little boys ever born; Esmond, with his golden curls and his pink cheeks and misleadingly angelic expression, was what his exasperated nurse called "a *grizzling grinding* baby"; we cannot have been a nice lot of offspring. I think we disliked our father, on the whole, or more strictly speaking regarded him

[1] For some mysterious reason, the packing of the genes seems to have changed radically between 1900 and 1903, and the three brown-eyed squabblers were succeeded by a blue-eyed trio—my sister, and my brothers Ormond and Richmond —whose tempers were by comparison angelic.

as a rather hostile natural force with which my mother had unaccountably chosen to ally herself, which was apt to erupt and when in eruption was best avoided ; but I cannot discover that we developed any Freudian complexes about him, or that our lives were in any way deeply shadowed. " Oo, I *do* love you," said Esmond to his mother in an ecstasy of affection ; " and I don't mind Dadda." That was about the size of it.

My mother's family was trading stock ; one side from the west country, and the other (the Le Lacheurs) from Guernsey, where their ancestry can be traced back to the seventeenth century. The Le Lacheurs ran ships to the West Indies, and I can remember limes and grapefruit coming to our house at a time when they were not common in the shops. My mother, Edith Allen, was one of the earlier products of women's higher education ; she and her younger sister went to the North London Collegiate School under the great Miss Buss, and she then proceeded to Girton at the beginning of the 'eighties, when the College had not long removed itself from the house in Hitchin where it started and only two blocks of the present building were in existence. Having come up as a mathematician because (I believe) the best teacher in the school at Camden Town taught mathematics, she soon turned to classics and thus came into contact with one Dr Postgate, ten years older than herself, who from time to time instructed young ladies greatly in awe of him. Long after, when I was at boarding-school, a junior classical mistress who had been at Cambridge confided to my house-mistress that it made her nervous to teach Margaret Postgate, " because she looks at me under her eyebrows just like the Doctor." (I know that upward glance very well ; it is generally seen on the faces of quite mild Highland cattle.) One of the young ladies, however, was not overawed ; it is on record that she " cheeked " her preceptor, and he seems to have responded in a wholly natural manner. They were married, after a courtship of which my mother said that his letters were so charming that she was never sure whether she had fallen in love with his letters or himself, in 1891 ; it was not so very long after the lifting of the ban which forbade Fellows of colleges to marry, and Cambridge was full of young wives and young mothers.

It is far more difficult to characterise my mother's family than my father's ; they are various and unaccountable. Some, like my great-uncle, John Allez Le Lacheur, the head of the Guernsey importing business, who had a big house and garden in Tunbridge Wells and begat twelve children, were very well off ; some were pretty much of a failure. Some were highly respectable, like my grandmother, who was a staunch Nonconformist and along with most of her relatives refused for years to speak to one of them who had married an Anglican clergyman; some as unconventional as a cousin of my mother's who could not bear to be well-off but found no way of supporting herself—even cobbling shoes—that did not pander to the demands of the rich, and eventually emigrated to New Zealand. What they all were, especially the Le Lacheur lot, was highly individualistic, not to say eccentric at times; when anyone says of my family—as they do—"the Postgates are all mad," it is the Le Lacheur strain which they are observing. They have queer bits of private knowledge (not always the same queer bits); they are generally untidy without being scatter-brained; they communicate with one another in strange, spontaneously arising private language, which bears no relation to current slang;[1] they *enjoy* life and are very resentful of being bored; and they are always liable to utter very disconcerting comments in very audible voices. Not many, however, have really lost their senses.

My mother was—and is—the most *individual* person I have ever known. She came of a handsome family, her brother, T. W. Allen of Queen's, the Homeric scholar, being the Adonis of his day at Oxford, and as a young woman she was very beautiful. She must have had a tough time, bringing up six Postgates under circumstances of some stress, but we never knew anything about that in our youth. She was the unquestioned sun in the sky to all her children, however much they quarrelled—I remember at one time the males of the family were on such explosive terms that she had to go for four separate walks on most days, once with her husband, once with each of her elder sons, and once with the two little boys who could be relied on to behave. It would not be correct to say we adored her; we were not an adoring tribe. But what we should have done without her is inconceivable.

The foregoing paragraphs show pretty well the kind of social milieu into which we were born. We were of the middle-class—my father, after a good deal of saving and pinching, as I have mentioned, left £30,000 when he died. Inside that middle-class we belonged to a special group, that of the professional academic, and we lived in a university town. The importance of this is that we were brought up in an atmosphere of comparative equality. The range of university salaries is not—or was not—enormous;

[1] My brothers once compiled a "Mrs P. Glossary" of words and phrases used exclusively by my mother and some of her children. I have it still; it has over a hundred and fifty entries, which must surely be unusual. I never attained her heights of verbal coinage; but to this day my husband insists that Richmond and I are unintelligible when we talk to one another.

and few of the parents with whose children we went to school and parties had noticeable private means. There was some difference, of course ; and our family was rather on the low side as regards expenditure. Other children had more or more expensive clothes or holidays than we had ; and I vividly remember my mother explaining to me when I was about eight that I could not have a rocking-horse " like Aurora Hutchinson " because we couldn't afford both a rocking-horse and little brothers. I was furiously angry ; I had never been consulted and would much have preferred a rocking-horse to horrible little brothers. But the difference lay in the frills, not in the essentials ; we all had nurses and servants and seaside holidays, and all went to upper-class schools and had dancing and drawing classes. None of us was in a position to exploit or to despise socially any of the others, and I think this early experience of an equalitarian society, even within so narrow a compass, has given me a natural bent towards equality, ante-dating any Socialist conviction, which will never be eradicated. If there were wealthy people among the townsmen, we never met them—there has never been a Nuffield Works in Cambridge ; as to the poor, we read about them in moral stories, even in books like Richard Whiteing's *Number Five John Street*, which came out in 1899 ; but we never thought about them as anything to do with the cobbler or the postman in Cambridge. We grew up outside the old conception of Victorian, Lady-Bountiful charity, and the newer conceptions of social service had not yet reached us.

Chapter Two

UNTIL I was sixteen and my youngest brother a year old we lived in 54 Bateman Street, an uglyish house with a front-door portico trimmed in coloured glass, in a street just beyond the bottom end of the road leading from the station. It was four storeys high; two maids slept in the attics; on the floor below was the spare room with its double bed—in which my father's idiosyncratic cat, Boo, once hid her kitten and then forgot where she had put it, and it was not found for some weeks. Boo—her real name was Boom, after the song, "Ta-ra-ra-Boom-deay," which was the vogue in the year of her birth—was a highly intelligent but very disagreeable cat. She adored my father, and obeyed him in all things; when he was away she would come and deliver unmistakable lectures to my mother, whom she apparently considered responsible for having mislaid him, and she was very jealous of the children and would wait for a chance to nip into the nursery and scratch them in their cots.

On the same floor was a bathroom which let out its water with an immense gurgling roar which frightened every infant in turn—and from which it was possible to climb out on to the roof, though I don't believe my parents ever discovered this—my father's inviolable and appallingly untidy study, and my own small bedroom, to which I was promoted after the night nursery became overfull. I was alone on that floor after I had gone to bed, and on many nights lay terrified because I was convinced that a burglar was climbing in—an unlikely eventuality, seeing the great height of uncreepered wall he would have had to scale. Children's terrors are curious things. I was not brought up to any extent on grisly stories. I was forbidden to read *Dracula*,[1] though I read it none the less, and was duly paid out by trembling at the inevitable attack of a vampire in the night; but I was able to extract terror from the most unexpected sources, *Uncle Remus*, for example, which one would hardly think would frighten anyone, and some American children's picture-stories called the *Golliwog Books*. But much the most effective of the terrifying agencies was a book of "noble deeds," principally rescues from shipwrecks and burning houses, which was responsible for many hours of agony. Even to-day I cannot read the words "blind alley" without a faint reminiscent

[1] Also Poe's *Tales of Mystery and Imagination*, and *What a Young Mother Ought to Know*. Otherwise, except for a ban on trashy magazines, my reading was uncensored; as I read all that was forbidden it did not make much difference.

shudder born of a story, whose details I have entirely forgotten, of people fleeing from a burning building into a blind alley with the flames at their heels.

These were not nightmares, properly speaking ; I was not generally asleep ; but before my shut eyes in the dark, when the candle was out, there came unescapably a vision of some familiar place—it might be the bit of Coe Fen bordering on the Trumpington Road, or the wild tangle of bushes which then masked the end of Brooklands Avenue—where I *knew* a lion, or Brer Wolf, would certainly appear in a minute or two. In these waking dreams I could not move forwards, only backwards, so that I could not turn and run, but must keep staring at the terrifying object ; and as it was not a true dream there was no chance of waking up. I had to endure until I really fell asleep. I do not know whether modern upbringing has succeeded in reducing terrors of this kind, and if so, how. They certainly seem, as far as I can judge, to be less common ; but as I can find nothing in my own upbringing that could account for them, I do not know how I should set out to prevent them for others.

Below my room lay the rest of the house, of which I remember best the nursery, with its wide window looking to the then unpollarded trees of Brooklands Avenue across a wide stretch of subsidiary gardens, called " allotments," though their contents were much less severely utilitarian than those of modern allotments—ours contained raspberries and strawberries and an extremely bumpy tennis-court with a tape slung across it until my father was persuaded to buy a second-hand net, and thus to remove one at least of the many causes of quarrels. The window was a fine setting for skyscapes.

There was also the drawing-room, an icy cold room with a grand piano in an even icier projecting alcove in which I had to practise—ugh !—and a gloomy sunless dining-room with a wallpaper of gigantic yellowish-brown poppies. (The nursery had a Kate Greenaway paper.) There were a good few books about, mostly, as far as I remember, things like Dickens and Thackeray in sets, but some others—some Kipling, some William Black, Marion Crawford, and other late Victorians which seemed to have been acquired rather at haphazard ; and children's books for us, George Macdonald, Lewis Carroll, Lear, Hans Andersen, the Andrew Lang collections, Juliana Horatia Ewing, who wrote *Jackanapes*, Mrs Molesworth, and later Evelyn Sharp and E. Nesbit, and " small ones' " books like *Little Black Sambo*, *Peter Rabbit*, and *Pigling Bland*. We had *Little Folks* bought for us, and later that wonderful compilation, Arthur Mee's *Children's Encyclopedia* ; and I browsed in my mother's bound volumes of the earliest *Girl's Own Paper*, with pictures of girls and women in the ridiculous clothes of the 'eighties, all bits and pieces, fichus and collarettes, bustles and bows, and highly moral stories about girls who insisted on higher education and neglected their little brothers so that they fell downstairs on their heads and became idiots for life—that one was called *Decima's Promise* and was written by Rosa Nouchette Carey, a prolific lady in her day. We were not, however, a bookish household ; I never remember hearing any literary discussion at all, and when we played talking or writing games, as we often did, they were not literary games, but tested knowledge of spelling, geography, astronomy, botany, or the dates of kings, or the flags of all nations, or Biblical history, in which we were very expert, having been brought up on the *Peep of Day* series, little books of Old Testament history called *Line Upon Line*, *Lines Left Out*, and *The Kings of Israel and Judah*. Esmond was always a safe winner on Palestinian monarchs.

I always *read* with enormous voracity. I cannot remember ever learning to read, and I read while eating, minding the baby, washing, or lacing my boots for skating ; but I read unguided, except when my mother observed that some of the story-books I borrowed from small friends were rubbish. (They were.) I don't think, on the whole, that I liked " great " literature, except Dickens ; I much preferred the second part of the *Pilgrim's Progress*, with Christiana and her son who ate the green apples, to the first, and I liked Walter Scott and company better when summarised, as they were in the *Children's Encyclopedia* and in W. T. Stead's penny *Books for the Bairns*. But I loved any sort of history (not historical novels, which seemed to me neither the one thing nor the other, until I found *The Cloister and the Hearth*) ; and of course I read everything over and over again, or I should soon have run out of reading-matter. We bought, when we could, twopennorths of the cheap reading, *Puck*, *Sexton Blake*, and *The Magnet*, of which George Orwell long afterwards made so portentous a sociological study, and I read all the " boys' school stories," from *Tom Brown* and *St Winifred's* onwards, that I could lay my hands on—and secretly wrote some myself.

This dream-literature of boys' boarding-schools is an odd temporary phenomenon in the education of the English middle-class, and as yets awaits explanation. No other country's literature displays it ; in no other country will you ever find females, old and young, interesting themselves passionately in the prefects, the (invariably large and unruly) Shell or Remove, the inky fags, and the final dramas of cricket match or rugger match—never by any chance soccer—in which Old Boys of the school go behind the pavilion and weep because "Caesar held the ball safely in his lean brown hands."[1] There was a connoisseurship in these stories. The real fans disliked irrelevant intrusions, as of a French or at a later date German master who turned out to be a spy, as much as your true detective fan dislikes irrelevant intrusions into the classic march of a detective novel. Indeed, I think that the English—not the American—detective novel may possibly be regarded as a slightly more sophisticated version of the public-school story; at any rate, we know on the best authority that Lord Peter Wimsey was a cricketer, and that when a match was all but lost he—having allowed himself, like an authentic public-school hero, to be sent in near the tail of the batting list—"opened up wrathful shoulders and whacked the ball to the wide."[2]

We were not read aloud to much. Possibly there was no time; more probably we were too restive. But in partial compensation, we had a good deal of singing. My mother had a small true voice and could play accompaniments that were not too difficult, and we learned an enormous number of carols and the simpler folk-songs and nursery songs of Scotland, France, and Germany as well as of our own country. My collection of books of songs (which alas! I cannot sing when anyone is within hearing or play except with a couple of fingers) is still extremely dear to me. Of "real" music, apart from the Christmas Eve carols and some anthems at King's, we knew nothing at all.

Our house was a coldish house—as indeed were most houses of the day; there was no central heating, no gas-fires, coal fires in a few rooms only (none in bedrooms unless someone was very ill), and a hot water system whose pipes for some mysterious reason ran *outside* the house, so that in winter the bath-water had plenty of time to cool before it reached the bath. I think, indeed, that warmth in winter is one of the principal changes which our stratum of the middle classes has gained in forty years. We were so often cold; we had dripping noses and chilblains on our fingers and toes. On winter mornings getting up was a horror; I, having no nurse to watch me upstairs, frequently dressed under the bed-clothes and did not wash at all. Sundays were worst, because

[1] Vachell, *The Hill*. (Of Harrow.) Girls' schools, in spite of the late Angela Brazil and her imitators, never achieved the same epic literature. Girls cannot play rugger, or even cricket very well; nor can they be believed to "rag" with such efficiency.

[2] Dorothy Sayers, *Murder Must Advertise*.

there were clean woollen underclothes, cold and prickly, to be put on. We were often caught out sneaking back into our last week's greasy, friendly combinations ; and one of my earliest recollections of going to church is the adjuration, " You're not to *scratch* during the sermon." Jaeger is kinder to children nowadays.

The house had about a quarter of an acre of garden, with a great old mulberry tree in the centre, and round the sides thirty-two pear trees planted by Bishop Browne of Bristol, a former tenant. The mulberry tree was our friend as soon as we could climb ; it is a dirty kind of a tree, and ripe mulberries stain deeply, so that if we were once safely in it we could not be called down to shake hands with visitors. The pears provided much food, but also much labour for my mother, who had to make muslin bags for the big ones so that they would not drop prematurely and smash themselves, and to pick those which were going to ripen in the winter and lay them in the attics—and then go up night after night to turn them over and see whether they were going bad. Pears are a maddening fruit ; whole rows of them can look quite unready for eating one day and all turn sleepy overnight—and there is no pleasure to be had from a sleepy pear. We had far too many pears ; we gave baskets of them away, had pear pie and pear dumplings and stewed pears where other households used apples. I got so sick of them that for many years I never wanted to eat a pear ; even now I feel it is preposterous to be expected to *pay* for one. But the pear trees bore lovely resounding names—Williams' Bon Chrétien, Beurré Superfin, Pitmaston Duchess (a huge creature), and something which sounded like Léon de la Clerc de la Valle.

On the surrounding walls one or two climbers struggled to fruit ; there was a nectarine, I remember, which in good years produced one jealously guarded offspring, and a Victoria plum-tree which sometimes rose to a couple of dozen. This plethora of trees meant that the garden grew few flowers, except in spring time before the leaves had developed ; my most vivid recollection, in fact, is not of flowers but of aromatic plants, rosemary, sweet southern-wood, which we knew as " Old Man," and lemon verbena. Of these, combined with roses—white Nephetos, pink cabbage, and cream-and-orange William Allen Richardson, which came to early flowering in a cold greenhouse—we made nosegays and peep-shows under a sheet of glass ; and even to-day my sense of smell, which is I believe, the most atavistic and long-remembering of all our senses, annihilates fifty years when it detects the aroma of any one of these.

I do not think that Edwardian Cambridge was quite so idyllic a place as it is painted by Mrs Kathleen Wallace, who seems to remember it as a town of blue summer days and perpetual blossom populated by the most angelic of children ; my picture of it adds a lot of rain, walks behind and around a pram wheeled by a cross nursemaid who, day in and day out, *always* pushed it along the Trumpington Road, and a remarkable number of spiteful, quarrelsome little boys. But in many ways, that Cambridge was a good place to be a child in. It was of manageable size to begin with. Nine-year-old legs, as soon as allowed out alone, could walk wherever anyone could wish to walk, though naturally not in the poorer quarters, the dismal little streets of Romsey Town, for example. (But one could go to a nearer slum, the ironically named Coronation Street, to take boots to the cobbler's or buy lovely crumpets—the shop proclaimed itself Patronised by Royalty, because Edward VII bought some crumpets there when he was an undergraduate.) One could walk to the open market which even in austerity days is still a feast for the eyes every Saturday morning—in June 1945 I saw carts and carts coming in loaded with nothing but strawberries—and spend a penny on seeds for one's garden ; and, if the grown-ups were kind, return home in The Tram, with a knife-edge top, which one old horse drew from the Post Office to the station ; it was just quicker than walking. One could get to any shop one wanted, to the dancing class held in the Liberal Club, with the proud and/or anxious mothers sitting round on the cold worn leather seats wondering whether Dolly or Muriel or Margaret would manage to get the waltz step right this time, or succeed in pulling the skipping-rope through twice to one jump without tripping, or whether Mrs Wordsworth, the terrible chief with the lame leg, would elect to pay a visit and call out Dolly or Muriel or Margaret to perform, and in all probability to disgrace herself, since Mrs Wordsworth's presence was enough of itself to petrify any normal child. The dancing-classes were a great social centre, and prowess there carried the prestige of athletics in a public school. How I envied, alternately, good dancers like Dolly Lock and children like Blenda Morgan, daughter of the Master of Jesus, who was allowed to wear *scarlet* dancing sandals !

Secondly, there was a really immense quantity of open space available. There was Coe Fen, since ruined by the by-pass road, which has dwarfed its size and uncovered all its mysteries ; no one will now believe that we were forbidden to go on Coe Fen unattended, for fear of tramps. There was the wide expanse of Midsummer Common, where great fairs were held in past centuries ; and there were the Botanic Gardens, only a few hundred yards from our own front door. I do not suppose that those who laid out the Botanic Gardens realised what a fine play-place for children they were making ; in fact, I am sure they did not, for I have more than once been turned out by keepers for using the Gardens for the purpose for which they were so obviously designed. Nevertheless, I can assure their makers that they shall be remembered in heaven for providing us with so much enjoyment—the small rivulet among the chestnuts where we hunted alligators, the trees to swing and jump on just over the duck-pond, the tunnel by the rockery where the smugglers lived, and that great pegged-up conifer (is it a larch ?) under whose artificial screen we made believe to build our camp-fire before we marched off for the wars.

Thirdly, it was beautiful. I do not think we were in the least conscious of that at the time ; but you cannot be brought up within a mile of the Backs and the Bridges, seeing year by year the huge weeping willows coming into leaf and the spring flowers waking in St John's Wilderness, or be taken, even occasionally, to King's Chapel when the morning sun is shining through the clear reds and blues of the east window, or even walk to school along the gracious curve of Trumpington Street, without some sense of beauty seeping into you. You have, as I think citizens of old medieval towns must have had, some innate standard within you which will tell you, without your asking, that ribbon-built suburbs are ugly, and that Glasgow and Sheffield (to pillory two cities out of many possibles) have made potentially lovely sites into a nightmare of ugliness.

Finally, it was alive and amusing ; there were pageants and acting shows, indoor and outdoor, got up by energetic people to amuse and employ the children every winter and summer—I have been a kitten with a lovely furry tail made out of somebody's mother's tippet, an elf in spangled tights and a pointed cap, Julius Caesar, and—of all things—Racine's Athalie ; it gave me an illusion that I could act which was not dissipated for many years. There were Christmas parties for which we had real dance programmes and stayed up sometimes until nine or even ten o'clock, having been put to bed for the afternoon in preparation ; there was Punch and Judy and the Midsummer Fair and the Christmas pantomine where I heard Wilkie Bard proclaim, " I want to sing in Op-op-op-opera ! "—fell violently in love with the principal boy, and dreamed of saving her from drowning or burning ; and there was the perpetual bright-coloured rivalry of college blazers in the streets, at Fenner's, and on the river. May Week, when we could go by push-boat—no punts then to speak of—or by train and footpath to Ditton Paddock, was the most exciting week of

FOUR GENERATIONS OF WIVES

Amelia Le Lacheur (Mrs. Allen)

Edith Allen
(Mrs. Postgate)

Jane Cole
(Mrs. Abraham)

Margaret Postgate
(Mrs. Cole)

BROTHERS AND SISTERS

Thomas and Edith Allen
1867

Margaret and Raymond Postgate, 1897

Margaret—and sugar mouse, 1898

the year, only marred by the fact that I, by birth a citizen of Trinity, had to be on non-speaking terms with my chief school friend, whose father had the bad taste to be attached to Trinity Hall.

We went to school in the top half of the pavilion on the University rugger ground. There, in two rooms and a tiny coat-lobby approached by an outside staircase—the men's changing rooms were underneath—Mrs Berry, wife of a don at King's, conducted a small private school, mainly for the children of the University. The big children were taught in one room, the small ones in another, and for playtime we had the whole of the football ground ; there were two assistant mistresses and a stout lady with a red face and hairs on her chin who came to teach us part-songs with the aid of a tuning-fork. Mrs Berry was no beauty—a tall woman with a skin like thick yellow parchment, yellow teeth and an inordinately long upper lip ; it was a little unfortunate that when dressing for a garden-party—a great feature of Edwardian Cambridge—she fancied a white tulle hat with a wreath of pink roses. Her sense of humour was not her strongest point, and we were rather frightened of her. But I am very sure she could teach. Our school hours were from ten to one on five mornings in the week, and there was very little homework ; but Mrs Berry's children easily surpassed those from other establishments. (The shortness of the hours was a source of annoyance to some parents, who complained that they did not pay school-fees to have their children around practically all day !) I cannot, however, recollect much that I learned there, except the history of Ancient Egypt, but it must have been a good deal more than I learned in the four years after I had left.

These short hours meant that we had a good deal of time on our hands, part of which we employed in improvising games. I had to invent a good many of these for my juniors, some of them immense serial games which went on for months. I regret to record that I used one of these to bribe Ray and Esmond to go to bed ahead of their proper time, so that I could get on with my private concerns. (" One of the trials of youth," remarked my uncle Tom Allen, himself the eldest of a family, " is the regrettable laxity of one's parents about the younger children's bed-time ! ") With my school " chum " I played endlessly at " hospitals " and " illnesses " —psychologists will no doubt say that this was an early outlet for sexual feelings, and I think it probably was ; it was certainly no real desire to emulate Florence Nightingale. But for a good deal of the time I was by myself, and used to walk up and down at the back of the garden or somewhere else where I could not be seen, telling myself endless stories which I sometimes wrote down.

I " commenced author " very young, before I could write. No one took down my efforts ; I wish they had, for the title of one of them which has survived, *The Melon Who Drove Too Fast*, excites my curiosity.[1] Later I wrote quantities of stories on the backs of London Matriculation papers which my father had received for correction ; but too much reading of other people's fiction, *e.g.*, from the twopenny library, choked the budding muse. After reading Lester Arnold's *Phra the Phœnician*, which I admired immensely, I wrote the chapter-headings—long and elaborate chapter-headings—for a novel which would show its hero translated, as Phra was translated, through every period of history with which I had any acquaintance ; but when the chapter-headings were done they looked so beautiful that it seemed unnecessary to write the book, and that was the end of my novel-writing.

For holidays we went away *en famille* for three weeks or a fortnight in September (then cheaper than August) to some place on the Norfolk or Suffolk coast, which meant a shorter rail journey than any other stretch of seaside. I think the best part of these holidays was, as so often in life, the anticipation, the arrival of the station growler, the train and dinner-on-the-train with a hard-boiled egg, the first sight of the sea, and the first removal of one's shoes and stockings on the beach. For seaside holidays should be all sunshine, especially for families living in seaside lodgings, and so often they were not ; and bathing on the East Coast, with an east wind blowing and whipping sand and shingle against one's legs, can be plain purgatory. To be just, though, I can remember lovely days spent exploring woods and cornfields near Cromer or jumping with nets and poles over the rock-pools, and particular joy when I was promoted to wear a sailor-suit of red Turkey twill with elastic round the bottom of the blouse into which the skirt could be tucked, and knickers with similar elastic so that they could be pulled up when one went paddling. The fear of " getting wet," which meant that Nurse would be cross and that one would have to wear wet clothes full of prickly sand until dinner-time, was an ever-present menace. There was no thought of spending hours in a bathing-suit slipping in and out of the water ; nobody, indeed, could have wanted to spend more than the minimum of time in the voluminous blue serge object, complete with skirt, in which I was encased for

[1] My youngest brother followed in my footsteps, but *he* had an amanuensis to write down his pithy masterpieces. One of them has so surrealist a touch that I cannot refrain from quoting it here :—

" Once upon a time there was a Piece of a Mouse. And he had a Djink (drink) and some Pudding. And he did Djink *all* his Djink. And (very impressively) He - Might - Have - Coughed."

bathing and pulled right under water by my father as soon as I had emerged from the bathing machine. But paddling was always allowed, and we were not *forbidden* to get wet ; this would have been impracticable to enforce.

I think the lodging-house life must have been uncomfortable and hard on my mother, who had to buy all the provisions, deal with the landlady, and keep the children reasonably quiet and clean indoors ; it is only quite recently that our society has addressed itself to the problem of providing family holidays, with some rest for the mother, for families who cannot afford hotels—I never entered an hotel until I was eighteen and then only as guest of a friend. Mr Butlin would not, I think, be quite my cup of tea ; but there is not the smallest doubt that he is fulfilling a deeply felt want—one only hopes for the rapid growth of similar ventures which are not quite so determinedly sociable. We, however, did not notice the lodgings ; if there were books in them we read them (when we were not having to amuse the babies), and, if not, played some of the many variants of Happy Families, or a board game like Ludo, when we had to be indoors.

There was very little either of politics or religion in our youthful lives. Our household was " non-political," that is to say Tory,[1] and my father's strong political views did not impinge upon us, partly because we did not eat much with our parents, until his opinions clashed violently with those of his eldest son. The first public event that I can remember at all was the death of the Queen, at which my mother—who must surely have been taken a little off her guard—said to me when I asked what sort of a king Prince Albert Edward would be, " Well, I think he'll be an improvement on the silly old Q." I was surprised and rather shocked, more so by not being allowed to wear black sashes and hair-ribbons, as many Cambridge children did. But I think that some of the writers who have described the veneration in which the aged Victoria was held by her people have forgotten the heavy burden of conduct and behaviour which standards derived from Albert the Good imposed, as long as she lived, not merely upon the Court but on people like my mother's acquaintances who never went near Court circles. People thought that with Edward VII calling the tune they might have a little more fun—and they did.

The South African war I remember well. We had halfpenny-

[1] That is still the meaning of the word in a good many circles. How often have I read in a review that it is a pity that the Coles " drag politics " into their detective novels. Politics of the Left, is what these reviewers mean. So did the Housewives' League of 1947 angrily claim that it was entirely non-political—only opposed to the Government.

sized medallions of the principal British generals—Roberts, Buller, French, Baden-Powell, Sir George White—to pin on our coats. When my brother Esmond was a tiny baby I was sent in to my mother's bedroom to say to her, "Cronje's surrendered," and we knew that Kruger was a very wicked man; after the relief of Mafeking there was a lovely great bonfire on the Common, to which (though I did not know this at the time) many Cambridge householders unwittingly contributed wooden gates and fences. We learnt from our nurses to sing the wartime songs—"Dolly Gray," "Tommy Atkins," "Soldiers of the Queen," and a dreadful barrel-organ drone called "Goodbye, my Bluebell"—thank goodness the B.B.C. has never picked that up, as it has picked up "Daisy Bell" and other songs of my childhood.

Of course, we had no idea that there was anything discreditable to Britain about the war, and we did not know, or even know of, anybody who had gone to it. Apart from the facts I have just stated, I remember it chiefly as the setting for innumerable sentimental stories about camp-fires and gallant young soldiers—the hero of *The Hill* perished nobly on the Veld, as did "Raffles," the gentleman-burglar who played country-house cricket and won so many hearts. It is a little odd that, because of the unpreparedness and the disasters of the early months of 1900 which made it necessary to call upon the youth of England for voluntary sacrifice, that inglorious imperialist scuffle should have become the last home of *roman militaire*—the kind of thing which Sir Henry Newbolt used to celebrate in verse. Even in the actual fighting, it seems, there was an element of adolescent romance which never came again (except perhaps in the case of the airmen in the Battle of Britain). You can find it in Deneys Reitz's brilliant *Commando*; and I remember Field-Marshal Smuts telling me, years afterwards, a story of riding down a young British sniper in a cornfield who clutched at his stirrups and cried, "Don't kill me, sir! Think of my mother!" At any rate, for some years popular literature thought it was *dulce et decorum* for the hero to be slain by the Boers; it was a great shock to me, long afterwards, to see from memorial tablets in cathedrals what a huge proportion of the gallant volunteers in fact died of disease—all those years after Florence Nightingale.

After the South African war my next public memory—unless you count the hanging of Dougal, the Moat Farm murderer, in which I was much interested—was the 1906 election.[1] Of the

[1] I *ought* to remember the Russo-Japanese war, but all I recollect is that we had two kittens who were called Togo and Kuropatkin after the rival admirals. I never heard of the Duma.

issues, which, goodness knows, were confused enough, I had no idea, though I have a vague memory of a big loaf and a little loaf on a poster. But we had a fine wall-map—in those days elections went on for weeks—on which we stuck blue, red, green, and yellow squares (green for the Irish Nationalists and yellow for the frightful Labour Party) as if we had been recording a war. All we knew in the end was that our side had been crushingly beaten ; it was as bad as if the Trinity boat had gone to the bottom of the river.[1] " I think," my mother said to me, " that the new people will make a dreadful mess of it." Maybe, in the end, they did ; but the end was a long way off.

As to religion, we were brought up orthodox C. of E. We had to say our prayers—I heard the babies' prayers on the nurse's evening out, and well remember Ormond reciting earnestly, " For thine is the kingdom, *the pirate*, the glory "—and grace before Sunday dinner, though not at other meals. We learned by heart, at least I did, collects and verses of Psalms, and we were taken on Sunday morning to Great St Mary's, where Archdeacon Cunningham (the same that wrote *English Industry and Commerce*) preached sermons whose content was far above the heads of the young. I was dreadfully bored, and did not possess Ray's convenient trick of bleeding at the nose, which often caused him suddenly to be withdrawn, so during the sermons and the Lessons[2] I occupied my mind in (*a*) trying to calculate the date of next Easter by the Golden Numbers, in which I was invariably unsuccessful, and (*b*) evolving schemes for climbing up the inside of the church by means of its variegated mouldings and columns—a curious fantasy for one who has no natural aptitude at all for climbing of any kind. I also attended, for a time, a Sunday afternoon Children's Service at St Edward's in Pease Hill, where we were given a good deal more of personal exhortation and what I can only call sentimental gush about Christ crucified. I absorbed it enthusiastically, but I believe my parents appreciated it less. At all events, when I showed a desire to become a " Golden Sunbeam," Golden Sunbeams being child subscribers to a cheap periodical who enrolled themselves as willing to bring the word of God to a child in another district—the East End of London, probably—I was very firmly discouraged ;

[1] Not " bottom " in the sense of being drowned. " Bottom of the river," means last at the end of the May races ; it is a fate far worse than mere sinking.

[2] Speaking of Lessons, what extraordinary extracts Anglicans do listen to unquestioning ! I still remember my attention being momentarily caught by the story of Abimelech, who slew his *seventy* brothers ; and when I was at boarding-school I had myself to read in chapel St Paul's spiteful remarks about Alexander the coppersmith.

and when, having read an appallingly sentimental book entitled *Bruey : A Little Worker for Christ* (she died, of course, at an early age), I tried to follow her example, I found that Little Workers for Christ were definitely at a discount in the home circle. My father, I discovered long afterwards, was an unbeliever who thought religion good for women, and I suspect that my mother's faith was not strong. I, however, unquestioningly accepted the fact of God, and did not even criticise him as more intelligent children (*e.g.*, the young H. G. Wells) did, though I was very disappointed in him on one occasion, when I fervently prayed overnight to become a boy, went to sleep in happy confidence, and woke up still a girl. Later I was persuaded to believe that such simple trust in the Almighty was not religion but blasphemy.

At the beginning of 1910 my father accepted the Professorship of Latin at Liverpool, a job which was near to pioneering, for the University was inclined to regard the arts as frills compared with serious subjects such as naval architecture, in which it was pre-eminent, and he had an uphill fight to obtain adequate recognition. We children were parked in various places while the furniture went on its laborious way by goods train, and on a cold damp January day found ourselves in a large four-storied house in Princes Park Terrace near Sefton Park.

I had already been two years at boarding-school when we moved, and Liverpool never took the place of Cambridge in my heart. I have a certain mild affection for it, sufficient to feel sorry when I heard that it had taken a week's heavy pasting in the spring of '41, when the Luftwaffe was trying to knock out the harbours of Britain ; but that feeling does not go deep, and I have never been back to it since, on my father's retirement, my family returned to Cambridge after ten years' exile. I do not think any of us liked it very much ; we were Easterlings to the core, and never got on terms with the grey dampness of Lancashire, the dirt and the harsh voices. You were warned not to keep your clothes shut up too long in wardrobes, in case they mildewed, but to put them out in the sun—only there never seemed to be any sun ! There is, it is true, a sea-wind from the Mersey, strong enough at times to blow small children off their feet, which dissipates the smoke from the Widnes soap and chemical works and other factories, and prevents the grimy fog which overhangs Manchester from lying so long in Liverpool ; but in compensation the salt in the air seemed to induce the particles of carbon to coagulate in lumps. I have never seen such *enormous* smuts as there were in Liverpool ; you could watch them drifting towards you, and dodge them if you could ; if you failed they spilt themselves down your nose. That same smoke, however, produced a murky beauty which was not to be found in Cambridge, lurid red and purple sunsets which we could see from the top windows of the house in Princes Park when the sun went down behind the dark line of the Clwyddian mountains on the far side of Dee. We were told by patriotic Liverpudlians that Turner practised his sunsets on Merseyside.

Liverpool introduced us, also, to ships and mountains. We were not encouraged to roam about the dock area, which was dirty and supposed to be full of dangerous characters ; the dock population was in fact mixed and pretty rowdy. But anyone could take a tram—if you had the little ones with you, a first-class tram [1]—to Pier Head, and watch the liners come in and the tenders fussing to and fro between the landing-stage and the big Cunarders, the *Lusitania* and the *Mauretania*, which even then were too big to stay alongside, but lay to the south in the wide and deep Sloyne opposite Garston. You could take one of the ferry-boats to Birkenhead or Port Sunlight or New Brighton, and walk across the Wirral peninsula to the Sands of Dee, or round it past Hoylake golf-course looking to see what jetsam the sea had thrown up. Wrecks played a distinct part in the economy of Liverpool. I remember picking up quantities of onions and oranges which had come ashore from a Spanish boat ; the mammoth stores like Owen Owen's were constantly announcing " salvage sales " (from fire as well as water), and once the wreck of a ship full of paint caused great pieces of the city to appear in new coats of a peculiarly ugly bluish-green. From Pier Head, too, you might one day take a holiday steamer to Llandudno, to the Isle of Man, or even to Ireland.

For one of the chief attractions of Liverpool was, I fear, that as others have said of Manchester, it is " so easy to get out of " for week-ends or summer holidays. The family finances no longer confined us to Hunstanton, Sheringham, Cromer, and the other repositories of shingle and east winds, and sea that remorselessly eats the land away. (The Atlantic rollers make a much more spectacularly threatening noise and foam, but the West is defended by granite and limestone ; it is the North Sea which is really wicked, the North Sea which comes up on a winter night, and devours great chunks of the soft sand-and-chalk, houses, churches, and all. Villages that I knew in my childhood are now under the sea, along

[1] About one in three of the cars from Sefton Park to Pier Head had an upholstered lower deck on which double fare was charged. I have never met this particular form of class distinction anywhere else ; it did not prevent my small brother getting lice in his hair and infecting me, to my infinite shame, in my first term in college.

with the seven drowned churches of Dunwich in Suffolk.) Instead, the shortest and cheapest holiday journey was to North Wales, and staying at Penmaenmawr on the Holyhead road I had my first experience of mountains, of walking over heather and bilberry and rough grass and rock up to the toothed ridge of Tal-y-Fan and beyond it to the mountains which look over towards the heights surrounding Snowdon. I found there what it is like to climb up and watch the view of sea and valley unfolding beneath you, and the lesser hills sinking into significance as you rise higher and higher ; I saw morning mist melted by the sun into rolling banks of cottonwool like those described in *The First Men in the Moon* ; and I learned that river-water can be clear bright brown, and run fast (instead of crawling like the Cam and getting choked up with weeds), and tumble and leap into heaps of foam like whipped thick cream. I learned to take a conscious pleasure in the beauty of natural things. But for some time I could only do this for a fortnight in the year. During other holiday weeks we stayed in Liverpool, and for eight months of each year I was at school—at Roedean.

PART TWO

EDUCATION

Chapter Three

I HAVE never quite understood why my parents sent me to Roedean. To remove me from the home was understandable ; the educational demands of Mrs Berry took too little of my time, and rather much of the remainder tended to be occupied in acting as a supplementary nursemaid. My mother tells me that at four years old, not long after Ray was born, I protested against this service, remarking that " You're always telling me to mooze the baby, so I can't do my own fings." It must have been about the same date that I started to howl after a tumble in the garden ; and when a visitor was prevented from coming to the rescue, picked myself up and observed with injured dignity, " *Once* when I cried all people used to run." Such are the pains of growing up ; but by the time I was fourteen I had no conscious rebellion against nursemaiding. I accepted it as the normal lot ; but I could think of more interesting occupations than amusing the baby or wheeling the baby or rocking the baby[1] or even teaching my young sister to read. Moreover, my mother had a strong and not altogether unjustified feeling that daughters growing up in the home were liable to quarrel with their mothers. So it was not unreasonable to send me away—but there were so many other girls' schools that might have been chosen.

I still find it difficult to write with detachment about the Roedean of my youth ; and must, therefore, make it perfectly clear that I am not in any way referring to present-day Roedean which may, for all I know, be as different from mine as chalk from cheese. Also, I have no doubt that at fourteen I was an awkward child with many unattractive traits, who might have found some difficulty in fitting into any community. I do not for a moment suggest that my experience at school was all the school's fault. But considering that up till September, 1907, I got on reasonably well with my contemporaries, that I left my home perfectly prepared

[1] None of this service included doing the really difficult things, such as bathing an infant at the stage when it is quite helpless and slippery, and its head feels as if it were certain to come off. Consequently, when I had to cope with a baby of my own I was as terrified as though I had never had a younger brother. We had too many servants to learn " mothercraft "—or even cooking, except making toffee. The cook was generally far too cross to let children into the kitchen—and on her evening out there was an equally cross deputy.

to like school and to like my schoolfellows, and that as soon as I got away from school to college I found it perfectly easy to get on with my contemporaries there, I cannot accept that in September, 1907, I turned abruptly into the kind of creature with whom it was impossible for any normal human being to enjoy associating.

My early terms were almost pure misery—the kind of misery which no one can realise who has not had the experience of being thoroughly unpopular, not by reason of any defiance or independence of your own (which would at least provide a martyr's crown) but simply because you cannot fit the pattern, because, as small boys would say, " you *stink* " ; you do not know why, and your best efforts seem only to result in making you stink worse. It is far sharper in a residential community without private rooms where you can never, for thirteen long weeks at a time, get away from seeing your own personality mirrored in the eyes of others—and watching them move away from the vision in repulsion. To have no one—no one at all—who wants to speak to you, to giggle with you, or to be seen alive or dead with you ; to find any group to which you try unobtrusively to attach yourself melting mysteriously away, leaving you in naked and patent quarantine ; to hear voices saying, " *Margaret Postgate?* No, thank you ; not with a barge-pole ! " ; to dread the week-ends, when you had ironic liberty to sit where you liked and next whom you liked, and to pray for Monday morning, when at least you had your desk, a place assigned to you by authority, and could not be roughly or politely asked to move out and make room for some more desirable Dorothy or Nellie or Sybil—all this is enough to make a pretty average hell for a poor dog who only wants to be liked. And in a thirteen-week term there are 130,000 odd minutes to be got through, somehow. I know ; I used to calculate it out and scratch them off in batches.

What I did specifically to turn me into a pariah dog I am not very sure. I know I was a bit unintentionally uppish ; I spoke before I was spoken to—to prefects, for example—and though one of the least attractive of a batch of seventeen new girls I piped up in full assembly and asked for a part in the house play. (That I performed it quite well made matters no better.) But the main cause was not anything specific, but simple general distaste. I was the wrong sort of cuckoo in a horridly alien nest. As Samuel Butler says, " the cross was too wide."

The cross was too wide, and Roedean was, emphatically, the wrong sort of school for me. But I would go further and say it was not a good sort of school at all. It was, for those days, very expensive ; I only got in as the winner of the single annual scholarship. It was founded by a formidable group of sisters, the Misses Lawrence—it would be ridiculous to call them spinsters, for the massive Penelope, Millicent, and Dorothy,[1] the three that I knew, had certainly never thought of doing anything so acidulating or humdrum as spinning—as an imitation of the second-rate imitations of the " great " public schools. I do not mean, of course, that the founders put it to themselves or to their clients in exactly those terms ; but that was in fact its purpose. The school did not put on a polish or train up young ladies for real Society ; I do not remember any titled girls, though we did have for a couple of terms the daughters of the Chinese Ambassador, the younger a lovely child. Nor was it devoted to learning ; though we spent the best part of seven hours a day in school, and Saturday morning as well, very few of us went on to Universities, and the standards achieved would have shocked Miss Buss and Miss Beale and the founders of the Girls' Public Day School Trust. Perhaps this was because the Lawrences themselves, though first-class organisers, not to say advertisers, were no good as teachers and therefore probably not very good pickers ; perhaps they were just giving their rich bourgeois clients what they wanted—some instruction, adequate Christian training for all but the Jews, discipline partly self-administered (by a prefectorial system and *plenty* of house and team spirit), and a frill of culture, *i.e.*, concerts and lectures, sometimes with lantern slides, on Sunday evenings. There was also a small school library at one end of the main assembly hall, where girls in the top forms were allowed to read. I forfeited this privilege when I was caught reading Macaulay's *Essays* in the time allocated to French preparation, because I had finished my French. A friend of mine, a sub-prefect, whose desk was near mine in the prep-room, saw me and reported the sin to the head of the house, with the result that I lost my own sub-prefect's badge as well as the access to the library for the rest of the term.

The clientèle of the school was, as I have said, well-off though not aristocratic. (The less wealthy were many of them Unitarians, owing to the connection of the Lawrences with the Martineau family, relatives of the great Harriet ; we envied them because they only went to chapel once on Sundays.) We had a large number of daughters of the business bourgeoisie from Birmingham, Lancashire, Newcastle, and Scotland, as well as from London and the south, and there was a considerable aroma of money about the school. To give them their due, the Lawrences did what they

[1] There were at least two more, of whom one presided over the out-boarders and the other founded the Johannesburg Roedean ; there may have been others.

could by sumptuary laws to prevent any overt display. The width of the hair-ribbons securing our plaited locks was regulated by tape-measure ; we were forbidden jewellery other than a couple of " quiet brooches or tie-pins," and we were dressed until tea-time in a regulation uniform called a djibbah, a waistless knee-length garment of thick blue serge topped with golden brown canvas with RS monogrammed on it in red silk—it was remarkably unbecoming to girls with the " developing figures " of mid-adolescence—long woollen stockings, black for indoor and brown for outdoor wear, and hard straw " sailor " hats. In my second year, in order to leave still less scope for sartorial extravagance, we were made to discard all ordinary frocks and dress ourselves for evenings and the week-ends in a coloured djibbah, in which we were at least allowed latitude as to length and hue. (Mine was a warm red, and the blouse worn inside it cream-coloured ; I thought it pretty and possibly it was, but it was not much use away from school.) Whether by choice or compulsion—I never knew which—the staff took to djibbahs at the same time. I remember my maths mistress, one of the comparatively few of the staff who exercised real authority, appearing suddenly in a purplish red one which swept the floor, just as I was endeavouring to give in my overdue arithmetic prep without being noticed. She was well over average height ; in her djibbah she looked like Tall Agrippa out of *Struwwelpeter*, and I fully expected to be plunged in the ink like the naughty boys.

Nor was " lavish expenditure " in other directions encouraged. We had to hand over all our pocket-money at the beginning of term, receiving instead small " cheque-books " and penny account-books in which to enter up the counterfoils for periodic inspection. The possession of coin of the realm was a crime and as only a few of the Brighton shops would accept our paper currency control of our expenditure was easy enough. (One of the ludicrous pictures which memory brings up is of sniffing girls in chapel, after a moving appeal from the pulpit for missions to somewhere or other, borrowing pencils to alter, through their tears, the 3d. written on their collection cheques to 6d. or even 9d.) Our food was pretty adequate, considering how hungry life on top of a cliff exposed to the Channel gales can make one, but certainly not luxurious ; and we were strictly forbidden to receive any edibles from outside. If any arrived, they were confiscated and given to the children of the school mission. Only one exception was allowed ; on the occasion of a birthday and a birthday party we were allowed to have a cake, but not sweets on any account. There was one terrible scandal when my friend, Phyllis Reid, had agreed to have a joint birthday party with another girl, and the other girl brought in sweets. The crime was discovered, and our house-mistress waited tensely for Phyllis to come and give herself up. When she came—as she did immediately she heard of the rumpus—bearing her own share of the illicit food, they wrestled together in prayer for a while and finally consigned the offending chocolates to the mistress's sitting-room fire. Our reading was censored ; unsuitable story-books were confiscated and not returned till the end of term—if necessary with a note of warning to the parents. I don't think we were allowed to receive picture papers or anything of that kind.

The trouble about all this restriction was that besides being humourless—as I think all restrictions and regulations are bound to be at some point or other[1]—it was all negative. It did not prevent in the slightest degree the conversation of rich girls turning on all the things which money could buy—or the pupils stuffing themselves dramatically when their relations came to see them and take them outside the school boundaries to lunch at the Royal Crescent Hotel—the Metropole was out of bounds ; nor did it provide any new set of values. The positive values of Roedean were supplied from three sources—games, the prefect system, and religion, in that order.

I put the games first because their value was absolutely unquestioned, and without some sort of proficiency it was difficult for any but a very exceptional character to gain popularity—or " influence " enough to reach the first rungs of the ladder leading to authority. We were *obsessed* with games—team-games, lacrosse one term, hockey in the next, cricket in the third, standing in highest repute, though one could also obtain half-colours (I had almost written " a half-Blue ") for swimming, gym, dancing, etc. We all played the team-games, compulsorily, every school-day afternoon, the whole school being divided by the games mistresses into about eighteen elevens which played one another on three days in the week, and house elevens which played on the two others. The full list of elevens, written in pencil, hung in the long corridor

[1] A good Roedean example was the attempt to prevent the use of slang. A kind of Hays Office code banned a list of words like " ripping" and " rotten," and forbade one girl to call another by an animal name, *e.g.*, " pig " ; the results were not always those intended. One visiting parent asked her daughter, "Why *do* you keep calling things ' obscene,' darling ? It's such an ugly word." " Because we aren't allowed to use slang," was the reply.

On another occasion a new chum innocently addressed a sub-prefect as " lamb," and was promptly served with a discipline mark ; the rule had certainly been broken. But in latter days Government Departments and People's Commissars have initiated prosecutions every bit as silly.

between No. III and No. IV Houses, and at intervals the sight of the senior games mistress advancing upon it, india-rubber in hand, collected a crowd eager for first news of promotions. There were at least four elevens which played outside matches ; there were also four to each house, competing for house cups. " Fielding practice " or its equivalent, between breakfast and morning school, was compulsory ; " watching matches " on a Saturday afternoon all but compulsory until the Girl Guide Movement (Heaven bless it !) was introduced and provided alternative recognised occupation with the additional chance of getting outside the place ; when we beat Wycombe Abbey in the great match of the year we had a school holiday. It was all like the Boys' School Story raised to the *nth*. I have no personal objection to games as such ; in after years I enjoyed both playing lacrosse and watching cricket, when I was not forced to ; and only mildly regretted the fact that, as there were only three tennis courts for a school of three hundred, I had gained no proficiency in a game much more socially useful than those which require twenty or more other participants. But I do feel that the games-worship at Roedean gives some support to the complaints of anti-feminists that women ought not to be allowed to do the things that men do, because they have no sense of proportion and drive everything to death.

The same element of caricature was to be found in the system of punishment and authority. We were punished by bad marks, order marks, punctuality marks, and discipline marks (one of the last equal to four of the two former, and awarded for such crimes as using slang, talking after lights out or in the corridors where silence was the rule). There was also a menace called a " conduct book " lurking in the background. I was told that a girl had received one for smoking, and that if you got two you were expelled, but was never able to verify this. Until you were free of discipline marks and reasonably free of order marks you could not obtain any position of authority. When you were, if you were otherwise a fairly desirable creature, and particularly if you were an athlete filled with team spirit, you were created a sub-prefect (there were twenty or so to each house), with certain minor privileges and the duty of being a minor spy ; you had to report to higher authority, for example, anyone you overheard using slang, or saw breaking a rule, with the result of depriving the reportee of her office if she had one. This form of discipline, in the hands of a conscientious Christian girl, could be a poisonous thing ; I do not believe boys would have been sheep enough to submit to it. If all went well, you would become in due course a house prefect, with a share of a study and the right to go to bed later than the rest of the house; and finally a School Prefect with a silver badge or a Senior Prefect with a gold one. Again, it might all have come out of a School Story; it was sanctioned by considerable social pressure, buttressed by the Church of England. Our religion was not in any way "enthusiastic"; we had two chapels on Sunday, were confirmed as a matter of course and prepared for it according to rule; we had Scripture lessons to which we mostly paid little attention, and a certain amount of exhortation. But I think we had no doubt that God was a kind of Super-Senior Prefect.

The worst gap, however, was the great lack of any intellectual interest. Roedean may not have been the stupidest school in England, but it certainly ranked high. The action of punishing a girl for finishing her preparation too quickly by depriving her of access to the Library seems to me indicative, and intellectual achievement rated in public opinion just nothing at all (by which I do not mean that it was maltreated); we did not follow the School Story example and persecute our "swots" or "sweats." Nobody minded if you were top of your form, which was very easy to achieve; but it was no advantage to you. And no one—or practically no one—discussed the subject-matter of lessons (as distinct from the awfulness of the sums or the unfairness of the piece of translation set) outside the class-room, or indeed any cognate subject such as politics. We had no debating society, and the only reference to politics (other than a joke or two about suffragettes) which I remember was when a young and untried history mistress suddenly observed in the middle of a lesson, "Now we are coming to a man about whom I cannot trust myself to speak calmly!" The monster turned out to be Disraeli; we looked up in mild surprise, but did not pursue the matter. We talked about other things—games, theatrical stars such as Lewis Waller (no film stars then), and male athletes, and places for summer holidays. Also about who was "keen" on whom; it was customary to have an emotional attachment to a senior girl, or to feign one if you had not. But we never imitated the "scandalous" side of public school life faintly, nor did we resemble the characters of Colette. One or two girls sometimes told slightly vulgar stories, but our language and our behaviour was otherwise clean as a whistle.

This general attitude must have been discouraging to any educational enthusiast, and I fancy this was the main reason why the lessons I listened to were so uniformly uninspiring. Taken by and large, mistresses were far less important than prefects or games captains. We had some terrifying ones, like Tall Agrippa and the senior French mistress, who rammed algebra, grammar, and historical dates down our throats by sheer force of personality and lashing tongue ; but we had very few who thought of making subjects interesting. I would make an exception in the case of one very shy mistress who took me for Latin, and encouraged me to find beauty in Virgil and Lucretius which I never lost again, and another—alas, a shocking disciplinarian, which made her classes confusion—who introduced us to the Lake poets and really encouraged us to write ; but these belong to the milder end of my schooldays.

For adolescent misery does not, thank goodness, remain at the same pitch of intensity. One can get used to anything in time ; one can learn to change one's spots to a certain extent. More important, the environment itself gets accustomed to the alien object and accords it a place of sorts ; one gets office eventually by lapse of time, and is included in a house eleven ; one can talk with those who three years earlier would have fled one's approach. And always there was an exception or two, such as my friend (who is still my friend) Phyllis Reid, who arrived, with reasonable athletic and other qualifications for popularity, a term after me, and seemed unaccountably to be able to endure me. I should add that this was a form of " slumming " on her part ; I knew that her other friends told her quite plainly that she would be well-advised to drop the connection. But there were a few others, whose numbers increased as time went on.

I also found, gradually, some literature, most of which I read, as in my childhood, over and over again. Macaulay's *Essays* were a prescribed book—for history preparation time—and from a shelf in a little-used class-room I " borrowed " volumes of Hazlitt, etc., and smuggled them up to my bedroom concealed in a large embroidery bag, since reading—though not sewing—in one's bedroom except on Sunday morning was prohibited and rated a discipline mark if one were caught. I also found unprescribed poetry, which was not marred by horrible notes on " Milton's use of the word *alchemist* " to be memorised for examinations, and learnt a great deal of Kipling and Browning by heart ; I even wrote an enthusiastic imitation of Kipling's *Sussex* about my own Fen country.

Moreover, as soon as I had acquired sufficient detachment to look at it, there was a good deal of beauty for the eye. Not in the school buildings themselves, which were adequate but no more, though even so I have caught my breath, at half-past six on a summer morning, to see the eastern sun making each pebble of

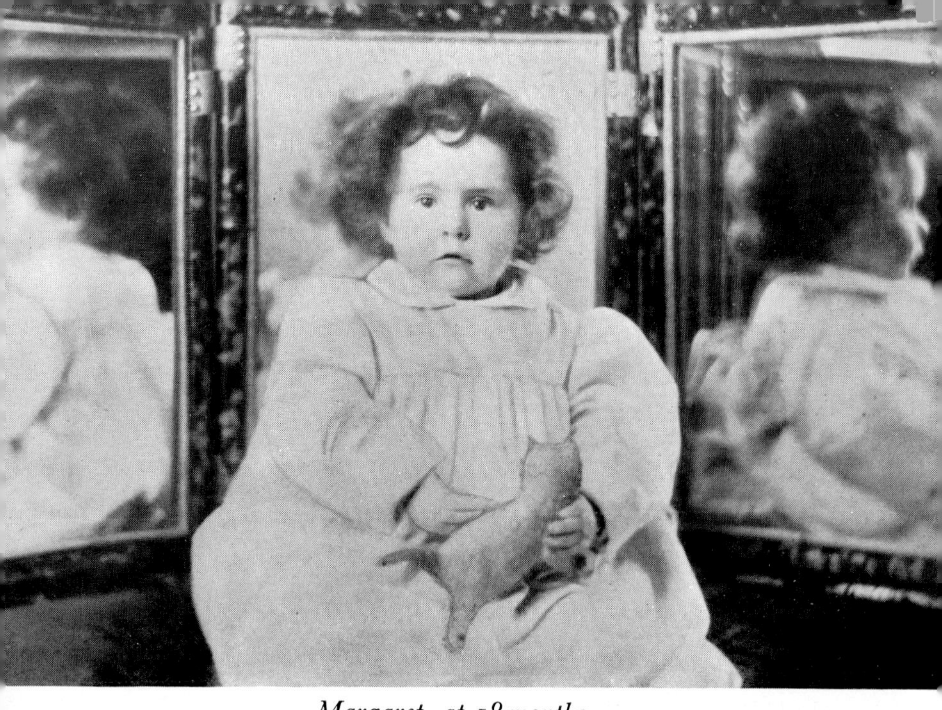

Margaret, at 18 months

Margaret, Raymond, Esmond and Ethel, 1904

Unexpected Treat for School

ROEDEAN SCHOOL, 1910–11

House Group—The author is second from the left in the last row but one

their rough-cast covering throw a thin dark shadow on the brilliant wall; but in walking the South Downs, on Girl Guide business bent, savouring the thyme and the trefoil and the long sweeps of sheep-mown turf; and above all, on an evening of thunderstorm, watching the blue sheet lightning on the far horizon changing to orange forks, and the long rods of rain marching towards us across the sea and the same sea rolling in with great green combers edged with white. Our truest religious emotion, I am sure, was at evening chapel on a stormy winter night, when the gale which was even then pushing thin streams of salty water through the casement windows of the school howled round and shook the building, and we sang from our hearts *For those in peril on the sea.* It was my misfortune to have wasted three years, more or less, before I was in a condition to accept any of this experience.

Chapter Four

Looking back and trying to evaluate, I find that the basis of my criticism of my school régime is general as well as individual. In general, it gave us no training or understanding either of the world we lived in or the problems which an adult creature, be it never so " non-political," would have to face. It was not until well after I had left school that I became in the least aware, as any fifteen-year old in a modern school is deliberately made aware, that anything worth noticing was happening in my own country, to say nothing of the world outside. And though " foreign affairs " were not noticed by the vast majority before 1914, the England of Edward VII was in fact full of public excitement. When I first went to school the last (before 1945) great Radical Government was in full reforming tide ; within a couple of years it brought in old-age pensions, minimum rates for the worst-paid, a little feeding of school-children, and made strikes possible again after the Taff Vale Judgment—all reforms which sound modest to-day but made Edwardian Tories foam at the mouth ; before I left it had begun to check and stumble. Lloyd George, the Radical whom a later generation of Radicals learned to hate so bitterly, in the famous Budget of 1909 tripped over the stubborn and sometimes plainly greedy prejudices of the last powerful generation of landowners,[1] and abused them in the fierce " Limehouse language " which makes anything that Emanuel Shinwell says in an incautious moment sound like cooing. The women found, slowly, that a Liberal Government was determined to deny them the vote, and that their Irish supporters would acquiesce in the hope (vain hope) of obtaining Home Rule for Ireland ; and the manual workers, whose support had contributed so largely to the huge 1906 majority, discovered that Parliament would or could do nothing to sustain their meagre standard of living against the insidiously rising prices, and in exasperation broke into the great 1910-1914 strike wave which in the month after I had left school loosed what was almost a small civil war in my new home of Liverpool.

I could not altogether fail to notice the Liverpool Dock Strike. I remember a broiling August, so hot that a piece of chocolate

[1] Memories are short in revolutionary times ; but if Press commentators had known a little more of rural history, of the pressure of Church and landlord on the labourer, they might not have been so naïvely astonished to find that the words " tied cottage " in 1947 still had the emotional power to make a Labour Conference turn down its leaders.

laid on a chair by Ray's bedside—he had heart trouble and was fainting with the heat—itself fainted and drooped limply towards the floor. I remember the stench of the unscavenged streets—the Corporation employees came out in sympathy—and of the truck-loads of vegetables rotting at Edge Hill station. I remember bits of broken bottle, relics of battles down by the Docks, the rain-patter of feet walking the pavements when the trams ceased to run and clank, the grey *Antrim* lying on guard in the Mersey, the soldiers marching through the streets, special editions of the evening papers coming out every half-hour, and American tourists, decanted from the *Baltic*, sitting at Pier Head on their Saratoga trunks with no porters to carry them away. I gathered from my father's thunderous noises that it was the beginning of the end of the world ; but as to what it was all about I had not the slightest idea—I had to read my husband's first book to find out.[1] No one had ever told me or my schoolfellows ; and after the storm had passed I went to Llandudno to spend a week-end with one of them—in a *real* hotel—my only concern being that my newly " put-up " hair kept tumbling down or ejecting cascades of hairpins. As to the other " public events " I knew nothing of them at all.

Nor was our ignorance confined to public affairs ; we were not prepared for any sort of life. One common criticism of the older " public school " system is that it produced boys and not men, creatures kept adolescent for so long that when they reached Oxford or Cambridge they could not be trusted to behave themselves without a quantity of regulations and disciplinary officials which made Continental students giggle : this was even truer of the girls. We learned nothing of home-keeping or how to conduct ourselves with the opposite sex, and came out of school—this, I believe, was as true of the products of the " serious " high schools as of those from Roedean, Wycombe Abbey, or St Leonard's—the most innocent greenhorns in the world.

I was a greenhorn, and a very timid greenhorn. For one result of my school experiences was that I did not want to leave and even begged my father to let me stay on. This is not so odd as it may sound. I had, by lapse of time, secured my niche ; if I stayed on another year the machine would have had to make me Head of the House, and so my existence would have been justified. If I left, I would be thrown again naked into a strange environment, a new hen ripe for the older hens to peck ; and I had had enough of pecking. (I think I have never forgotten what it is like to be well

[1] G. D. H. Cole, *The World of Labour* (1913). But I did not read it until some years later.

and truly pecked; and I hope it has been of some service to me as a writer and in my human relationships.) But my father did not believe in wasting time or money;[1] I had won a middling scholarship to Girton College, and to Girton I duly went in October 1911. The fact that my family had moved to Liverpool meant *inter alia* that my father could not be my university preceptor; and though he kept an eye on my studies—generally, it appeared to me, urging me to read authors such as Lucan, whom I disliked as much as Macaulay did[2]—he was too much occupied and had too many younger children to supervise me in detail.

I can never be sufficiently grateful to Girton College and the University of Cambridge for the part they played in transforming an unpresentable tadpole into a moderately decent sort of frog. The carping can, of course, find things to criticise in Girton. The mile-and-a-quarter which separates it from the centre of Cambridge is a bit of a nuisance, and was more nuisance in the days before 1914, when there were no buses and we had to cycle to and fro or journey to lectures in Cox's decrepit old cabs—there was a legend that the bottom of one of them had once dropped out *en route*, leaving the students to run along inside keeping pace with the horse—and when we were not allowed to go to meetings unchaperoned, so that before the closing of the debate or whatever it might be we had to rise and go home with our nurse, as it were, in order to get in before the Lodge gates closed. (The most unintentionally dangerous chaperone, in such a case, was our junior mathematical don, Miss Cave-Brown-Cave, who was both an enthusiastic stargazer and an indifferent cyclist, and if she caught sight of a pet constellation while climbing Castle Hill would curvet wildly about, head in air, to the great peril of all her charges.) The red-brick building, with its lopsided tower over the main gate, was not beautiful; I cannot honestly say that the pinkish modern additions are much of an improvement, quite apart from their having wantonly cut out the view of woodland from my own old windows in Chapel wing.

Many of the dons of my day were funny old things, and not the least funny was the Mistress, Miss Constance Jones, a woolly lady with a lisp who professed philosophy and was said to be tolerated by the administrators because she was so distinguished a philosopher

[1] He could not, to speak truth, have had any idea why I wanted to stay. I never confided my school troubles to my parents; this was due less to stoicism than to shame at being a failure.

[2] "Read Lucan for the fourth time—found him as dull as ever." (Macaulay's diary).

and by the philosophers because she was so good an administrator. " Oh, Mith Pothgate," she said on an occasion when she had come upon me behaving with undue exuberance in the passage, " if we *all* whithled and thang in the corridorth, where *thould* we all be ? " We were hedged around with regulations which were pretty ridiculous even for that date. I was rebuked for going cycling without a hat, and we were not allowed to entertain in our own sitting-rooms unchaperoned any male but a father or an uncle. During my stay, this privilege was by public notice extended to grandfathers, but the position of a brother *in statu pupillari* was always very uncertain.[1] As to other young men, they could be entertained only in a grim lecture-room, and when Miss Jones was asked to grant leave for one to be shown round the lovely College grounds and gardens she refused with the unanswerable observation that "thome of the thudenths might be lying about in all thorts of unthuitable attitudeth." It was with the greatest misgivings that she at length gave permission for us to play games in tunics instead of calf-length skirts. But she was a kind old body, for all that, and interfered with us very little.

And that, immediately, was what mattered. My first impression of College was one of freedom—freedom to work when you liked ; to stop when you liked ; to cut, even, lectures which turned out unhelpful or uninteresting ; to be *where* you liked *when* you liked, with *whom* you liked (subject to not making too anti-social a racket) ; to get up and go to bed when you pleased and if desirable to go on reading, writing, or talking till dawn. " I wept as I remembered how often you and I had tired the sun with talking and sent him down the sky "[2] ; the Greek anthologist caught that ineffable freedom of the undergraduate, and indeed, as Herodotus said, the Greeks were always boys. How often have I, drunk with talk or poetry, crept or staggered great distances back to my own room (Girton contains, I should think, a good long half-mile of corridor), seeing through the windows black fingers of cloud against a blue-green dawn sky, or groping in the dark to avoid the heavy fire-proof doors which closed in certain corridors at night ; and, careless of essays to be written, or any other academic chores, rolled happily into my bed for a couple of hours sleep before the new day. This

[1] My seven-year old brother Ormond, being under no ban, once came on a visit and was a crashing success with the girls.

[2] —*ὡς δέ με δάκρυ*
ἔρρυον, ἐμνήσθην δ'ὅσσακις ἀμφότεροι
ἥλιον ἐν λέσχῃ κατεδύσαμεν—
Johnson Cory made a good shot at translating the untranslatable, but the English still sounds too sentimental.

freedom, as I have admitted, was enjoyed within a framework of regulation which modern Cambridge might well think only a slight improvement on a concentration camp ; but to creatures fresh from school it was next door to Utopia.

My second immediate impression was of *friends*. I had come up with only one friend from school, Sigrid Pearson, daughter of that distinguished and alarming Rationalist and biometrician, Karl Pearson—she remained a close companion throughout my college days—and two acquaintances dating from my Cambridge childhood ; but from the moment I got inside the College I never lacked company. Our year numbered fifty-nine, ranging intellectually from the brilliant historian Rosalind Smith,[1] daughter of the great A.L., then Master of Balliol, to a small carrot-headed goose who was sent down in her second year for inability to pass Little-go ; it would have been a difficult girl who failed to find congenial company among them. And if that were not enough, there were a hundred or so others, from Second, Third, and Fourth Year, who were not, like school prefects, unapproachable by their juniors. Violet Stuart, the present impressive head of Sherborne School, was one of those whose friendship I courted admiringly in my first year. And you did not have to aspire to be a Senior Student (spokesman for her year), or a captain, or secretary of anything in order to gain recognition. You could be yourself.

The amount of sustenance provided for a starved young personality was enormous ; and I—and others, of course—was equipped with every possible variety ; nodding acquaintances, hail-fellow-well-met companions with whom one indulged in exercise or a mild female variety of ragging, kindred spirits with whom one discussed Literature and Life, close personal friends, and—so that the picture should not be too rose-coloured—a few Haughty or Dislikeable types, and a very personable Jewish girl, who wore picturesque flowing frocks and a necklace of great fire-opals, with whom I fell passionately and fruitlessly in love. The vast majority of this good company I have never seen again ; I have met perhaps a dozen ; I know the after-careers of some others and could know more if I studied more carefully the College Records. But on the whole I would rather not ; I have always found anything like Old Girl Reunions painfully depressing ; and I prefer to think of my contemporaries as girls between eighteen and twenty-two, dressed, not very aesthetically, in shirt-blouses with high collars and ties, ankle-length skirts secured to the blouses with vast safety-pins which sometimes gave way and left a hiatus, and woolly cardigans,

[1] Now Mrs Murray Wrong.

full of eagerness and problems personal and impersonal, and all together building up the picture of Cambridge as it was before the wars. I wish them all very well, and hope that if they remember they may do the same for me.

In this congenial atmosphere I grew quickly, and not merely as a person. Cambridge also turned me intellectually into something more like an adult ; incidentally, it was only then that I discovered that I had book-brains better than the average ; from my father I had always gathered that I was a semi-imbecile, and Roedean provided no one to measure oneself against. In my own subject I learned really to enjoy literature, history, and the study of civilisation. Alfred Zimmern's *The Greek Commonwealth* had just come out ; I sucked that great book dry as an orange and all but learnt it by heart, as I did many of Gilbert Murray's translations. To those two scholars, who have both loved the civilisation of Greece as though it were a new and delightful discovery laid on their doorsteps—and to Jane Ellen Harrison, J. L. Myres, and that erratic but brilliant genius Arthur Verrall—I owe more than I can say ; on the Roman side[1] I must pay a belated debt to Terrot Reaveley Glover, afterwards Public Orator, whose first-year lectures on Roman history were a revelation to one who had never known that history lessons could be anything but material for 10 or 20 questions to be answered in writing "with your books shut," and handed to the next girl to correct. Glover, that ugly and uncouth man with the harsh voice, believed in relating the subject-matter of his lectures to whatever happened to be interesting him at the moment. In 1911 he had just returned from Canada, and his lectures, therefore, contained a good deal of comparison of things Canadian with things Roman. Realising this, he on one occasion observed in half-apology that " it is a poor subject that will not get into a lecture on Roman history " ; when the remark was repeated to Miss Katharine Jex-Blake, our Director of Classical Studies, she observed acidly, " It is certainly a curious subject that does not get into *Dr Glover's* lectures on Roman history ! "[2]

[1] I once, but only once, heard A. E. Housman lecturing, on the astronomer-poet Manilius. I was gate-crashing then, because the lecture was meant for specialists ; it told the audience little about Manilius, but much, in most caustic terms, about rival commentators upon him.

[2] Miss Jex-Blake (" Kits " to Girtonians) had a gift of acid speech delivered in a dry precise voice with a slight curl of the nose which always suggested to me the kind of wit known as " judicial." But she was no hanging judge, and I think often appeased her wrath with her own phrases. During one Long Vacation term, a student who had been allowing night-rovers to climb in through her ground-floor window—a pretty flagrant breach of rule—was rebuked in the terms: " Understand, once and for all, Miss B., I will not have you privily conniving at illicit practices ! " —after which satisfying rotundity no more was heard of the matter.

But he was a great teacher, and whatever matter he introduced he made ancient Rome a reality to us before he had done.

Through these and others I learned to be a good classic, to enjoy and to understand Greek and Latin and Greek and Roman civilisation *at leisure*. There is point in the words italicised. For one of the best defences of the old classical education, which is all too seldom made by stupid people who talk nonsense about the " discipline " of Latin syntax and Greek irregular verbs, is that the amount of prose and verse written in Latin and Greek of the classical period is limited, and there can be no more of it. No one is likely now to find the lost books of Livy, not that they would take up a great deal of space in comparison with, say, one volume of the *Cambridge Modern History*, if they did turn up. The result is that anyone with reasonable brains and good early grounding could read without much difficulty practically the whole of the literature of the period, re-read any that appeared worth re-reading, and—even allowing for a certain amount of time wasted in " composition," *i.e.*, in reproducing English prose and verse in babu Latin and Greek which would undoubtedly have made Cicero or Euripides dissolve into guffaws—could get an appreciation of the *whole* of the civilisation he was studying, its history, its politics, its philosophy, its art, and its architecture, and still have mental leisure to think about it. We classics, in the days of the unreformed Tripos, when Part One took three years to pass and provided a degree [1] and only specialists took Part Two, may have spent rather an excessive amount of time on linguistic problems, including philology, but we had an infinite amount of leisure compared with the slaves of many other subjects, with the scientists, for example, sweating the good daytime hours away in their laboratories, and the historians writing endless " time-papers " to test their knowledge, and both alike panting eternally in a vain effort to master even a proportion of the masses of *facts*—ever-accumulating facts—connected with their subjects. We had a limited subject ; but, though limited, it was not narrow. The whole of human life, within the dates set, was its province. It dealt with human beings dead long ago ; but it dealt with them as humans in the round, not in bits and pieces. And that, and not cant about " discipline "—you can get more " discipline " from the dreadful traditional medical course, much of which is about as educational as learning the London

[1] Or, in the case of the women, a " Degree Certificate " which did not confer membership of the University. Not until 1947 did my alma mater abandon its last-ditch stand and grant to its women the equality which Oxford had given over a quarter of a century before.

Telephone Directory by heart—is the real reason why a classical education can claim to be cultural in the best sense of the word.

If you have leisure to think about Roman society and Greek society, it is improbable that your thinking will stop there. My curiosity led me into other subjects, to put in an enquiring appearance at lectures on non-classical philosophy and history of later date which strictly speaking were no business of mine ; it also took me into wider fields. In those three years I became—or, to speak more correctly, discovered that I was—an atheist and a Socialist, two intellectual faiths from which I have never wavered and do not suppose I ever shall. These conversions took place with incredible ease. For the first, when I came up to Cambridge I was a practising Christian simply because I had never known that it was possible to be anything else. When I discovered—I cannot remember how I discovered—that it was not necessary to believe in God or hell or personal immortality or the Fall or the doctrine of the Atonement, that there were many real people, intelligent people, who did not, I felt the burden of religion slip from my shoulders exactly as Christian's slipped from his, and with the same sensation of joyful relief. I did not ever, like the hero of Mrs Humphry Ward's *Robert Elsmere* and other earnest works, suffer from " religious doubts " ; as soon as religious doubts appeared upon the horizon I gladly yielded to them, and it is possibly for this reason that, though an atheist, I have never felt any urge to be a militant atheist. I have to accept that a large number of people do not feel as I do ; and if they do not, if they do not become atheists of themselves, as it were, I see no hope of converting them and am not inclined to interfere. I do not mean that I would urge people *towards* religion ; I could not have my own children baptized or tell them what I believe to be untrue. And I am well aware that religious—or, to speak more correctly, sectarian—intolerance is at best a drag on social progress, and at worst a cruel and dangerous obsession which has been responsible for a very great deal of human misery ; no one who has read any history can deny that. But there it is. Some people are, and always will be, really religious ; many more are slightly superstitious. But no religious sectary is so frightful a thing as a Nazi.

In much the same way, I slipped into Socialism—the non-dogmatic, idealistic English Socialism of the early twentieth century —as easily as a duck slips into water. The first step in my conversion was a little book called *The Science of Wealth*, by that generous profound, and long-neglected thinker, J. A. Hobson. It was a book on economics, not Socialism ; but when I read in it the statement, almost casually thrown out, that a certain number of unemployed without wages, living in the last resort on charity and the Poor Law, were a necessary condition of capitalist industry, I was outraged. It must be remembered that in 1911 there was no State unemployment insurance at all (and very little before 1920) ; long spells of sickness or unemployment did mean recourse to the Poor Law, and " the workhouse " was pretty real to anyone who knew anything of nineteenth-century popular literature. I might not have read Beatrice Webb's *Minority Report of the Royal Commission on the Poor Law* ; but I had read and re-read *Oliver Twist* and Mrs Henry Wood.[1] In this mood of altruistic indignation I picked up H. G. Wells's *New Worlds for Old*—under the misapprehension that it was another scientific romance like *The First Men in the Moon*, which had fascinated me years before—and tumbled straight into Socialism overnight.

I was not, of course, the only one so to tumble, though Girton contained few Socialists and I never came across the Cambridge Fabians, who were burgeoning so fiercely during my college days ; I knew nothing of the battle of ideologies, in which my future husband was a protagonist, which was then raging in the Socialist movement, and had no conception that, some time before I got hold of his book, Wells, in an explosion of rage, had flung himself out from the contaminating contact of Shaw and the Webbs and their Fabian fellows. I was just one of the many young who over three generations at least took their hope of the world from that vivid, many-gifted, generous, cantankerous personality,[2] and accepted, not merely once but again and again over forty years, his eager conviction that the ideal of Socialism, which included world government, the abolition of all authority not based on reason, and of all inequality based on prejudice or privilege of any kind, of complete freedom of association, speech and movement, and of an immense increase of human welfare and material resources achieved by all-wise non-profit-making organisation of economic life, both could and would save humanity within a measurable space of time. We also read, of course, and thoroughly enjoyed Bernard Shaw's devastating clowning with the moral and social

[1] The sentimental sensationalism of books like *East Lynne*, combined with her passion for deathbeds, which may be compared with Trollope's obsession with inheritance problems, has obscured the real gift of Mrs Henry Wood for social description and character-drawing ; but readers who doubt it should try *The Channings* or the *Johnny Ludlow* stories. She is due for a revival.

[2] I have paid my own tribute to him in *Makers of the Labour Movement*, and many paid theirs at his memorial gathering. Only, I think, at the very end, when he was all but on his death-bed, did H. G. give up hoping for humanity.

precepts on which we had been brought up, recognised, delightedly, our fathers, uncles, and schoolmasters photographed in Butler's *Way of all Flesh*, enjoyed G. K. Chesterton's scornful attacks on money-power and his thunderous defence of strikers—" The Song of the Wheels, written on a Friday and Saturday in August 1911 " is the best English poem ever written about a strike. We appreciated, too, the writers and essayists of the Liberal-Radical left, men like C. E. Montague of the *Manchester Guardian*, Lowes Dickinson of King's, and E. M. Forster, whose *Howard's End* (a best seller in those undergraduate circles) probed more subtly than the Socialists the make-up of English class society, and contained *inter alia* this passage which I copied out then and have never forgotten :—

> " I'm tired of these rich people who pretend to be poor, and think it shows a nice mind to ignore the piles of money that keep their feet above the waves. I stand each year upon six hundred pounds . . . and as fast as our pounds crumble away into the sea they are renewed. And all our thoughts are six-hundred-pounders, and all our speeches . . . "

We read Noel Brailsford on *The War of Steel and Gold*, and learned from Norman Angell that wars do not pay the victor ; a conclusion which then seemed to indicate plainly that wars would not happen ! But our major prophet, the man who really seemed to want to get somewhere with us, was Wells.

Being a Wellsian Socialist, I naturally became at the same time a feminist ; there, again, however, by so easy a passage that I had no spur to become a militant. I had never in my own life felt any acute sex disability other than the youthful and inescapable one of being a girl in petticoats. My father did not hold with Votes for Women—of course not. But he did not restrain his daughters any more thoroughly than he restrained his sons, and though he strongly opposed the admission of women to degrees at his own University, he paid for their higher education.[1] Nor did I, at this stage, feel any yearning for the sexual freedom demanded by Wells's *Ann Veronica*, whose adventures were then setting the dovecotes to such wild fluttering.

Ann Veronica was the only novel of H.G.'s to receive really abusive reviews, and Beatrice Webb's *Diaries* show that (in spite of the earnest preoccupation of some of the early Fabians with

[1] He wished me to finish at Liverpool, so as to get a degree ; and he sent my young sister to Oxford when degrees for women were obtainable there ; he was not a perfectly consistent man.

"free love") she regarded it with grave reprobation. It is, therefore, both ironical and an important fact of social history that of all the crusades which Wells embraced this one alone has been really successful. His Ann Veronica went off with a married man who in due course became free and made an honest woman of her, and in 1909 this produced a fearful hullabaloo; in 1925, another Wellsian heroine, Christina Alberta, lived a far looser life and the reviewers did not even trouble to mention it. In 1947 I read in *Punch*, of all unimpeachably respectable sources, that "religion apart, there are few who object nowadays to a certain amount of extra-matrimonial truancy"! Taking this casual remark with the doubling of the illegitimacy rate between 1938 and 1946—not a war year—and with the reports of social workers on the proportion of babies conceived before marriage and the number of spinsters who have had sex experience; and comparing it with the great Press agitation of 1914-15 about a probable flood of War Babies which never happened, one can only observe that in this aspect of life, at any rate, a revolution has taken place, and has practically been accepted. "Immorality" among women, in the Victorian sense of the term, is unquestionably far more prevalent than it was thirty or forty years ago; but it is almost impossible to get up any public excitement about it. So *Ann Veronica*, alone of its author's social novels, is covered with the dust of antiquity.

I was not, as I said, at all personally concerned to secure the kind of sexual freedom demanded by Ann Veronica. I had little knowledge of men and met hardly any male undergraduates; the nearest I came to having a boy friend was in my last year when a kind and rather dull young man whom I had known as a small boy took me out to dinner and an A.D.C. performance of *The Alchemist* (which I thought an unduly heavy joke) subsequently came to a stiff chaperoned tea in my rooms, and after I had gone down telegraphed me the news of my First. We corresponded at rather long intervals for a while until he, like so many others of 1914 Cambridge, was killed in France; but beyond a slight feeling of pleased vanity, I cannot say that the association meant anything to me. My emotions were far more deeply stirred by the Jewish girl I mentioned earlier; and this state of mind was true of many more of the 1914 inhabitants of Girton, and even of Newnham,[1]

[1] "Even," because Newnham is only a quarter of a mile from King's Parade. Men were that much more accessible to the Newnhamite. But see M. A. Hamilton's *Remembering My Good Friends*, for an account of an earlier, but equally sexless Newnham.

than anyone coming to maturity after 1918 would believe. We were, for the most part, only schoolgirls grown a bit bigger, not yet young women.

So propaganda about free love meant little to me. Nor did propaganda about The Vote mean very much more. I thought that the anti-suffragists were wrong and their arguments, if taken seriously, insulting ; but I had not then learned to be exasperated, as Virginia Woolf and Rose Macaulay, to take two out of many examples, were exasperated, at the attitude adopted by our society to women in work and in public life. This attitude, which has not changed nearly so much as the attitude to sexual freedom, derives, I believe, from a combination of Athenian democracy, with its contempt for women, Roman patriarchal law, and Christian asceticism drawn from the Near East, with the material conditions under which women entered paid employment during the Industrial Revolution. It is not easy to explain to a man, even an intelligent and sympathetic man, why the habit of regarding women as something odd, irrelevant, incomprehensible, tiresome—anything but ordinary fellow-creatures with whom one could co-operate in matters other than Love and the Family—should be so infuriating, and in a brief paragraph I shall not even try.[1] I would merely observe that it *is* infuriating, and even in 1947 was strong enough to cause the creatures to receive with grave scepticism the explanations, however economically impeccable, that the Labour Cabinet could not accede to the Labour movement's demand for the instant fulfilment of pledges about equal pay ; rightly or wrongly, they heard behind the arguments the echoes of earlier tergiversations, and saw the face, not of Dr Dalton, but of Mr Asquith forty years earlier explaining just why Liberal pledges about the Vote must be broken. Whatever generalisations can be made about women being unsuitable for this and that—and among all the nonsense that is talked and written there are some that are sound—it seems to me that the attitude *as a whole* is both wrong and maddening, very different, for example, from that of the Soviet Union, which has not gone back to any extent from the equalitarian line it took up at the Revolution.[2] In 1911-1914 I was opposed to this attitude, and supported where it came my way the right of women to work at anything they chose and hold any offices open to men ; but it did not come my way very often.

[1] I have said something more about it in my book on *Marriage* (1938).

[2] Whether this is " Communist policy " or " the Russian character " does not much matter ; the point is that it is *possible* to have a different national attitude.

I was more concerned in growing up in other ways—in " commencing poet " and being taught about clothes. My mother had taught me little—as even those who have loved her best will admit, she had not much knowledge to impart. I had now an Allowance of £20 per annum, all in, and bought an Inexpensive Silk Evening Frock fastened with press-studs (instead of the multitudinous and elaborate hookings which meant that you could not get dressed or undressed without assistance) which leapt undone in one single popping when I spoke too eagerly in College debate ; and as poet I was able to add to it by winning some prizes in that great nursery of young Edwardian *littérateurs*, the Competition Page of the Saturday *Westminster Gazette*. I won my first two guineas for a new poem in the style of *The Shropshire Lad*, and under the guidance of a senior friend used the prize to help in the purchase of a new outfit—a grey suit with a " hobble skirt " of ankle length, *grey* stockings and shoes instead of black (very daring), a round grey hat with a thin upstanding feather some eight inches tall, and a grey veil dropping to the tip of my nose. Earlier veils were black ; they covered the face and were knotted under the chin, which was awkward when one had a sneezing cold. Looking back, I should say the outfit was pretty ugly, and the hobble skirt one of the most ungraceful fashions ever known ; but at least I did not have to buy a great whale-boned corset with steel busks. The fashion for a wasp-like waist with bulges above and below died out while I was still at school; late Edwardian women could retain their own lines, more or less.

The stiff high collars had gone, too, together with the ridiculous bits of metal called " collar supports," designed to make neck-pieces of lace or other soft material stand up to one's ears as though they were stiff ; and the starch which had made the summer cotton frocks of my childhood a source of much pain was losing its sway. Colours, for everyday as well as " best " clothes, were becoming much more variegated, though the triumphs of rayon and coal-tar dyes which have brought the working-class girl so much nearer to the sartorial level of her better-off sister were still in the future ; no one, for example, had yet thought of a brightly coloured raincoat. Games and cycling had loosened tight clothes and shortened skirts, which no longer needed to be " held up " when crossing a muddy road. Tennis shorts and sunbathing suits were still a long way off ; the female skin was not yet judged suitable for public exhibition except in the evening, when a great deal of it was regularly exposed. Girls in the years before 1914 wore a great deal more clothes than girls of to-day ; but they were not wadded and padded as their mothers had been.

PART THREE

WAR AND MARRIAGE, AND POST-WAR

Chapter Five

I LEFT Cambridge in June 1914, having rejected a suggestion of my father's that I should stay for a fourth year, for no better reason than that my friends, including the Jewish girl, would nearly all have gone down, and I could see nothing but dust and ashes in the prospect of returning in October as one of a handful of "has-beens." (I was then just twenty-one.) I retired, as it seemed to me then, from active participation in the world to a quiet domestic existence, varied by the writing of long letters and very minor poetry,[1] in Liverpool. My father then proposed that I should do a year's Geography at the University (Why Geography? I don't know) and so get a degree there. I thought the prospect most uninviting; but I was spared the necessity of a battle. For in August I wrote to Miss Jex-Blake at Girton, asking if she could find me a job; and when in September a telegram arrived at Criccieth, where the family was holidaying, inviting me to fill a gap as junior classical mistress at St Paul's Girls' School, no patriotic parent could reasonably stand in the way of his daughter's going out to work.

The last weeks of that July I spent at a farmhouse at Thornton-in-Lonsdale, with my brother Ray. After our squabbling youth, he and I had become deeply reconciled, largely, I must admit, through the influence of Phyllis Reid,[2] who had stayed with us on more than one occasion. Phyllis, who was always far more attractive, in every conceivable way, than I was, who possessed in abundance what we had not yet learned to call either S.A., or It, or Oomph, was ready to take on anything in trousers,[3] and, much to my surprise,

[1] I *like* what poetry I have written. But others, save a few of my friends, do not; and Naomi Mitchison (who should know) once explained to me why it wasn't poetry at all. So I suppose it isn't.

[2] Ray, on reading this, remarked that the change was at least partly due to the effect of Confirmation, and that he was very much disconcerted when a pious kindness began to replace the guerrilla warfare to which he was accustomed. If that is correct, my Christianity must have gone for a while deeper than I recollect.

[3] Her kind, friendly, and determinedly feminist mother later charmed my most unfeminist father to the extent that he invited her to Witness His Will, and offered to Show Her How. Mrs Reid, business manager for many women's societies, considerately restrained her amusement.

treated my fifteen-year-old brother as a social asset rather than a nuisance. This opened my eyes to his possibilities ; it also naturally caused him to fall in love with her in due course. They had a charming brief idyll on the Welsh hill-tops, conducted partly by means of mutual instruction in foreign tongues. Ray taught Phyllis how to say in Greek, " There are nine lecherous young men waiting for me in the market-place " ; and she reciprocated with some equally suitable phrase in German. The idyll was brief ; Ray was far too young and Phyllis far too well-provided with admirers for it to come to anything. But while it lasted it was good for the Postgate family, at least.

These two Postgates walked from their farmhouse through the Yorkshire dales, up to the great saucer which is the top of Ingleborough, peered apprehensively down the deep " pot-holes " in the limestone explored by spelæologists, returned of an evening to the enormous meals which Yorkshire housewives then thought suitable—" I'm sorry you didn't like your pudding," said ours of a monster on which four helpings each had made no apparent impression—and talked continuously about poetry, life, Socialism, and the world. Ray was by that time a full-blooded Socialist, far better informed on the texts than I was myself ; and he was educating me. We agreed that the British Admiralty's offer to stop building ships if the Germans would also was an obvious attempt by a stronger power to trap a weaker one, that war was wicked, ridiculous and unprofitable, and should be prevented, preferably by general strikes of the working classes. We had no idea that, when we came down from our fell-tops and back to Liverpool, we should walk into a world that was all but already at war.

The stunned astonishment of the population of Britain in August 1914 has been time and again described ; but every year it grows more difficult to believe. The generation of 1939, provided by newspapers and radio with year-to-year and month-to-month pictures of the Nazi and Fascist forces literally striding towards a pre-announced attack on the rest of Europe, shown by horrific books and horrific films that the war which was coming would be immeasurably worse than the last and would destroy the whole of civilisation in agony, so that Neville Chamberlain's broadcast on September 3rd came almost as a relief from tension, notwithstanding the immediate wail of the sirens all over London—how can they possibly imagine a situation in which people of all sorts went off for their Bank Holiday week-end with no idea that anything bigger was at hand than another " outrage " of militant suffragettes or, at the worst, a totally unnecessary civil war in Ireland caused by the blind obstinacy of politicians and their reckless invocation of unreasoning nationalist passions whose calamitous nature we did not really discover until many years afterwards?

There must certainly have been some, other than denizens of the Foreign Office, who saw the danger—men like Brailsford, for example, who had had experience of the Balkan cockpit; but their words did not reach even the fringes of the general public. What did reach it were "German scares" in the newspapers. I remember "WE WANT EIGHT [DREADNOUGHTS] AND WE WON'T WAIT" as a headline, and a serial in the *Daily Mail* by William Le Queux about a German landing in England, which would have been more impressive, even as a scare, if the same writer had not written up much the same plot a dozen years earlier with the French as villains. We treated them all as fairy-stories, and so did the "serious" journals which we read. When, at the end of June, I went to stay in Donegal with the Ernest Franklins in their lovely summer house of Glenalla, set high on the wooded and boggy hills between Lough Swilly and Mulroy Bay—my first experience of country-house life—the papers carried little but the disputes about the third Home Rule Bill, the Government's suggestion to leave Ulster out for five years, and "stories" about the antics of the rival Irish armies,[1] and the chief concern of my hostess was that, as I was to go home on the twelfth of July, Orange Day, the anniversary of "Boyne Water," I should not get damaged in a fracas at Omagh or Belfast. And that was fourteen days after the murder at Sarajevo—I assume I must have seen a report of the latter, but do not remember paying it any particular attention.

When the war did come, this ignorance bore fruit in the wildest confusion of thought and action. People were violently somersaulted from one opinion to another. It is often forgotten that up to the very last moment about half the Cabinet and I should think over half the country, including almost the whole of the organised Labour

[1] I and my friends were Home Rulers, naturally; we felt sympathetic and guilty about the oppression of Ireland by Great Britain, and were rightly shocked at the behaviour of those lunatic anarchists, Edward Carson, "Galloper" Smith who became Lord Birkenhead, and Andrew Bonar Law, who died an ex-Prime Minister with his responsibility for Irish (and English) blood conveniently forgotten. But I was not a very hot Home Ruler, because I could not believe in the coercion of Ulster. This was partly due to my knowing a Belfast girl at college and discovering with my own eyes and ears the wild impenetrable glare and the fierce intransigeant language of your whole-hearted nationalist. I have met it many times since, like it no better and fear it more than I did in 1913. But I think that if I, at twenty, could recognise that Ulster could not be coerced and that it would be both wrong and hopeless to try, Asquith and Lloyd George might have recognised it also.

movement, was against war. Horatio Bottomley's *John Bull* produced a poster which screamed "TO HELL WITH SERVIA!" and the Labour Party, trying to act up to its pledges as part of the International Socialist movement, summoned a great conference to consider ways and means of stopping the war. By the time that conference met, it found itself considering, instead, ways and means of upholding working-class standards of life in wartime; and, only a few weeks later, *John Bull* was screaming with no less fervour "TO THE TOWER WITH LANSBURY!"—the pacifist. For in the meantime the Germans had invaded Belgium; King Albert had sent us his dignified and moving S.O.S., and the great majority of those who at the beginning of August were pacifist or "non-interventionist" now eagerly *wished* to go to war. If of military age, they rushed to recruiting-offices ludicrously ill-equiped to receive them—the more eagerly since they all wanted to get at the wicked Germans right away, to be in Belgium within the week, and in Berlin before Christmas. Hardly any of them heeded Kitchener's sombre warning of a three-year struggle, or doubted that Britons, half-trained or totally untrained, could teach barbarians, and murderers of Edith Cavell [1] a good lesson, once they had made up their minds to fight in a just cause. It is easy to smile at them, drilling in their workaday clothes with bits of wood to simulate rifles, and singing "Tipperary" and "Keep the Home Fires Burning," in shocking ignorance of what was in store for them; but it is not very seemly in a generation which managed to persuade itself that Hitler had missed the bus and drivelled about hanging its washing on the Siegfried Line.

The percentage of recruiting in the early days was certainly highest among the young men of the middle class, the university and public-schoolboys, who joined up instantly,[2] and who perished

[1] Who, in 1915, was shot for the undoubted offence, under military law, of aiding soldiers of the Allied Armies to return to the front. But in those far-off days women were not shot by civilised Powers, and the Germans had a very bad Press. See the chapter on Edith Cavell in my *Women of To-Day* (1938).

[2] Some, if Rupert Brooke is to be trusted, found in the call to arms a psychological release from the sense of purposelessness which was generated in sensitive minds by the social troubles of pre-war England, and which could not be assuaged, as once, by reading libertarian verse from *Songs Before Sunrise*. "No more," wrote Sir Henry Newbolt, a much-recited poet in his day:—

"No more to watch by Night's eternal shore,
With England's chivalry at dawn to ride;
No more defeat, faith, victory—O! no more
A cause on earth for which we might have died."

Brooke and his contemporaries found their cause; nowadays causes to die for, and men who die or kill for them, are distressingly common. But the sentiment was real enough.

in such numbers as subalterns at Loos, Hill Sixty, or in the early battles of Ypres, as the University Air Squadrons perished in the Battle of Britain. (Had I been a man, I should almost certainly have been carried into the army on a surge of emotion.) It was pretty high, indeed, in all classes; the number of miners, for example, who went into the army and had afterwards to be got out again, with great difficulty, in order to keep the war industries fed with coal, was very impressive. But, in contrast to 1939, the feeling was not universal, even after the invasion of Belgium, although there was no Communist Party to lay down an opposition line. In all classes there was some resistance. In the Cabinet, John Morley and John Burns resigned their posts, and put an end to their political careers, sooner than take part; at the other end of the scale a good handful of the working men, particularly engineers on the Clyde and miners in South Wales, who had been especially class-conscious before the war, felt that, whatever statesmen might say, one government was pretty well as bad as another when it came to looking after the ordinary day-to-day interests of the people, and that, whoever won, the workers would be the losers unless they stood to their rights meantime—in 1939, of course, it was as plain as the nose on your face what would happen to anybody's rights if Hitler won. With them stood the religious pacifists, Quakers of the left, Christadelphians and odder sects, "straight" pacifists such as Philip Snowden, Fred Jowett, and Clifford Allen, and some middle-class Socialists like my brother Ray, who had taken seriously the resolutions of the International, and believed that the war was an Imperialist war on both sides and that it was the duty of Socialists to refuse to vote war credits or to serve in any way. So far as I remember, only Karl Liebknecht in Germany, and of course Lenin and his Bolsheviks—who had not the smallest temptation to die for the Tsar—reciprocated.

Out of these groups came the conscientious objectors of later years. Conscription did not arrive until 1916, after every expedient, including solemn promises *not* to introduce conscription, had been used to man the armies with volunteers; but right from the start any critics of the war suffered a good deal of sporadic persecution by victims of war hysteria. They were booed and pelted, served with white feathers by excited young women, and subjected, particularly as the news of Mons and Charleroi began to come through and it appeared that our army and the French armies were not marching on Berlin but rather running away from it, to a barrage of untrue and idiotic "atrocity stories" about children with their hands cut off by the Germans, priests tied upside-down to the clappers of their own bells, dead bodies boiled down for fat, and the like. (It was a misfortune that the subsequent exposure of *all* these stories as lies conditioned some muddled souls into rejecting any atrocity story whatsoever and so led them to deny or to discount up to the last any reports, however factual, about the doings of the Nazis.)

This, as I say, was mostly hysteria, the simple reaction of people whose world had tumbled to pieces and did not look like putting itself together in any reasonable time; and, on looking back, I find that one of the greatest differences between the first and the second world wars, in England, is the comparative lack of hysteria in the latter. In 1914, people, in their ignorance and astonishment, seemed literally not to know what to think or what to do, except join up. The Government closed the banks to prevent a panic run on them. It was a good thing they did; but it did not prevent a panic run upon grocers' shops by a disgracefully large number of the well-to-do, who thought they were in danger of starvation and rushed off to lay in stones of flour and sides of bacon, much of which, I am glad to say, went bad in the hot August weather. Some, with more reason, thought that there would be widespread unemployment and distress—there was some, until the war industries had got into their stride—and hastily got up Funds and started workrooms; some, with equal goodwill but more romanticism, offered to take in any number of Belgian refugees, and often repented very quickly when they discovered that their guests were not heroes but ordinary rather unattractive creatures who grumbled at English coffee and the heating in English homes. Others developed spy mania of the most ludicrous and/or pernicious kinds, breaking the windows and looting the stocks of small shopkeepers who had the misfortune to bear foreign names, denouncing German governesses to the police, and smelling out mysterious signalling stations. One such lady, a friend of my mother's, visiting a soldier nephew who was quartered in the Tower of London, caused him acute shame by loudly asking the Beefeater at the entrance where she could see Prince Louis of Battenberg,[1] who, she averred, was locked up there. Others believed and passed on the wildest stories, of which the Russian army corps which was *known* to have travelled the length of Britain " with snow on their boots," and the angels who appeared at Mons, are the best remembered, and the most socially revealing the " war baby " scare, when virtuous people predicted that within nine months there would be a flood of illegitimate children and got up a fund for them.

[1] Father of Earl Mountbatten.

For there were *no* war babies—or practically none; the illegitimacy rate did not rise nearly as much as it did during the late war, when there was no public outcry. But the apprehensiveness of those good ladies discloses an attitude to the working classes—it was the wives of privates who were going to have all the bastards—which has completely passed away. Emissaries of the War Office, in 1914-15, put East End soldiers' wives through insulting inquisitions about their morals before they would allow them to draw their legal separation allowances[1]; they would not have been allowed to do that in 1939-40. Nor would employers, and the well-off generally, have dared, as they did in 1914, to think and talk of the workers, particularly the organised workers, as though they were all potential traitors and would sabotage the war effort if they could, and get as much as possible for themselves out of it, if they could not. Hence came the tales, endemic throughout the war, of the wives of miners and munition workers who *wore fur coats and bought grand pianos*; generally told by people who, apart from the awful and increasing shortage of cheap maidservants, were doing very well themselves; hence, too, pontifications like this of *The Engineer*, a journal of the engineering employers, when discussing dilution of labour :—

> " The fact of the matter, is, really, not that women are paid too little, but that *men are paid too much* for work that can be done without previous training. Everyone knows now that . . . *the whole argument of high wages based on long training has gone by the board.*"

If this remark, produced at a time when the Trade Unions were vainly struggling to secure a minimum of a pound a week for the women dilutees and when great numbers of the men who were " paid too much " were away fighting in France, is not an incitement to class-war, I do not know what is; and it did not stand alone by any means.

Not everyone, of course, was afflicted with hysteria, or we should never have got on with the war at all; and the first frenzied manifestations died down as people gradually adjusted themselves. But all through, or so it seems to me, hysteria was very near the surface and liable at any moment to break through. Pacifist speakers always ran a risk of being mobbed; Bertrand Russell was summarily deprived of his fellowship at Trinity. Trade Unionists and shop stewards were always enemies of their country. And there sprang up from time to time fantastic nightmarish

[1] See Sylvia Pankhurst, *The Home Front* (1933).

stories, like that of a mysterious Black Book containing the names of *forty-seven thousand* traitors and perverts (including Mr Asquith !), which fired the weak head of one Pemberton Billing, and actually wafted him into Parliament on a wind of popular excitement—though neither the Black Book nor even a page of the entries in it were ever produced in public. Even at the very end, the rejoicings at the Armistice had a wild note of unreasoned shrieking which was not heard again until the days of Munich.

It must be remembered, however, that on Armistice Day, unlike VE Day, we did really believe that war was over and could never return, because its fruits had been so patently terrible. The immediate impact of the casualty lists was quite enough to turn anyone hysterical. In 1914 there was no cushioning period of Sitzkrieg or phoney war ; almost at once there began to appear the long ambulance trains, the cripples in hospital blue, and the lists of killed, wounded and missing which took up columns of small print in *The Times*. (The French, of course, were killed in much larger numbers—a fact which deeply affected the policy of French governments right up to 1940 ; in this last war, as we should not allow ourselves to forget, the Western powers were much more economical with their human material, and it was Russians who died in millions.) Nor was there then the insulating factor of distance between home front and battle front, or security silence about destination. " Leave-trains " from Victoria, packed with soldiers, were seen off by wives and sweethearts bidding what might easily be a last farewell, for within forty-eight hours you might receive the War Office telegram announcing that the man was dead.[1] This narrow margin between vigorous life and muddy and gangrenous death produced an atmosphere heavily charged with emotion—for many years afterwards I could not hear a gramophone playing " Pack Up Your Troubles " or " Ev'ry Little While " without a catch of the breath, so often had they been put on " once more before it's time to go." And this emotional charge, it seems, transferred itself easily to other issues where the emotion was not direct and authentic, but forced ; hence the terrible recruiting speeches, the nauseating letters to the Press from people who wanted to " give their sons "—or other people's sons—to shoot strikers, or to send conscientious objectors to the Front, and

[1] " Embarkation leave," this time, had nothing like the same poignancy ; one did not know when, or whither the embarker was going, or indeed whether he was going at all. One friend of mine, arriving home on his *third* embarkation leave, was constrained to apologise for being so like Dame Nellie Melba making her positively last appearance.

shocking statements by prominent gentlemen to the effect that the war was a " crusade of Christ against the Devil." It must be remembered, too, that in that war the general public never really feared defeat, not even in the black " back to the wall " days of March, 1918, when the German army made its last great break-through ; they never even contemplated it. There was nothing like the sharp and evident peril of 1940 to steady the nerves and silence the screamers.

Chapter Six

1.

IN my own life, the war is not one period, but two—the first when I was still an adolescent, though on the surface a school teacher supporting myself in London, and the second, after Ray had gone to prison, when I found my political home, gave up school-teaching, and got engaged and married all within a couple of years.

The first period began in September, 1914, when I travelled up from Criccieth to a not-yet-darkened London,[1] to St Paul's Girls' School. Though very much alarmed at first by trying to discipline a form of girls of fourteen to sixteen, who seemed to me so little younger than I was myself, and who very much resented the disappearance of my well-beloved predecessor, I did not dislike teaching in itself—in fact I liked it very much. I was regarded, I believe, as a very promising starter, and discovered in myself an incurable didacticism. In one form or another, I have gone on teaching ever since.

I found St Paul's, with its high scholastic standards, infinitely superior to Roedean. But I did not like the atmosphere of staff-rooms. I must believe that my colleagues were not all infinitely old, though several of them were certainly on the elderly side ; but to me they seemed, with one or two exceptions, to be rapidly qualifying for their old age pensions, and their war-knitting and their conversation about patriotism, the need for turning taps off in wartime, and the progress of the girls under their care, extremely tedious. The staff were encouraged to develop a maternal attitude to the girls ; in my time you stayed in charge of the same form for four years on end, as they went up the school ; and on one occasion a mistress of unusual unsophistication, observing the father of a member of her form seat himself opposite her in a bus, leaned forward and greeted him brightly with the words, " I think you're the father of one of my children ! " I was too young to feel maternal to the Paulinas ; in fact, I was altogether too young and coltish for the staff-room, and was always getting into mild trouble for lacking dignity, sitting on the table while talking to girls, and so forth.

[1] It never became " blacked-out " ; but later on we were supposed to curtain our windows and the London street-lamps were shaded, with rather beautiful effects when they swung among trees on a windy night. Only in the eastern counties was it really black after dark—I once got completely lost in Cambridge, my own home-town, and ended up in the police-station, which had the only light showing !

I was very conscious of this, particularly when at the end of my first term I exhibited my youthfulness by catching *measles*, of all things, and being despatched by an indignant landlady to the London Fever Hospital, which was then suffering either from incompetent running or an early war-shortage of staff.

I ought to make it clear, however, that I had nothing really to complain of. None of the staff were unkind, not even the die-hard old French mistress with the squint and the peculiar voice, who wore her superannuated tweed jacket *underneath* her blouse in order to keep warm ; and some did much to enlarge my horizon. Ethel Moor was a Fabian and a free-thinker ; she took me to her week-end cottage in the Chilterns, where we ate nuts and cheese in the company of a short square woman with a bright red face and a determined manner—Miss Mary Hankinson, teacher of games and gymnastics, who for so long managed the Fabian Summer School, captained its cricket team and did her stern best to force its more unruly elements to go to bed by eleven o'clock. They described to me a wickedly subversive young man who was doing his best to ruin the Fabian Society and thwart and hamper the great Webbs ; his name, they said, was G. D. H. Cole. Lucy Macirone took me to concerts ; the mother of one of my " children," who is now Lady Beveridge, asked me out to meet Persons of Consequence, and once organised a unique evening picnic in the Port of London, when we ate our meal sitting on the lid of a barge outside Wapping Old Stairs and afterwards climbed up the tower of Limehouse Church and saw St Paul's dark against the western sky. Vera Volkhovsky, the slim dark fierce gym mistress, daughter of the great Russian revolutionary, Felix Volkhovsky—she had come to England at eight years old, hugging a vast doll stuffed with revolutionary documents—took me into her flat for a year, and taught me a good deal about life and literature ; she was, naturally, a radical herself in many ways, but lacked entirely the woolly sentimentalism which is unfortunately characteristic of so many British and American radicals. I had quite a lot done for me, and I was not deeply affected by the war. I had no close ties of affection with anyone who had gone to it, war restrictions bore lightly on me, and my 1914 patriotism had already almost faded away ; like a great many others, by the beginning of 1916 I simply wanted the war to be over, somehow. But I was rather lonely ; with the exception of Phyllis Reid, Stella Bowen, the artist from Australia who lived with her, and one or two others, I had few companions of my own age ; digs in London were dreary after dark, and I was getting tired of the classics.

2.

It was in the spring of 1916 that the change came. The Military Service Act was in force, and Ray, a scholar in his first year at St John's College, Oxford, was called up. Of course he refused to go, thereby reducing his father to apoplectic fury ; and, after he had failed to secure exemption and was brought before the magistrates as a mutinous soldier, I went up to Oxford to be by his side. At that date it needed a fair amount of courage to be a C.O. Though the Military Service Act allowed exemption on grounds of conscience, it was regrettably vague in its definition of either " conscience " or " exemption " ; and the decision as to whether a man had or had not a valid conscientious objection, and if he had, whether he was to be exempted from all forms of war service or from combatant service only, or something between the two, was left to local tribunals all over the country, who had no common standard or guidance, and generally—though not by any means invariably—took the view that every fit man ought to want to fight, and that anyone who did not was a coward, an idiot, or a pervert, or all three. Objection on religious grounds was for the most part treated with respect, particularly if the sect had a respectable parentage ; Quakers usually came off lightly, and were permitted to take up any form of service they felt able to do ; though Quakers who were " absolutists," *i.e.*, who refused to aid the war effort in any way whatever, were apt to be jailed after a long and futile cross-examination by the Tribunal on how they would behave if they found a German violating their mother. But non-Christians who objected on the grounds that they were internationalists or Socialists were obviously traitors in addition to all their other vices, and could expect little mercy. They would be sent to barracks, and thence to prison—and then nobody quite knew what would happen to them. There was talk of despatching them to France, unarmed, and shooting them there for mutiny ; this was entirely contrary to the provisions of the Act and was eventually prevented, though not until Gilbert Murray had made personal appeals to Asquith, the Liberal Prime Minister. They might be sent to a mild early version of a concentration camp, at one of which a C.O. had just died when my brother's case came up. They might get any kind of treatment, so far as anyone knew. Subsequently a sort of routine procedure was established, by which a good many who were not absolutists were released after a spell of imprisonment for work in bone factories, on the land, or the like ; but at the time it was a nerve-racking prospect for boys of nineteen who had never before been on the wrong side of the law.

Admittedly, the C.O.s were a difficult problem; the logic of their position was in effect anarchist, since they claimed the absolute right of private judgment. The British public, unused to positive compulsion of any kind but naturally law-abiding, had not understood the two ideas that by 1939 it had thoroughly grasped; first, that a man who is willing to risk prison rather than go into the army is not likely to be a very profitable soldier, and it is therefore uneconomic to try and compel him; secondly, that a modicum of anarchists, of people who simply say "I won't," and deny the most convincing arguments that their rulers can bring forward, is a political necessity, an indispensable leaven to maintain health in the State.[1] And as the C.O.s of 1916 were of so many differing types, and gave so many different reasons for their behaviour, it is not surprising that those who had to deal with them on the spot sometimes got very confused, and that some of them suffered considerable injustice, with the result that sympathy for their point of view and disquietude about the "war for democracy" steadily increased.

I did not realise, until I had heard the old man with the long beard hanging over the edge of the Bench pronounce sentence, and seen Ray disappear through a kind of pantomime trap-door in the floor,[2] what a large slice of England there was that was either actively opposed to the war or very doubtful about its conduct; but it is almost literally true that when I walked away from the Oxford court-room, with Gilbert Murray solicitously holding an umbrella over my head (though it was not raining), I walked into a new world, a world of doubters and protesters, and into a new war—this time against the ruling classes and the government which represented them, and *with* the working classes, the Trade Unionists, the Irish rebels of Easter Week, and all those who resisted their governments or other governments which held them down. I found in a few months the whole lot which Henry Nevinson used to call "the stage-army of the Good"—the I.L.P., the Union of Democratic Control, the Fellowship of Reconciliation, the *Daily Herald* League, the National Council of Civil Liberties—and,

[1] Germany for many years contained far too few anarchists; that is one of the reasons why a strong government in Germany has proved so great a menace. In Spain, on the other hand, anarchists appear to be over-numerous—on both sides the political blanket.

[2] Not to remain incarcerated for long, as it turned out. For, being a long thin, nervous creature, he fell ill shortly after his conviction. The authorities, not being Himmlers, suddenly took fright lest he die on their hands; it was suggested that the Bishop of Oxford might make a speech in the House of Lords; and after a brief interval for "saving face," he was released unconditionally and not called up again for a couple of years.

above all, the Guild Socialists and the Fabian, later the Labour, Research Department.

As on previous occasions, my intellectual conversion took place so easily that I cannot recollect even thinking about it ; once the State had taken my brother it lost his sister's vote automatically. But I very well remember the material circumstances. Ray had told me that, if he were taken, I must as it were, keep the flag flying, and that I should go and search out one J. Alan Kaye, an Oxford friend of his who was unfit for military service and therefore certain to be available. So I did, and was asked out to dinner in a small restaurant in Victoria Street. I arrived, somewhat keyed-up and expecting to meet a leader of revolt, who would look, I supposed, rather like Ramsay MacDonald—I found the ugliest little man I had ever set eyes on, three or four inches shorter than myself, with thick-lensed spectacles, thick lips, nails bitten to the quick, and a disreputable old felt hat. Anything less like a leader I had never seen.

After I had recovered a little from the shock, I found that the strange object was talking to me in a kind and friendly manner, was promising faithfully to fulfil whatever Ray's last commissions had been, and was inviting me to join in the good work, to come, when I was free of the class-room, and do some voluntary work at the Fabian Research Department. Of course I promised, and on a September evening I duly arrived at a dingy house in Tothill Street, Westminster (it has since been pulled down) labelled *Fabian Society*, walked up to the second floor, tentatively opened a door, and disclosed a small room filled with smoke, several very tall men, and one smaller man who said to me in a strong Scots accent, " Will ye come in or will ye go out ? Don't stand there like a Perri at the gate o' Paradise ! " Naturally, I went out, and remained downstairs until kind Kaye turned up to my rescue, and re-introduced the new voluntary worker. And that was my first acquaintance with " The Movement."

Two of the tall men were G. D. H. Cole, Honorary Secretary of the Department and adviser to the Amalgamated Society of Engineers—in which capacity, as someone remarked with amusement, he secured exemption from military service by doing his best to make the Munitions Acts unworkable—and William Mellor, later editor of the *Daily Herald* and then a C.O. on the run ; the little Scot was Robin Page Arnot, the paid secretary, who accepted his new recruit with tempered gratitude, and set her to work on a Gazetteer of Trade Union branches, which was being slowly and laboriously compiled by copying out from innumerable Trade

Union reports the names and addresses of branches on to sheets of paper geographically arranged. It sounds about as dull an assignment as anyone could have invented ; I will only say, as evidence of my state of mind, that I worked on the thing for many weeks, was immensely proud when by discovering that Finsbury Park was not located in Finsbury I caused the reorganisation of several of its sheets,[1] and that my pleasure in this work and in the comradeship arising out of it was so keen that before Christmas I had incontinently resigned from my safe pensionable teaching post and by New Year was employed by the Fabian Research Department on a job with no security and no prospects, and a salary of two pounds a week. When I handed in my resignation, Miss Frances Gray, the impressive High Mistress of St Paul's, asked me whether I had considered making provision for my old age. I had not, and at twenty-three I did not care. I had become part and parcel of " the Movement."

3.

" The Movement," which became my second University, taking up the major part of my time and thought, sleeping and waking, for the next few years, was a strange and live thing, vivid now in the recollection of anyone who was ever a part of it. It was neither a party nor a defined or organised society, but rather a nucleus of " comrades " (to use a word which has since become deplorably narrowed in its meaning) to which were loosely attached a great number of sympathisers. It had its being within an older and wider movement, of Socialism and Labour ; but within that movement it was clearly distinguishable by its own characteristics.

First, it was not merely Socialist, but Guild Socialist ; that is to say, it believed and preached the gospel laid down by A. R. Orage,[2] S. G. Hobson, Cole, Mellor, and others, for reorganising British economic life on " functionalist " lines, by establishing in each industry self-governing Guilds, based upon Trade Unions and working on capital provided by a socialised state.[3] All who

[1] Arnot, immediately after the war, succeeded in selling the *Gazetteer* to the Ministry of Labour which printed it in three large volumes. This is the only occasion on which I have contributed, even in the most indirect manner, to a Blue Book. But I never heard of anyone consulting it, either then or since.

[2] Editor of the *New Age*, that brilliant weekly which, besides its Guild Socialist contributors, published the writings of Hilaire Belloc, G. K. Chesterton, Arnold Bennett—who, as " Jacob Tonson," gave it some of his finest literary criticism—Michael Arlen, Ezra Pound, and many others. Later, alas, Orage embraced, first Major Douglas's Social Credit fantasies, and afterwards a form of spiritualism, and the *New Age* became, appropriately, the ghost of itself.

[3] For the fullest exposition, see G. D. H. Cole, *Guild Socialism Restated* (1920).

were in " the Movement " were members of the National Guilds League, a propagandist body which on a small and hand-picked membership managed to be immensely active, publishing a number of well-written and persuasive pamphlets, contributing articles with a Guild Socialist slant to any paper which would take them, sending out speakers all over the country, and inducing many branches of Trade Unions and even some national bodies to pass resolutions in favour of National Guilds and/or workers' control in industry.

This success of Guild Socialist propaganda in the later years of the war was not so surprising as it may sound. For notwithstanding the desire of upper-class persons to keep the workers in their proper place, the enormous growth of war industry had combined with the losses of man-power to give these same workers an importance in the country's economy—and a pay packet !—the like of which they had never possessed before. Their leaders were actually consulted by the Government and made members of official Boards, like the Wool Control Board, which were invested with effective power. Arthur Henderson, Secretary of the small and undistinguished Labour Party, was admitted into the War Cabinet—it is true that he was always treated as a poor relation, and in 1917, after he had presumed to disagree with his colleagues over the Russian Revolution, was allowed to resign without protest and without thanks ; but the precedent had been set. More than that, the wartime industrial truce, which forbade under penalty strikes in the industries covered by the Munitions Acts,[1] resulted in the emergence of local unofficial leaders, shop stewards, and the like, men such as Willie Gallacher, David Kirkwood, George Buchanan (both the last-named now Privy Councillors), John Maclean, the " Red Consul " of Glasgow, and Arthur McManus, later secretary of the Communist Party, who developed a great deal of power and initiative, who were mostly Syndicalist, Marxist, or Guild Socialist—on the extreme left, anyway—and were continually clashing with the Government. Kirkwood, who is now one of the mellowest members of the House of Commons, was deported from Glasgow in 1915, for leading a strike at Parkhead Forge.

Here, it seemed, was not merely official Trade Unionism admitted to a share in government, but spontaneously-chosen leaders from

[1] This did not mean that there were no strikes ; more days per annum were lost in industrial disputes in 1914-18, when they were illegal in major industries, than in 1945-48, when they were not. But it did mean that they could not be led by Trade Unionists in official positions.

mine and workshop arising to force it into insurrectionary if not revolutionary paths; and it did not seem to us at all fantastic or Utopian to think of such movements, with Cole and Mellor to act as their guiding philosophers, going forward to set up a Guild Socialist society. Certainly our view of the possibilities was much too optimistic, based on a wartime inflation which soon passed away, and our ideas much too schematic. I remember that one plan envisaged a "Miscellaneous Guild," as if there were any organisable group whose function was to be miscellaneous; nevertheless, however crudely we expressed ourselves, the problem which lay behind all we said, the need to give all working members of society opportunity to play their part in the running of it, remains unsolved to-day. We of "the Movement," needless to say, being young idealists with the minimum of practical experience, rejoiced in the shop stewards' or any other insurrectionary movement, used the *New Age* and Lansbury's weekly *Herald* to cheer on any strike, anywhere, about anything; and were very scornful of the slowness and stupidity, in our eyes, of all persons in official positions. When I first came into the Fabian Research Department, there was a crack current which said, "Trade Unions, like Gaul, are divided into three parts—the officials, the members (who were apathetic or voted the wrong way), and the rank-and-file (to whom we pinned our hopes)." If we had realised the essential truth of that epigram, instead of treating it as a joke, we might have saved ourselves much disappointment in the years to come.

"The Movement" was Guild Socialist; and most, though not quite all of it, worked in the Fabian Research Department, either for love or for very low pay, or as outside advisers. The F.R.D. was, originally, the creation of Beatrice and Sidney Webb. In the years immediately preceding the war, when their magnificent campaign for the abolition of the Poor Law had been "dished," as John Burns put it, by Lloyd George's Insurance Act, they decided that the older political parties were hopeless from their point of view, and that it was necessary to work out, preferably through the Fabian Society, a series of projects for turning Britain into a Socialist country. Beatrice Webb particularly had the idea that a Fabian Research Department would be a good way of utilising the ability of young University men such as Hugh Dalton and Ben Keeling (killed in France) and other Cambridge Fabians, whom she had met at the Fabian Summer School.[1] Unfortunately for her purpose, there had simultaneously entered the Society another group of

[1] See Beatrice Webb, *Our Partnership* (1948).

University young men, principally from Oxford, led by Cole and Mellor, who were Guild Socialists and violently opposed to the extreme State collectivism of the Webbs. Sidney and Beatrice thought "workers' control" pernicious nonsense, and said so; the Guild Socialists thought them wicked old bureaucrats, and staged magnificent ideological battles. I was not present at the historic meeting of the Fabian Society at which a deeply-stirred member of long standing moved "that Mr Cole be a cad," though soon after my initiation I was told the saga of that and other similar Homeric occasions; when I arrived on the scene the Guild Socialists, defeated in the Fabian Society itself, had nevertheless captured and manned the Research Department and had drawn into its orbit the most vigorous of the younger Fabians who had not been swallowed up in the war.

The F.R.D., however, strongly though it repudiated the Webbian philosophy, followed closely the Webbian example of hard work and steady collection of facts. On Trade Unionism, strikes, the course of wages in different trades, and the accumulation of profits, particularly in war industries, it did a colossal amount of work; in addition, it formed itself into an enquiry bureau for Labour organisations, national and local, of all descriptions—the headquarters of the Labour Party not being then equipped to do anything of the kind;[1] it produced a *Monthly Circular* of information on Labour questions which is still published by the L.R.D. of to-day; it read, annotated, and indexed masses of Trade Union and Labour journals, and it kept up an enormous file of press-cuttings whose classification no one but Cole and his assistant Walter Holmes ever really understood. Time and again did I work, pasting and annotating press-cuttings, until the last buses had all gone, and we walked home through the Park and up Regent Street through the shadows made by the shaded street lamps, wondering whether there would be an air-raid before we got home, but never doubting that we had to finish the job. Our task-masters were severe; we were expected always to get our facts right, and to have, at the least, the Webbs' *History of Trade Unionism*, Cole's *World of Labour*, and the names (and initials) of all the principal Trade Unions at our fingertips; and though Arnot had an occasional good word for a middling sort of effort, neither Cole nor Mellor nor Norman Ewer ever appeared to look for anything but faults. It was a good stiff training.

[1] Not until 1919 did the reorganised Labour Party set up a Research Department of its own and a set of advisory committees, of which G. D. H. Cole was for a time general secretary; even then, the cautiousness inevitable in any officially representative body slowed down its efforts.

It was something of an irony that all this anti-Webbian activity was conducted on the premises of the Fabian Society itself, in a nest, as it were, of vociferous cuckoos located between the first-floor office of Edward Pease, the shaggy, growling, elderly Secretary of the Society, and the residence of Mrs Herbert, the caretaker and provider of lunches to the Fabian Commonroom, at the top. We were the bane of both their lives. Pease objected to the noise over his head, to the burning of lights and creating of litter until all hours, and was inclined to accuse us of opening *his* post and abstracting or deliberately mislaying *his* postal orders. Mrs Herbert, with better justification, suspected us of raiding her stores and eating up " Mr Pease's jam " when we worked week-ends ; and there was a running feud between us and elderly Fabians who, having grown rheumatic in the service of the Society, came to sit quietly in its Commonroom and found something between a revolution and a romp going on.

The feud, nevertheless, was far less bitter than anyone attuned to the latter-day observations of Comrades Vyshinsky and Molotov would believe. We abused, but we did not hate ; nor were communications severed. Shaw and the Webbs both sat on the committees of the F.R.D., and Beatrice always displayed a very lively interest in its work. I did not immediately make her acquaintance—I think she was ill when I first took up my appointment. It was not until the early summer of 1917 that there entered the small room where Kaye and I worked side by side (with a desk behind us reserved for the use of the Honorary Secretary), a tall lady wearing a large and very ugly hat, with a beaked nose, a very thin pale face, a harsh high voice, and a bright commanding eye. I was introduced to " Mrs Webb." I thought she looked infinitely old and frail and would probably disintegrate if I sneezed or shouted suddenly (Beatrice, of all people !), and escaped from the room as soon as I decently could. (Long afterwards, I learned that she had sized me up as a possibly attractive young female, and had warned the Honorary Secretary—Cole—not to allow me to entangle the young men in the office.) I was, of course, thoroughly unjust ; my few months in " the Movement " had inoculated me against recognising her quality or her character at the time. I saw only a Bogie-woman, one who wished to deny self-expression to the workers and increases of pay to Fabian research workers ; there was a curious streak of parsimony in the Webbs which led them too often to exploit the willingness of the enthusiast to work for low pay. It was not until some years afterwards that I learned to appreciate either the greatness of the Webbs or their remarkable tolerance of those who differed from them. For the moment, they were on the Wrong Side.

4.

The strength of "the Movement" lay not in its numbers, but in its personalities. Its principal leaders were Cole and William Mellor, who combined to make an almost perfect pamphleteering partnership, Cole with his knowledge of facts—not then quite so overwhelming as it has since become—and his incomparably lucid style, being preserved from dullness or over-intellectuality by William's greater natural understanding of the working-man's mind and his gift for straightforward eloquence. William, bred originally for the nonconformist ministry, a black-haired, broad-shouldered six-footer, with an uglyish sallow face adorned, when he smiled, with the most incongruous dimples, and a magnificently resonant Yorkshire voice,[1] was for many years one of the most effective, though not the least temperamental, of the personalities on the "left." He was one of the original makers of the British Communist Party, and one of the first to leave it; for a time he was editor of the *Daily Herald*, until his innate nonconformity rebelled against the conditions which an official Labour paper, owned by Odhams Press, necessarily imposed upon him, and he helped to found the ill-fated Socialist League in 1932; he died, too young, of pneumonia in the early years of the late war.

Associated with them was Norman Ewer, now the *Daily Herald's* foreign editor, and then a C.O. employed as cowman on the Astor estate at Cliveden—where he was once nearly gored by a bull; he was distinguished from the ruck of us by owning a real establishment, a house in St John's Wood which his lovely Irish wife, Monica, daughter of a radical editor of *Reynolds News*, vainly tried to keep swept of pamphlets, tracts, and other Guild Socialist *débris*—and a whole live baby boy. There was also Rowland Kenney, a soldier, a fierce ex-Syndicalist journalist who had once edited the *Herald*, and is, so far as I know, the only genuine working-man (he was a navvy in his youth) ever to get into the Foreign Office; there was an indubitable scion of capitalism, Maurice Reckitt of Reckitt's Blue, distinguished at croquet, Christian theology, and as a writer of satirical revue. Maurice was our expert on Trade Union journals,

[1] In the autumn of 1938, when, as a member of the Parents' Committee of an impeccably respectable preparatory school, I was helping to present a scheme of evacuation to a mass meeting of parents, I was very much taken aback when a tall looming figure arose from the back of the hall and, wagging a menacing forefinger, announced deeply "That's naat the waay to do it!" It was William; and for the moment I thought I had gone back twenty years.

which he enlivened with clerihews [1] ; his sister Eva, chief organiser of the press-cutting department, later started the successful enterprise of Collet's Bookshops.

Of the " associates " there were an enormous number. I remember particularly W. H. Thompson, solicitor and "absolutist," who spent long terms imprisoned in various jails, which he always said had been of great value to him in his practice, since he had inside knowledge of the kind of treatment which was likely to fall to the lot of his clients. Harry Thompson was a tall handsome athletic fellow, excelling in all games ; he married Joan Beauchamp, a militant left-wing suffragette, and worked up a large and socially very valuable practice in the defence of Trade Unionists, strikers, persons accused of treason or mutiny—and above all in cases of workmen's compensation. He was one of the few men I have known who managed to devote his life to " causes " without ever losing either his sense of humour or his power of enjoying himself ; his death in the summer of 1947 was an irreplaceable loss to the Labour movement. An absolutist of very different type was Clifford Allen (Lord Allen of Hurtwood), the I.L.P.er, founder of the No-Conscription Fellowship, and one of the leaders of the pre-war Fabians of Cambridge. Allen, through his prison sufferings, became the hero of the pacifists ; his saint-like profile and moving eloquence —he, like Mellor, had been trained for the ministry—concealed, as I suspect was the case with more than one of the official saints of the calendar, a sound business instinct and a flair for political management ; he later headed the I.L.P. agitation for " Socialism In Our Time " which so upset MacDonald and caused him to believe that the I.L.P. which made him Prime Minister had also betrayed him. (Subsequently, however, Allen made his peace with his chief and in 1931 followed him out of the Party.)

Of other " associates " I remember Ivor Brown, now associate editor of the *Observer*, and from the *Herald* Will Dyson, its editor George Lansbury, and Francis Meynell ; it is indicative of the small part which our attitude to the war played in our lives that those three, with their very different views, could all work happily together. Dyson was a brilliant biting Australian cartoonist, whose sharp pencil attacked alike financiers, profiteering employers, " safe " Labour and Trade Union leaders, and German military men, with a bitterness unknown in British caricature since Gillray

[1] *E.g.* " The *Shop Assistant*
Is over-persistent.
I cannot trust myself to speak
Of a paper that comes out once a week."

" G.L.," not yet the Mayor of Poplar and leader of a movement to make the rich districts of London contribute to the upkeep of the poor ones,[1] not yet chief of the Labour Party or even in Parliament, was nevertheless set to become father-confessor and Santa Claus to all the most " ornery " spirits of the Left ; he was a strong pacifist on Christian grounds, and was occasionally worried by the eagerness with which his Socialist contributors greeted mild outbreaks of violence in industrial disputes. (His daughter Daisy married my brother Ray.) Francis, son of Wilfrid and Alice Meynell and named after Francis Thompson, was unquestionably the artist among us, in the widest sense of the word. This needs no proving now ; since his Nonesuch Press showed conclusively that lovely books need not necessarily be priced at levels which only rich collectors could afford, Francis has become so fully established as a front-rank printer and designer. He was a printer even then, but we thought of him more as a young man who loved with excitement all the *nice* things in life, who could read poetry and make a pig of himself over good food with more or less equal enthusiasm—the *Herald* once sent him to the Ritz to get copy for an article on how magnificently the rich could guzzle in the fourth year of the war, and nobody could have appreciated the assignment better ! When Francis went to prison as a Socialist-pacifist and hunger-struck, it seemed an emblematic protest of " the liberal arts " against war ; and I would only add a personal note of thanks to the first man who ever seemed to be attracted to me for myself alone—not because he had made a pass at Phyllis Reid and failed. Perhaps " burnishing the ego " of one rather shy young woman is part of an artist's business in life ; at all events it was most reassuring.

Among soldiers I remember, besides Rowland Kenney, Mostyn Lloyd, a few years older than the rest of us, who had served the Webbs so faithfully in the campaign for the break-up of the Poor Law,[2] and who afterwards became head of the Social Science Department of the London School of Economics and a pillar of

[1] This " Poplarism," for which G.L. and his fellow-Councillors went to prison in 1922, aroused great indignation at the time, even among some of his Labour fellows. But the Poplar Councillors won their battle, and twenty-six years afterwards the new system of allotting grants-in-aid in effect extended "Poplarism" over the whole country.

[2] Finally achieved through (*a*) Neville Chamberlain's 1929 Derating Act, (*b*) Lord Beveridge's Report of 1942, and (*c*) the Labour Government's legislation. The whole story is a fine example of what the Webbs' contribution to public life has been, and by what means achieved. People should re-read Beatrice's *Minority Report* to the Poor Law Commission to see for themselves how far her foresight went.

the *New Statesman.* Mostyn was one of the kindest and most charming people I have ever known, and invariably on tap for " good " causes ; but for some reason—possibly because the Webbs had given him too many soul-destroying jobs in his early years—he was deeply pessimistic about the future of any of them. " Oh, Christ ! " I think of Mostyn as saying wearily, " not *another* meeting. All right, I suppose I'll come "—and he always did. I remember Clem Attlee and Hugh Dalton—and a good few soldiers who never came back again ; also Frank Horrabin, the creator of " Japhet," the lifelong foe of Imperialism and the best draughtsman I know of maps for the geographically ill-equipped, who looks (when dressed for the part) exactly like the Mad Hatter, but is neither mad nor bad but sweet all through.

Of civil servants there were many. I recollect particularly Delisle Burns, the historian, who had a job in M.I.5, and used to sidle round our office door at lunch-time—he never lost the physical marks of his early training as a Jesuit—and murmur in a conspiratorial voice, " D'you know what X is at now ? "—X being a higher official in the same department. This was the best grist to our mill, for we regarded it as part of our job to nose out as much advance information as possible about the intentions of the enemy, *i.e.*, the Government ; and on one occasion at least a very valuable pointer for a wage negotiation was presented to us by the quite accidental tapping of a Ministerial telephone call. *Per contra*, we were occasionally favoured with the attentions of Government spies or *agents provocateurs* who, however, got singularly little reward for their pains, since we were not in fact traitors or conspirators or even in touch with conspirators. One such turned up on one occasion and asked to become a voluntary helper in the office. Arnot, who did not like the smell of him, put him in a room by himself and set him to copying out figures of Trade Union branch voting on all manner of issues during the past half-dozen years. After three days, it seemed, he decided the job was unproductive and vanished ; he was subsequently found shot dead in Ireland during the troubles. I assume he was following the same profession in more dangerous surroundings.

I remember leaders of working-class education—Arthur Greenwood ; Alfred Zimmern ; dear Jimmy Mallon of Toynbee Hall, who has never been on time for anything in his life (he broke his agent's heart when he stood for Parliament by always arriving in time for the meeting that had just finished) but who comforted me inexpressibly when I was taken with panic the night before I married ; and (I think) William Temple, who became Archbishop of Canterbury—at least, he was pilloried as a dangerous Bolshevik in a wonderful nightmare of a book called *The Red Network* which bore on its dustcover an enormous scarlet spider's web with Lenin in the middle of it. I remember Trade Unionists—Ellen Wilkinson of N.U.D.A.W., tiny and young and fiery as her hair, flaming with rage because the wife of the secretary of another Trade Union had insisted on "sitting-in" to his (purely professional) discussions with Ellen; a glimpse or two of Mary Macarthur,[1] the one really great personality and orator ever produced in the women's Trade Union movement, telling the world what she was going to do with Lloyd George when she next saw him; many meetings with an Executive member of the A.S.E., which called for tact because the Executive Member, when moved, had only two adjectives, neither of which were in 1917-18 considered suitable for female ears. So this female had in mercy to find an excuse to go out and sit on the landing for a period long enough for our visitor to get off his chest a reasonable number of f———s and b———s. There were many other Trade Unionists, such as Fred Dalley of the Railway Clerks (who has recently reported to the Government on Trade Unionism in the Colonies); Harold Clay, the tramwayman from Leeds, for long second-in-command to Ernest Bevin, and now a member of the Road Transport Executive; George Hicks of the Builders; George Thomson of the Draughtsmen (a strong Guild Socialist and 1946 Chairman of the Trades Union Congress); and many more.

In fact, I could go on for pages saying, "I remember," simply because in those days a very high proportion of Socialists and pacifists under forty, including many who have since become famous, were if not in "the Movement" at least sympathetic to it. There were exceptions, of course. The Webbs, though more friendly than we had any right to expect, could not have been called "sympathetic"; nor was Herbert Morrison, who then hated the idea of functional or any indirect representation like poison—one could hardly say to him, "Metropolitan Water Board" without producing an explosion. Nor were the more single-minded pacifists; Philip Snowden had very little use for us, and we were pretty rude to him, though we would always co-operate temporarily with the pacifists against an official Labour leader. But the generalisation is true on the whole.

[1] Secretary, first of the Women's Trade Union League and then of the National Federation of Women Workers, and chief campaigner against sweating and *causa causans* of the Trade Boards Acts. She died, alas! when she was barely forty; had she lived she would have been an outstanding leader.

These that I have listed were the Great, or the more-or-less great. Below them burgeoned the smaller fry, people like myself and one or two friends I brought in, a collection from the East End who were known as the Bow Brigade, some of Sylvia Pankhurst's working-class suffragettes (including several Lansburys), young C.O.s on the run, and anything up to a score of others, whose work in the Research Department was organised after a fashion by Alan Kaye, my friend and close colleague for two and a half years, and the gentlest and most idealistic of human creatures. Kaye's suicide, in the spring of 1919, because he was literally too good for this (political) world, was the first great personal sorrow I had ever experienced ; my only consolation has been that he was spared the brutalities of a later world which would have assuredly broken his heart if he had lived.

It was the Great who laid down policy, but we small fry who worked in the office and stewarded and sold pamphlets at meetings ; and dined in groups or *en masse* in Soho, selecting our restaurants according to the weight of our purses or to what we could borrow mid-week from the petty cash-box. When rich, we paid two shillings for a dinner with ice-cream *bombe* at Beguinot's in Old Compton Street ; when very rich, we added a nasty fiery drink called *cérises à l'eau de vie.* At week-ends (if the Great released us—I remember at least one Saturday morning when the female members of the staff used their long skirts to conceal under the table a cowering Kaye who rushed upstairs crying, " Cole and Ewer are going to send me to Beaconsfield ! ") we went on long walks in Surrey or Buckinghamshire and declaimed poetry to one another ; we closed all our meetings by singing the songs out of Chesterton's *Flying Inn*, satiric chants written by Cole or Reckitt, and the *Red Flag* to end up.

We had, it seems to me, a remarkable passion for poetry, mostly though by no means exclusively of Edwardian, *i.e.*, near-contemporary date, and I, who had then a good memory, was often called upon by Kaye in particular to repeat pieces from Flecker, Rupert Brooke, Housman, Masefield, Chesterton, and even Kipling ; for up-to-date news, as it were, we went to readings at the Poetry Bookshop started by Harold Monro in an alley near Southampton Row. Modern poetry was not then as *difficult* reading as it has since become ; it was Eliot and Ezra Pound, I believe, who (something like Browning long before them) began the practice of writing poems so allusive that they cannot be understood without a battery of glossary and footnotes. Only the other day a young man showed me his *chef d'œuvre* in which the references and overtones were all but lost on me—who am reasonably widely read. I have no means of judging whether they stir the imaginations of his contemporaries as Flecker's *Golden Journey to Samarkand*—to take a not very top-rank example—did ours ; me they make turn with relief to *John Brown's Body* and Benét's other poems and wish he were not dead.

It will have appeared that we were very young. The Movement proper contained, so far as I remember, nobody over thirty, and hardly any of its members had incomes of any size. As a result, we had scarcely any personal ties ; some of us had homes which we used to sleep in, others lived in digs—oh, those London landladies and their horrible furnished rooms !—or in cheap flats ; in effect, we lived as well as worked together, with our eyes on the job, and almost oblivious of the events of the war—even of air-raids. The air-raids of 1916-18 were, of course, a very different proposition from those of the Luftwaffe ; they were comparatively short, for one thing, and the destruction and loss of life infinitesimal, but they were noisy and sometimes alarming. Most of us took little notice, but Kaye was one of those who disliked them very much, and on the evenings I was with him (which was on the average half the time), when the maroons went off like outsize fire-crackers we would seek cover in some underground place—not the Tube, which was too crowded with frightened and odorous humanity, but in the bar of the Criterion, say, or Oddenino's—we once wrote an enormous poem in pencil on the marble tables at Oddenino's, and completed it before the raid was over. I only remember being really frightened once, in a raid which started just after I had left a girls' club in Stepney. All the lights went out instantly and I was left stumbling in black unfamiliar streets. Suddenly a door opened and framed in a square of light a woman who called, "Come right in, dearie." But I had visions of White Slavers, and stumbled on wildly until I reached the Mile End Road and fell gasping into the comparative safety of an empty stationary tram.

We were very young ; and we were as arrogant as we were young, and contemptuous of anyone with whom we disagreed even on the smallest points. Henry Massingham, the very distinguished editor of the *Nation*, was not the only one to refuse to speak to gatherings of Guild Socialists for the reason that they were such offensive critics. But I should in justice add that we were arrogant because we were public-spirited, deeply convinced that we were right and upholding a righteous cause against embattled might. Though we would not have called ourselves a " thin red line of heroes," being very suspicious of emotional appeals, we did really believe that it mattered enormously for the future of mankind that we should stick up the last press-cutting and check the last significant fact ; we were ready to spend ourselves up to the limit in the service we had voluntarily entered—and who is prepared to say that we were wrong ? Being so dedicated, we were extraordinarily happy, so happy that we never realised it fully, but worked ourselves into states of tremendous agitation over minute differences in the philosophy of Guild Socialism and its application to immediate problems of the day, such as the 1917 *Whitley Report* on Joint Councils for Industry. None of these controversies, however, went really deep ; what split " the Movement " asunder was, alas, the aftermath of the Russian Revolution, which at first we had all hailed with such delight.

5.

We were politically occupied most, if not quite all of our time—and if you have no family-ties and live in cheap digs or flats which you only use for eating breakfast [1] it is astonishing how much time there can be. But we had " leisure " interests. For some it was music, or the Russian Ballet with Massine, or Frederick Ranalow in *The Beggar's Opera* at Hammersmith—one of us saw that performance *nineteen* times—or the wartime revues with Violet Loraine singing " The Gipsy Warned Me," or Alice Delysia and Léon Morton (" *Imitations?* Yes ; somesing moins deesgusting "), or Lee White and Clay Smith in *Cheep*, with Beatrice Lillie singing about " the black-eyed Susans "—nearly all of those for whom we stood in the pit queue are gone now, and their songs forgotten, save for a few exceptions like, " If You Were the Only Girl in the World," which the radio has kept alive.[2] For myself, it was the people I met in or through the Kensington studio where Phyllis lived with Stella Bowen and gave spasmodic dancing lessons and even more welcome dances. There was to be found a magnificent variety of guests, ranging from the Baroness von Hutten, author of a once popular novel called *Pam*, whom I remember as about nine feet high and dressed in an accordion-pleated silk garment which fell from her shoulders to her feet and made her

[1] I remember once upsetting a frying-pan on the floor of my room, and retrieving an egg, which was all I had for breakfast, irremediably tainted with furniture-polish. I was frightfully, youthfully hungry, and fled to Kaye's flat, where there was a spare piece of bacon.

[2] I wonder whether the B.B.C. realises its responsibilities in giving immortality to one tune and condemning the rest to oblivion. On the other hand, it has certainly greatly reduced the time-lag between music composition and public appreciation of the composer.

look like a piece of archaic Greek sculpture (" early tree-motif ")—to T. S. Eliot, not then O.M., but the obscure author of an odd but curiously satisfying poem called *The Love Song of J. Alfred Prufrock.*

I listened eagerly, dancing whenever anybody had a mind to me—which was not very often. I was very little of a social success, in the ordinary way, in my youth ; I did not dance or dress well enough, and I was clumsy and unattractive in conversation ; this increased my gratitude to " the Movement " for giving me something else to think of than personal conquests. But I drank in all that was offered, particularly from a wild Irishman named Jack White (son of Sir George White of Ladysmith fame, and organiser of the Irish Citizen Army) ; and Ezra Pound. Ezra was then about thirty-two, and I believe at his best. His later ignominious appearance as the William Joyce of Italy has clouded his memory for most people, but at that time he was, not only a considerable scholar and a poet who looked as though he might do big things, but also a vital and vigorous creature with a face like a bearded faun, a hopping dancer and torrential talker prepared to initiate any young thing into the meaning of life, and a hierophant for many movements of literary and artistic revolt, much of it expressing itself in an American-printed *Little Review*, " Making No Compromise with the Public Taste." In this capacity he was a gateway to many experiences. Ezra's real gift, I think, was that of a preacher and initiator rather than as executant ; as teacher he introduced me to that brilliant draughtsman and sculptor, Henri Gaudier-Brzeska (killed in 1916), whose stag-drawings are now collectors' pieces, to W. B. Yeats and to other and wilder Irishmen and Irishwomen, including many of the Sinn Feiners then in London. Also to Ford Madox Hueffer, whom I came to know much better afterwards, when he was living with Stella Bowen. This studio connection was not a large part of my life, but at the time it was very important, not simply because it provided light, colour, and amusement, but also because it prevented one from becoming one-idea'd ; it reminded one regularly that there were people full of intelligence and character who cared passionately for ends that were not political in any sense of the word, for rightness in line or colour, in the sound of a chord or of a sonnet-sequence. My political friends, who, as I said, were by far the biggest part of my existence, thoroughly respected my " artistic connections " even when they did not share their tastes ; and, though Stella in her autobiography accused " the Movement " of not knowing how to live their personal lives nicely, I think she was unjust. We had the sort of personal lives that we wanted and enjoyed, while managing to appreciate other people's patterns. And, incidentally, our preoccupation with our kind of politics somehow seemed to preserve us from the ordinary kind of sex entanglement. We had plenty of emotions, and some of us were deeply attached to others ; but we had no necking parties, and when we stayed overnight at one another's flats it was simply because we had had so much to talk about that the last bus or tube had gone. When I took so sexual an action as to get married it was received with astonishment (and on William's part, at least, with wrath !) as well as congratulations.

6.

Up to this point I have written of my husband as " Cole " or " G. D. H. Cole,"[1] because that was how I thought of him until a new relationship made it imperative to discover and to use his Christian name—and I found calling him " Douglas " much more embarrassing than kissing him in public. I had worked with him, first as a humble volunteer, and then as an employee who gradually came to take more and more critical liberties with her employer, for about eighteen months before we became engaged. I had known *of* him, as I have said, for a good deal longer, both as a Frightful Revolutionary within the Fabian fold, and (from some very young Oxford Socialists) as a Possibly Reactionary Force in Oxford. All of which did not add up to very much, but—let psychologists make what they can of this—I very clearly recollect writing the words " Mrs G. D. H. Cole " on a piece of paper in the St Paul's staff-room and hastily crumpling it up ; and when I first set eyes on him—in the room of a friend of Ray's in St John's, the winter before Ray was called up—I thought that his face and appearance were exactly what I should most like to look at for the rest of my days. I set eyes on him then, but I did not actually " meet " him ; it was afterwards reported to me that, on being asked, " Would you like to be introduced to Postgate's sister ? " he replied emphatically, " No, I should *not*."

These were schoolgirl yearnings, no doubt, though they help to create in my mind the feeling that I was all but born married to my husband—at least, that there could never be any question of anyone else ; and they faded into the background when I went to work in the Research Department, and was on the one hand subjected to the severe discipline which I have described on an earlier page and on the other wildly excited by the content of my new life. I was not conscious of making any " passes " at the Honorary Secretary.

[1] Interpreted as " God Damn Hell " by his *New Age* friends.

But I suppose I did ; at least, as time went on, I seemed to find myself getting on to more and more human terms with the terrifying object, even by such absurd means as having a grass-green silk jumper (a notable extravagance on £2 a week) drowned in tea because the Honorary Secretary had suddenly elected to lob a large office india-rubber right into the middle of my teacup. I talked boldly to him ; I went out to dine with him, and even persuaded him to accompany me to a concert—on which occasion a Labour woman, as I afterwards heard, commented sourly, "Cole's going to marry that Postgate girl." Of these possibilities I was, however, quite unaware ; I merely thought that I was getting on better terms with the formidable fellow, and how nice that was for everyone. It was at the Whitsun holiday of 1918 that, having taken part in an Annual Conference of the National Guilds League, punctuated by air-raids, we decided to take a day off and walk in the Buckingham beech-woods around Hampden House ; and our behaviour (entirely unanticipated by me) was such that a shocked and indignant pigeon flew out in a great whirl from beneath the log on which we were sitting. Even than I was not quite sure what had happened, or if anything had. Douglas went fast asleep on the rail journey from Wendover to London, and bade me an affectionate good-night at Marylebone Station ; when, feeling quite unable to sleep, I called at Alan Kaye's flat to yatter to him and he said, " Are you trying to tell me you're engaged ? ", I could only reply, " I don't know ! " The following morning, when I arrived at the office and opened the post, the first thing that fell out was half-a-dozen or so photographs of Douglas taken by a comrade in Coventry. Two of them I sent to my mother, as a kind of breaking of the news ; her first and obvious comment was that he was amazingly handsome. The others I have still.

Of course it was all right, and I had no need to be apprehensive. Our walk in the beech-woods happened in May ; in August we were married—after our friends had got thoroughly bored with us as lovers and only wished we would get on with it—in a dingy room belonging to the St Pancras Borough Council, plastered with notices saying, " *No Confetti : Defence of the Realm Act.*" The registrar who officiated got back so late from his lunch that he was only just able to succeed in marrying us within the legal hours ; I remember walking up and down the pavement outside and looking apprehensively at Douglas's mother, a very kind but very properly brought up little lady, who would certainly have disapproved of our beginning our honeymoon in sin. I think that she was not at all sure what a Socialist girl working in London would be capable of suggesting ; for, though I never received anything but great kindness from Douglas's parents and his family,[1] it cannot be said that I was their sort of person. On our honeymoon, just in case we had forgotten the outside world, Douglas was called up for a second Military Tribunal, which, however, passed off without disaster because he had the sense to keep his mouth shut and let the A.S.E. officials plead his case. William Mellor, who insisted on making a speech to the Tribunal, was gaoled.

This is thirty years ago, as I write ; and the thirty years which have passed have done no more than deepen my conviction that whatever may have been the ups and downs met with in the co-operation of two very different—and obstinate !—personalities, neither of us could possibly have married anyone else. We are, in fact, pretty different ; though we happened to be " joined together " in the same depressing building as the Webbs, we are emphatically not complementary to one another in the same way as that unique partnership ; and the occasional descriptions of us as " another Mr and Mrs Webb " is only true in so far as that, politically, we have pursued broadly the same end—Socialism—by broadly the same means—writing, organisation, and propaganda—and that we have both worked pretty hard for it.

But there the resemblance ends. Douglas, besides being a first-class lecturer and teacher, and rather unexpectedly one of the best chairmen of committee I have ever known—business ability inherited from his father shows itself in an immense capacity for the handling of the organisational work which, of later years, partly through reasons of health, has become increasingly burdensome to him—is a natural writer almost to the point of disease. Sit him down anywhere, in practically any surroundings, lovely or squalid, still or moving—even put him to bed with a cold—and he will immediately start writing as though a plug had been pulled out, whereas an ordinary person would read a book, look at the view, or talk to his neighbours ; it is this urge to write, and to write continually almost without need to correct, which distinguishes him from almost all other human beings, even from other voluminous writers, such as Trollope, who have recorded that they had to force themselves to their desks of a morning. I should like to add here my personal opinion that the " lowest bottom level " of his immense

[1] My own father did not reciprocate ; after a single meeting and an ideological correspondence in which I think he got distinctly the worst of it, he severed relations, and refused to let my mother stay in our house, though he allowed me and my children into his. This was politics ; he also turned out his eldest son, and later disinherited both of us ; this accounts for the fact that from 1918 until after his death in 1926 I saw very little of any of my family but Ray.

output is astonishingly high—higher than Trollope's. I don't believe he has ever written a *bad* book, just as I have only once heard him deliver a really bad speech.

This means, however, that as a writer he cannot really collaborate, partly because his pace is much too fast for anyone else to keep up, and partly because the shape of his thought and the turn of his phrase resent being mixed up with anyone else's. I do not mean that he cannot take criticism—far from that ; but it has to be incorporated by him, at his discretion, in his own words and in his own way ; he does not want another mind interfering with and deflecting *his* book. The many books, including the detective novels, which bear our joint name, are the result of combination (one hand writing either the whole draft or a chapter or more) and criticism, rather than collaboration of the kind which produced, for example, the *History of Trade Unionism.* Douglas, with his immense fluency and rapidity and gift for tearing the heart out of documents and statistics—a gift to which I can lay no claim—coupled with his ability to maintain and express continuously his own personal view-point, should really have been a one-man encyclopedist, a kind of twentieth-century Dr Johnson. Some say he is.

I am no encyclopedist. I cannot remember—largely, no doubt, because I do not want to—the sort of facts which fill *The Intelligent Man's Guide* to what you will. The facts which stick in my head and illuminate the world for me are largely the odd, semi-personal facts, such as the prohibition, in the mid-seventeenth century, of the use of linen for shrouds,[1] of which the historian who can handle statistics and tendencies in the mass takes a poor view. Moreover, certain subjects are to me a closed book which I gladly keep closed. Banking and currency, particularly, strike me as a peculiar kind of unintelligible abracadabra which every now and then interferes fiendishly with the lives of ordinary people ; and when, a few months after our marriage, Douglas experimented with reading *Das Kapital* aloud to his wife, he speedily abandoned it as an unprofitable exercise. I think on different lines and far more slowly than he does ; I write much more slowly and with reluctance, generally putting off starting as long as I can. Moreover, I am very much dependent on outside contacts, which matter to him increasingly less and less. He is a far more Unsocial Socialist than ever Bernard

[1] Enacted in order to protect the English woollen manufacture. One trouble about this type of fact is that it is impossible to card-index it or keep it filed in any way. One has to rely on memory ; and as the number of *facts* grows with reading and one's memory weakens with age, the fact is apt to get lost altogether.

Shaw created ; apart from his own pupils, over whom he takes endless trouble, he gets very little out of personal association with outside people except definite pieces of information—and even then I think he would rather they wrote it down and put it in an envelope ! —whereas I am continually interested in people—individual people—in what they do or think, and in their companionship ; and if I cannot revitalise myself in having friends and meeting people, in many ways, even including such apparently arid groupings as the Special Services Sub-Committee of the Education Committee of the London County Council, I become slightly mad, very miserable and eventually of no use to myself or to anyone else. I have the kind of mind which seems to require quite frequent stimulation from outside sources.

The preceding paragraphs explain why we are not a new edition of *Our Partnership.* But of course it is not nearly the whole of the story. We have been partners in a very great many enterprises—the L.R.D., the Workers' Educational Association, the Tutors' Association, the revived Fabian Society, for example ; we have liked and cultivated the same friends and colleagues.[1] And while we cannot claim credit for founding abiding and monumental institutions such as the London School of Economics or the *New Statesman*, we have enjoyed ourselves together in many other kinds of work. I have mentioned detective novels ; I would add writing political satire and political songs—one of his which ends, "Keep the 'ell-fires burning for the bour-geoi-sie" has almost become a folk-song—making sixteen small books of selections from British poets, compiling an enormous biographical index to Cobbett's *Rural Rides*—a labour of love if ever there was one ; and, finally, producing and bringing up three very satisfactory children. All of this, and more like it, goes to make a range of common ground wider, I should think, than most married people could claim ; in comparison, differences of opinion about such things as cinemas, wireless, women's clothes, and American phrases—Douglas is a strong Tory in everything but politics !—count for very little.

[1] And to some extent made the same enemies. We have both upon occasion gained the reputation of being fierce and formidable creatures, and not unjustly, though I am, I believe, harder than Douglas in the last resort. Not everyone who has heard him inveigh against the wickedness and/or stupidity of the human race or some section of it realises how incapable he is of really doing harm to any living creature.

Chapter Seven

I.

In September, 1918, we began our married life at Number Twelve Bramerton Street, off the King's Road, Chelsea. Douglas's parents, while we were on honeymoon, had put the house in order for habitation, and our wedding-presents were there awaiting us. I remember many of them clearly—a black and white Spode dinner-service from Barbara Drake and her husband, and a breakfast service from Alan Kaye ; purple Bristol glass from Robin Arnot, and an old oak chest and tall oak cupboard purchased out of the Webbs' ten-pound note—what we should have had to pay for them to-day I cannot imagine. Alfred Bacharach, research chemist of Glaxo and encyclopedic authority on music and detective novels, gave us a full set of the one-inch Ordnance maps of the Home Counties—by 1948 the spread of the Wen and the cutting of by-pass roads has rendered parts of them of historical rather than practical utility, but at the time they were a highly valuable as well as an original present. Most impressive of all, there were in place Morris tapestry curtains and Morris cretonnes provided out of a subscription from ninety-three members and/or friends of "the Movement." Alan Kaye and Francis Meynell collected the money and Francis had all the names of the donors inscribed and illuminated in a roll, backed with red leather, which stands on a bookcase at this moment, looking from a distance rather like an infinitely superior wine-list. It was a nice warm feeling to come home and find visual evidence that ninety-three people wished you well.

A whole house was a new experience for me, who had spent four years in lodgings or single furnished apartments—the last being a lovely first-floor room in Mecklenburgh Square belonging to the poet H.D., with three tall windows, a balcony looking out on the plane-trees of the Square, very inadequate heating and a large population of mice. None of my close friends, except the Ewers, soared beyond a studio or a share in a flat ; but Douglas had to have a House. This was partly because he was better-off than any of us ; his earning power, even then considerable, was augmented by an old-time fellowship at Magdalen which asked practically no work of him, but provided him with three whole rooms with oriel windows in the beautiful New Building looking out on Magdalen deer park. But it was also because he was a man of leisure and of possessions—of leisure, in the sense that he had never had to shop or to wash dishes and could not be expected to begin to do so, and of possessions, because he is a born accumulator of good things, pleasant things, and above all of things that are permanent and take up a lot of space. Even then, he had more clothes and more books than my previous experience had led me to believe that any ordinary man could own ; he had a collection of English and Bohemian glass housed in cabinets of incredible weight ; he had a huge settee, a big wardrobe *and* a tallboy, and the most enormous mahogany bookcase I have ever seen outside a library proper. With all these—and there were a good many more—he obviously had to have a House.

The one which we rented, for £55 a year, belonged to J. R. M. Butler, whose brother Neville[1] had been at Cambridge in my time. When we came to look it over, the door was opened by an apple-cheeked lady in her 'fifties, shaped like a cottage-loaf, whose name was Mrs Farrant and who was caretaker there. As soon as we had decided on the house, Douglas asked her whether she would stay on as our cook, inhabiting the basement with her family. She promptly agreed, and, to cut the story short, remained with us when we bought the house, when we moved to Hampstead and afterwards to Oxford, only leaving us after ten years to get married for the second time—and unfortunately to die shortly afterwards. She was, of course, a grand windfall for a young couple who wanted to continue with their own outside work—and I would like to add here that, though there has never been anyone quite like Mrs Farrant, I have throughout my life enjoyed exceptionally good service and friendliness from those who have done my house-work, partly because of Douglas's remarkable gift for getting himself adored by nearly all who have ever worked for him.

I was never quite sure of Mrs Farrant's past history, of which she gave different accounts on different occasions ; and though I used to offer myself as an amanuensis to write down her reminiscences, she always shied when it came to the point. Sometimes she told us that her first daily job in life had been to undress and redress daily in freshly-brushed clothes the waxworks at Madame Tussaud's ; at others that she had started as a " tweeny " in Warwick Castle—and she had certainly lived in the Castle, for she told me a lot of obviously true facts about life in a large servants' hall, and

[1] Sons of the legendary Montagu Butler, headmaster of Harrow and Master of Trinity. I used to dine at Trinity Lodge in my undergraduate days, when the great man would take his guests on a personal tour of the portraits, saying, " Ah, that is poor dear Spencer Perceval ! " as if he had personally known the murdered Prime Minister of 1812.

how important it was for the maidservants to charm the men-servants in order to obtain assistance in the carrying of trays and coal hods ; and when Lady Warwick came to lunch at our house they had a great pow-wow together. Neither did I know much about her family at the time we took her on. They lived in the basement, into which I never ventured, but from which rose occasionally unmistakeable sounds of Mr Farrant in his cups ; when full rationing came in I was astonished, and rather apprehensive, to observe *seven* ration-books, in addition to our own two, lying in our letter-box. I wondered whether I should be arrested by the Borough Council for permitting gross overcrowding, but decided pusillanimously that it was no business of mine. (I believe that ours was in fact only an " accommodation address " for some of them.)

Mrs Farrant was born to be a family retainer ; she mothered and looked after us both—though she had a temper and a tongue which could be, and were, employed on occasion both upon her own family and upon later members of our staff. I ordered meals, under her supervision, and bought food sometimes, when I did not forget ; but she did the bulk of the shopping, as well as cooking and cleaning both for us and for the miscellaneous cuckoos who lodged from time to time in our nest. Arnot, for example, lived with us for quite a while ; so did Walter Holmes, and a young Serbian Socialist who drew upon us the attention of a plain-clothes man with unmistakeable boots, who used to stand against a lamp-post on the other side of the street, keeping a watchful eye upon the house.

In the late autumn of 1920 we entertained Ford Madox Ford (Hueffer) while his daughter was coming into the world in a nursing home ; this was a more serious business than it sounds, for the baby's appearance was delayed and the actual birth prolonged and difficult, and Ford was sympathetically brought to bed with some chest-trouble which according to him demanded very special dieting. I remember Mrs Farrant appealing in perplexity to Douglas because " Mr Ford " had said he could touch nothing but a devilled sirloin-bone (meat-rationing was still in force) ; and on another occasion receiving a pathetic request for clear soup with plenty of oysters—it was early-closing day in Chelsea and I sent Ezra Pound up town to buy them.

This was very like Ford ; the great suffering, which I do not for a moment suggest he did not feel at the time, and the preposterous demand for solace according to English country-house standards. Christopher Tietjens, hero of Ford's war saga, was not yet born in his author's brain ; but I am sure Christopher Tietjens, when ill, had to have devilled sirloin. It was one of the misfortunes which dogged Ford all his life, that the acts which he put on, his extravagant poses and gestures, were almost all out of timing with the currents of public opinion, and so earned him unpopularity. His war novels, for example, though treated with respect by the critics, came out at exactly the wrong time between the wars, and so fell flat ; he attacked prominent people and prominent tendencies, not at the moment of their greatest popularity, but what was worse, at a moment when nobody cared about them one way or the other ; and I think these recurrent disappointments made him more than ever of a perverse play-actor in private life. I certainly recollect feeling nothing but indignation when I regarded him wallowing in my spare bed, with his hooked nose, his thick pink fingers, his fat pinky-white face and quiff of yellowy-white hair above, like an obese cockatoo, wheezily demanding impossibilities at a time when we were all much more concerned about Stella and the baby. In many ways, he was an exasperating fellow.

None the less, he was a real artist, a passionate lover of literature as a living force—many years afterwards, when I had long lost touch with him altogether, I sat up till three in the morning reading his great *March of Literature*—a poet whose poetry, particularly his war-poetry, was finely individual and never appreciated as it ought to have been—and a lover of freedom. Even at the time when he was groaning and wheezing away in the spare-room bed, he was directing, with the co-operation of ourselves and Johnny Rodker, a propaganda campaign against the Black-and-Tans and the English occupation of Ireland, which had certainly nothing phoney about it.

It was a little before then, if I remember rightly, that J. L. Hammond took me to lunch with Erskine Childers, author of that fine pre-war thriller, *The Riddle of the Sands*, and soon to be executed by the English as a traitor, and I saw in his eyes exactly the same fierce intransigeance as I had seen half-a-dozen years before in the eyes of the girl from Ulster ; and a few months later that, reading with angry shame that Hamar Greenwood, Chief Secretary for Ireland, had appeared in the Commons on St Patrick's Day *wearing a shamrock*, I wrote a furious parody of *The Wearing of the Green*, which a Liberal journal accepted and then refused to publish.[1] One never knows quite how much influence is in fact

[1] It, with other political skits and satires, the majority written by Douglas, appeared in a small song-collection of ours called *The Bolo Book*—Bolo being a French spy who made headlines in 1918.

exercised by such rallyings of " the Good " as these ; the Irish war was ended, of course, largely because the bulk of the English public were ashamed of what was being done in their name, and quite unprepared for the real war which would have been needed to re-conquer Ireland ; but I think that anything which gives form to public opinion must be of some help. At any rate, the Treaty came next year, and the further fighting passed into Irish hands alone. Ireland rapidly ceased to be news, even in the *Manchester Guardian*, and as Yeats wrote—though this was not quite what he meant :—

> Romantic Ireland's dead and gone ;
> It's with O'Leary in the grave.

Others in plenty came to stay with us—Douglas's ex-Oxford friends as they came out of the army—I remember G. N. (" James ") Clark, now Provost of Oriel, Kingsley Griffith, afterwards a Liberal M.P., and the poet Sherard Vines. And, to anticipate a little, when we were living in Hampstead in 1923 we entertained for six weeks an uncouth gawky young Frenchman named André Philip, who was studying social and political theory in England and simultaneously teaching himself English by listening to the tub-thumpers in Hyde Park. In the latter endeavour, as anyone who met him during the last war as an ambassador of *La France Combattante*, will recognise, he was abundantly successful ; but when, after twenty years, I listened to him on the radio and heard the unmistakeable *snort* with which he opens his speeches, I said at once, " That *is* André Philip who lived with us and frightened my young Jane into tears with his odd growling manners."

With Mrs Farrant there, and with the bulk of our meals eaten out, we suffered very little from rationing or war-scarcity, unlike responsible housewives such as my mother, who had a nervous breakdown as a result of trying to feed and cherish a young family in Liverpool ; even the great price rise after the war did not come home to us except as an annoying increase in the weekly bill which Mrs Farrant presented. I do remember being outraged at having to pay eightpence for an egg ; but generally speaking the 1919-20 inflation served me best as ammunition for election speeches in 1945. Twelve Bramerton Street was insulated from the storm.

It was not, however, a nice house. Barring its location off the King's Road, it had nothing whatever of " Chelsea " in it ; it was an ugly jerry-built object in a street of similar objects, with sham pillars in front, walls made principally of rubbish and pervious (as we soon discovered) to any sort of weather, and rooms all the wrong shape. It had no garden, but a grimy backyard full of cats; when I wanted to take the baby out into a bit of green space I had to push the pram for what seemed miles over the bridges to Battersea Park; and the neighbourhood was damp and foggy. Except for the *Cross Keys* round the corner, whose landlady was 'Orribly Murdered of a Sunday morning, creating great local excitement, it had nothing of the traditional Chelsea mateyness, and I had no regrets when, early in 1922, after an attack of pneumonia, Douglas was advised to move away from the river, and we bought a vast square house of yellow-grey brick in Thurlow Road, Hampstead. (It cost £900 for something like a thirty-year lease, and except for a few weeks after Anne was born, we never needed to use the top floor at all. Those were the days.)

2.

This section has taken me forward well beyond the Armistice; and not without reason. For whatever November the eleventh may have meant for the pure pacifists—and indeed, for the great majority of the people—for us of the Left it was no more than one incident in a story which began in 1916-17 and finished only in 1922-23, when the post-war boom was long over. (I must admit that, as owing to influenza I took no part in the mafficking of Armistice Day, I may tend to minimise its significance; nevertheless, I am sure that what I am saying is broadly true.)

The time during which I was being initiated into "the Movement" was, as near as I can judge, also the time when the first war enthusiasm finally died, drowned in the blood-baths of the Somme battles, and many people began to ask themselves, "When is it going to *end*?" and, more gradually, "What is it all *for*?" Those who remember only the quick shifts and spectacular changes of the second world war must try and imagine the dismal oppressiveness of the middle years of the first one, when nothing seemed to happen but "successful advances" by the Allies, followed by lists and lists of casualties, and a line finally stabilised very much where it was before. If there had been radio in those days I cannot imagine what the nine o'clock news would have found to say. The winter of 1916-17, in spite of the brief excitement of Lloyd George ousting Asquith, which seemed much more a manœuvre of the high-ups than such a stirring of the nation as the fall of Neville Chamberlain, was extremely gloomy, with the war machine eating up more and more young men every day; round about Christmas, news of "a German peace offer" filled the press, but few believed either that it was genuine or that if genuine it would even be discussed by the other side ; the war was just going to go on and on. The minds of writers began to turn away from the mood of Rupert Brooke to that of Sassoon's biting sonnets about "scarlet majors at the base," and Henri Barbusse's terrible novel *Le Feu* (published 1916).

Upon this situation there burst the news of the Russian Revolution of March, 1917. On the way to the office we bought our newspapers and read with incredulous eyes that the Russian *people*, the workers, soldiers, and peasants, had really risen and cast out the Tsar and his government, who were to our minds the arch-symbols of black oppression in the world—far worse than the Prussians. On that day we did no work at all in the office ; we danced round the tables and sang, and went out to celebrate. Nor was it merely our small group that was delighted ; throughout Britain everyone with an ounce of Liberalism in his composition rejoiced that whatever might come next tyranny had fallen, and thousands of them gathered in the Albert Hall and wept unashamedly as they paid tribute to those who had suffered in Siberia or in the Tsarist prisons. The people of Russia had risen, and not merely the Russian Socialists and Liberals, but the oppressed nationalities, the Poles, Finns, Letts, etc., were to be free at last.

The news of Russia put immense heart into the left-wing forces all over the country. It seemed as though there might be something good coming out of the war after all ; for if the Russian people could overthrow their government, could not the Germans and the Austrians—or the French, or the British ? We went about declaiming Chesterton's lines :—

> "It may be we shall rise the last, as Frenchmen rose the first,
> Our wrath come after Russia's wrath and our wrath be the worst."[1]—

and savouring Soviet as a new political term of enormous significance. When we learned that the Russians were appealing to the Socialists of all countries to join them in holding discussions of possible peace terms at Stockholm, our excitement reached fever-heat ; a conference "of Soldiers and Workers" was held at Leeds, at which even those Socialists, like MacDonald, who were entirely out of sympathy with "workers' control," were fain to put in an appearance ; we thought for a brief while that the "war to make the world safe for democracy" might actually result in a world democracy very different from the ideas of those who had coined the phrase. It

[1] G. K. Chesterton, "The Secret People," (in *Poems*, 1915).

became of even greater importance to get the press-cuttings finished, to bring out the *Labour Year Book*—one of our largest enterprises—and to spread the gospel of workers' control through the restive ranks of miners, railwaymen, and munition-workers.

This enthusiasm was scarcely even damped when it became clear that nothing of the sort was going to happen immediately, but that those in power on both sides intended to fight to a finish, when the Stockholm Conference was forbidden and Henderson frozen out of the War Cabinet as penalty for his part in it, or even when, after Lenin and Trotsky had made the Revolution of October, the weight of the German Army was turned against the Russians and they were forced to sign the (for those days) barbarous treaty of Brest-Litovsk. For in our hearts, I believe, we had expected nothing else ; we had imbibed enough romantic Marxism, through books like *News from Nowhere*, to be certain that the purpose of capitalism was to keep the working class down, and that this purpose was hardly likely to be deflected as the result of a strike or two or a demonstration or two. Something very much tougher, very much more violent and bloody, would be needed—and, as not everyone will remember nowadays, something very much more violent and bloody very nearly did happen. I quote from the Diary of the L.R.D. *Monthly Circular* for December, 1918[1] :—

Nov. 1. Austrian Revolution.
,, 6. German Naval Revolt.
,, 7. Bavarian Republic.
,, 9. German Revolution. Swiss General Strike.
,, 10. Dutch Labour Disturbances.
,, 13. Danish ditto. Spanish movement to Revolution (*sic*).
,, 14. Labour Party Leaves Coalition.
,, 17. Hungarian Republic.
,, 18. Portuguese General Strike.
,, 23. London Labour Demonstration Refused Albert Hall.
Dec. 1. ,, ,, ,, in Albert Hall.

—the last two items recalling a glorious bit of fun when the Electrical Trades Union coerced the scandalised proprietors of the Albert Hall—who had refused to let it for a Labour celebration—by threatening to cut off the lights for its Victory Ball. The *Herald* celebrated the climb-down in a special issue with a cartoon of a huge electric bulb on its front page and a caption THE LIGHT THAT FAILED.

[1] The "month of revolutions" was scarcely less exciting than the Year of Revolutions (1848). It was, however, much sooner over.

With all this happening or about to happen, it is not so surprising that we made little note of Wilson's Fourteen Points, proposals for the League of Nations, or even the sweeping victory of reaction in the " coupon " election. We did not believe that salvation would come out of capitalist America or from an association of nation-states (unless they were Socialist states) ; and though we opposed as economically idiotic as well as vindictive the idea that defeated Germany could somehow be made to pay the whole cost of the war to the victors, and were often applauded by large meetings of the already partly convinced, we were not really surprised at our electoral beating—only at its size.[1] We wanted a revolution, like the Russian one—though it must be recorded that the Bolshevik success made the first rift in " the Movement," which had survived differences over the war without splitting. Neither the Christians nor the strong anti-Germans amongst us could stomach the atheism of the Soviets or their peace policy, and they found themselves in momentary agreement with those like Snowden and the Webbs who disliked equally the Russian experiments in workers' control (very soon abandoned under the stress of invasion and civil war). Partly as a consequence of this, the Soviet supporters became gradually more Marxist and intransigeant and began to employ on their " comrades " hate-terminology learned from Marx and Lenin ; it was a sign of things to come.

3.

We took the coupon election so calmly partly because the element of anarcho-syndicalism in our political upbringing had prejudiced us to believe that all existing governments from autocracies to parliamentary democracies were bad, and not one of them except the Tsar's much worse than any other—we had not really faced up at all to the problems of political power. But the Coalition Government of 1918 onwards really was pretty bad, and it is a discreditable episode in our history that Lloyd George, a great man who came into public life as a great Radical and who, as his later history showed, retained so much of real radicalism in his heart, should at that moment, of all moments, have chosen to hang on to personal power at the price of giving way to the worst elements in the community—only to be cast out by the Tories like an old shoe, when he had served his purpose, killed the Liberal Party,

[1] 1918 results : Coalition (" coupon "), 509 ; Labour, 61 ; Liberal, 27 ; Others, 4. Douglas and I read them in a large gloomy room in a pub at Farnham, where we had gone to recuperate from 'flu. The weather was vile, and the chimney smoked ; it was an appropriate setting.

and deceived the working class so thoroughly that they would never trust him again.

I should not like to suggest that Lloyd George had his tongue in his cheek when he sponsored all the "reconstruction" activities of the last years of the war—the Homes for Heroes, the Fisher Education Act, and all the less well-known projects which went down the drain.[1] I am pretty sure that he had the intention of creating a better world after the war, and of making a just and lasting peace. But between the signing of the Armistice and the closing of the election campaign he discovered, or thought he discovered, that Premier Lloyd George could only stay in power if he said yes to those who shouted loudest and looked most dangerous—and he let his aspirations go. The result was an enormous personal majority for him,[2] Liberal and Labour oppositions from which most of those capable of really standing up to him were excluded—and a Government which pursued a definite but impossible policy abroad, and at home gave way to profiteers and mutineers when either looked menacing.

I do not want to dilate long on the Treaty of Versailles, whose cloud-cuckooland economics finally destroyed all that was good in it, partly by giving English liberals, led by J. M. Keynes, such bad consciences about their treatment of Germany that they helped to smooth the path of a new tyranny far more terrible than anything Prussian. (Keynes's *Economic Consequences of the Peace*—published towards the end of 1919—was an eloquent and very influential book; but everyone can see now that it proved far too much.) Even without the lunacy of reparations and war-debts, which in effect were never paid but served to poison all international relations right until Lease-Lend and beyond, and even without the continuance of the war for two years against Soviet Russia and the subsequent efforts to freeze her out of existence, I doubt whether the Wilsonian policy of setting up sovereign states all over Europe and trying to pretend that they were parliamentary democracies with English or American or even French traditions behind them would ever have worked. Wilson, Virginian by birth, was presumably a Jeffersonian and advocate of States-rights; but he acted

[1] See Robert Pollard's able Fabian pamphlet, *Reconstruction Then and Now*, for an account of most of them. A minor incidental tragedy is that people who remembered their history were inclined to be chary of making "reconstruction-plans" for the second aftermath—with the result that there were far too few made.

[2] Which majority, however, brought him to heel as soon as he tried to make a peace which, in his own words, "should leave no *casus belli* to Germany." The interview (March 1919) in which these words occurred produced the notorious telegram from 370 M.P.s demanding the last pound of flesh from the Germans,

as though he had no knowledge of the painful manner in which his own Union of forty-eight States—homolingual, at that!—had been built. But nobody should deny that the drafters of the Treaty tried hard, that they worked out machinery, such as the Mandates system, which under happier circumstances might have borne good fruit, or that they mapped out excellent areas of international co-operation in minor fields; anyone who is disposed to condemn the Treaty out of hand should at least read it first. But reparations and the *cordon sanitaire* against Russia were its dark angels from the beginning; we Socialists used Keynes and the U.S.S.R. as touchstones, were only mildly tolerant of the "Genevan apologists" of the League of Nations Union, and when D'Annunzio, for example, seized Fiume by force, or Mussolini defied the League over the Corfu incident (1923), we only murmured "What did you expect?"

For some years, in effect, we were not interested in "foreign affairs," under which heading we did not, of course, include the U.S.S.R.; our eyes were on the situation at home. There, as I have said, my general recollection of Government policy is that it had none, except to yield to any pressure, from either side, that looked as though it might be dangerous. Naturally, the strongest pressure came from the side of the employers, the profiteers, "the hard-faced men who looked as though they had done well out of the war."[1] With indecent haste the Government abandoned its reconstruction plans, removed the wartime controls as fast as possible, sold the war factories for a song and allowed masses of "war surplus goods" to be disposed of to dealers at knock-down prices. With price control gone the cost of living rushed up and up; fantastic profits were made, and even more fantastic capital gains by people who bought up businesses and sold and resold them to mugs at ever-increasing rates until, towards the end of 1920, the war-impoverished world could no longer afford to replenish its stocks at such soaring cost, and the brief price boom broke. Then the engine promptly went into reverse; coal mines were decontrolled and miners' wages left to the "free market"; housing expenditure was cut clean out; the operation of the Education Act (including the raising of the school-leaving age) postponed *sine die*; the ludicrous Geddes Committee was set up to recommend millions of pounds worth of cuts in social services—among them the abolition of the Labour Exchanges and the turning of all children under six out of the schools, etc., etc.

[1] Keynes, *op. cit.*, on the members of the 1918 Parliament. See also Pollard, *op. cit.*, for the whole story.

At the same time, however, as it was yielding to the profiteers, the Government was mortally afraid of the burgeoning working classes. I have spoken of " mutineers " ; and there were in fact actual mutinies among the soldiers, to which the Government replied by hastily scrapping its own schemes for orderly demobilisation, hurrying the men out of the army anyhow, and (necessarily) passing legislation to give all who could not find work 29s. a week [1] and to forbid employers from prematurely cutting wages. Mere stabilisation of wages, however, was not enough, particularly with prices beginning to soar. The workers were in an explosive mood ; there were strikes and riots on the Clyde, in Belfast, and elsewhere (even among the London police, those symbols of law and order, who left work, and that before the war had ended !) ; railwaymen and miners were demanding not merely wage increases but nationalisation of their industries—with " workers' control "—and threatening to strike for it, Churchill having in an incautious moment expressed himself in favour of railway nationalisation ; building workers were starting to organise Building Guilds [2] ; throughout the country workers in widely differing trades were asking for higher wages, shorter hours and (ominous phrase) " improvement of status." With real revolution bursting out all over Europe and the need for strong-arm tactics appearing in both Ireland and India,[3] the situation looked very ugly. The Government resigned itself to a wave of strikes, and left most of them to the employers to deal with ; but it met the gravest danger by a number of improvisations, of which the most important were, first, persuading the principal Trade Unions to enter a National Industrial Conference with the employers (chairman and secretary of the workers' side, Arthur Henderson and G. D. H. Cole), whose recommendations were quietly shelved when the crisis was past, and secondly, buying off the Miners' Federation, its most formidable foe, with a Statutory Commission presided over by Mr Justice Sankey and given a roving mandate over the whole organisation of the industry. The

[1] An unprecedented amount. This was the original " dole," and it alone fairly deserved the name. As soon as possible the amount was reduced to a " reasonable " level, but it could not be taken away altogether. Unemployment insurance, for the bulk of workers, had come to stay.

[2] The Building Guilds of 1919-21 were a real experiment in Guild Socialism in a section of an industry ; working for local Councils under the first Government housing scheme they won a great deal of credit for enthusiasm and performance. But when the scheme was abruptly terminated they perished from lack of capital. For the full story, see G. D. H. Cole's *A Century of Co-operation*, (1944).

[3] The first Sinn Fein Dail appeared in January, 1919 ; the massacre at Jallianwallah Bagh, which did more than anything else to establish the Congress Party in India, took place in April.

Government, in a reiterated pledge, promised to implement the report of the Sankey Commission "in the spirit and in the letter"; but when they received the final documents, with Sankey and six others recommending nationalisation, they took refuge behind a technicality, refused to act at all, and handed the coalfields over to the twenty years of bitter class-struggle whose fruits we are reaping to-day. The immediate danger, those short-sighted politicians felt, was over; the rest of the Labour world would not fight for the miners, and the coalowners could deal with them at leisure. Their calculation was right; when the boom had broken and the owners presented demands for slashing wage-cuts, the two great Unions of railwaymen and transport workers who were supposed to be partners of the miners in the Triple Industrial Alliance, bared their teeth in a snarl—and then refused to strike. This was Black Friday (April 15th, 1921), our first crushing post-war defeat.

What all this amounts to is that the immediate post-war saturnalia, the dancings and junketings, etc., of which so much was made, were conducted against a background of growling class-war of which we in the L.R.D. were not merely conscious, but an actively co-operating part. Like the Government, we concerned ourselves with profiteers and mutineers, but with the emphasis on the latter. For the purposes of this book, I have recently re-read the whole of the monthly journal of the L.R.D., which I edited more or less continuously from 1917 to 1925, and have noted with surprise its steady concern with industry, to the exclusion of politics. To take a few examples only:—the 1918 Conference of the Labour Party,[1] which entirely reorganised the Labour Party and equipped it for the first time with a real (Socialist) policy, is mentioned in the Diary of the Month, but nowhere else; there is no report of a Labour Conference until 1922—and that only an isolated one; of an I.L.P. Conference only one, which seems to have got noticed because it was debating a resolution on workers' control; there is regular news of Trades Councils, but not of local Labour Parties. The 1918 election is not mentioned at all; the reports on Parliament, which begin to appear after a while, are the dullest possible chronicle of Bills and White Papers, with no attempt to synthesise or to evaluate. There are articles on the elections of 1922 and 1923; but they state no issues and confine themselves to analysis of the *industrial* interests represented among the M.P.s; even in 1924, the year of the first Labour

[1] I attended this, and heard Maxim Litvinov make a speech of fraternal greeting from the Russian Communists.

Government, there appears nothing more than a few coldly factual contributions about its doings. Only in the "International Section," edited by a Communist—of whom more hereafter—is there any attempt made at political comment, or, I would add, anything of any *political* interest at all.

On the other hand, there are masses about employers and Trade Unions. News of dividends and of watering of capital appear regularly. Any official report on profiteering—and, to do us justice, there were plenty of juicy scandals presenting themselves for comment—gets full space; any blatant statement by any body of employers, like the quotation I reproduced earlier from *The Engineer*, is delightedly publicised. At the other end of the scale, strikes and "forward" movements are seized upon and given front-page space; a resolution from a Union branch or a Trades Council rates more highly than any political event save the imprisonment of Lansbury and his Poplar Councillors—and that, I suspect, more because the official Labour Movement repudiated Lansbury than for any other reason. We had a case to make out in industry, and we made it out as advocates. I myself, as late as 1924, produced an elaborate calculation, published by the L.R.D. under the title *The Condition of the Working Classes*, which proved, by a combination of the official cost-of-living index with the official index of unemployment among Trade Unionists, that the working classes had been getting steadily worse off, materially, since the beginning of the century. My arithmetic was all right, so far as it went; the only misfortune was that the conclusions were wrong, as I could have seen for myself if I had used my eyes and my commonsense instead of barking up an ideological tree.[1] The conditions of life for the working class had not steadily worsened; they had in fact improved —though with a set-back just before the war—and were to continue to improve through the operation of a number of factors, such as public hygiene, the fall in the birth-rate, and changes in production, for example, of which my crude calculation took no account. But they improved against the clamour of a vocal upper class which was always ready to shout against any improvement. Press and public comments upon the rates of unemployment benefit at almost

[1] This technique, of using unquestioned but carefully *selected* facts to establish a decline in working-class standards, has been employed by other writers, of whom one at any rate has gone so far as to show that the British working-class has been getting steadily worse off ever since the Industrial Revolution. On which one can only comment: "If you can believe that you can believe anything." I am not proud of this performance of mine; I will only plead that greater minds than my own have been guilty of special pleading under the influence of strong emotional ideas. Keynes, for example.

any time during the 'twenties, in the aftermath of the General Strike, and in the 1931 election, had all the note of people fighting a war, and go far to excuse, if they do not wholly justify, our attitude of permanent indignant hostility.

4.

The point, however, is not so much that we had an unbalanced view of the social development at the time, for plenty of groups of intellectuals have similarly suffered throughout history, but that our view was shared by a great number of the more vigorous personalities in the working class itself—who like ourselves were very doubtful about the value of politics. We were not living in any ivory tower ; nor was any eccentric person of wealth financing us ; we were earning our livings out of affiliation fees paid to the L.R.D. by a whole host of Labour bodies—Trade Unions which paid ten pounds a year, Trades Councils and Trade Union branches which paid ten shillings, pamphlets and booklets and our monthly journal which we sold among the members of these bodies, and special fees, charged on a piecework basis, for special work done. And neither Trade Unions nor their branches could afford to throw money away ; we gave them what they wanted, and we thoroughly earned our salaries. Day by day, we answered their questions, provided them with ammunition for agitation, gave them legal advice, hunted up the profits of firms from whom they were asking a wage increase, and worked up full briefs for them when there was a serious dispute pending. I can remember a dozen or so of such occasions ; but the one which was most spectacular and got us much the most public credit was the 1919 railway strike.

In brief, the Government, which was then still running the railways, in September of 1919 decided upon drastic wage-cuts, and the workers struck. The National Union of Railwaymen was one of our affiliated organisations ; and after some discussion its executive decided to make an unprecedented effort to mobilise public opinion on its side, to set aside a large appropriation for publicity purposes, and to give the L.R.D. the job of running publicity. We took on the job, and a wonderful time—the adjective is carefully chosen—was had by all.

We had never in our lives had so much money to spend on our work ; we hired space in the newspapers, and filled it with statements of the railwaymen's case, and refutation and denunciation of the Government spokesmen—as it was the Government and not a corporation that we were attacking there was no risk of libel actions. We held press conferences and gave hand-outs to newspaper men ;

we arranged meetings and posters and broadsheets ; we did our best to convey to the public of the United States and the Dominions the news that the British Government was trying to stamp on the faces of the railway workers. We ran the whole business, under Arnot's main direction, as a campaign, and brought innumerable people into it, small and great ; perhaps the high-water mark was when Bernard Shaw offered to write an article to appear under the signature of J. H. Thomas (the N.U.R. Secretary). We had enormous fun, and, what is more, we were successful. The tone of the newspapers, which at the beginning of the strike were writing about the railwaymen as though they were Germans or Bolsheviks, was sensibly affected within a week ; the Government had recourse to arguments, and its arguments were not good. It was not prepared to face widespread unpopularity, and it gave way all along the line. It was a substantial Labour victory, only surpassed the following summer when the whole movement sprang to life at the news that Lloyd George was sending arms and possibly armies to Poland to fight the Russians, and by threatening a general strike stopped military intervention in Russia once and for all.[1]

None of our efforts was so spectacularly successful as the railway strike ; in the long and bitter mining struggle which followed Black Friday there was nothing we could do, no possibility of bringing a public opinion to bear on the mineowners. Indeed, after the boom had broken, our scope was much restricted, for Labour was on the down-grade and unemployment—the unemployment which never fell below the million level until the coming of a new world war—was beginning its disheartening effect. In the big engineering lock-out of 1922, for example, the good case we made out did not save the workers from complete defeat. But in other less noticeable instances the L.R.D. did effective *ad hoc* research work for Unions which had not reached the point of establishing research departments of their own ; and it certainly never ceased trying, attacking capitalism continually and drawing attention to its weaknesses and its failures—a tendency which was naturally intensified after 1924, when it came under Communist control.

This was a gradual process. For when the Communist Party of Great Britain was founded in July, 1920, few people realised

[1] This achievement of the "Councils of Action" was only made possible, of course, by the fact that all but the extremists were heartily sick of the futile attempts to break the Revolution by force of arms and quite unwilling to embark on another major war. What happened when a general strike was called for an object with which the middle classes were not in sympathy was made plain enough six years later.

exactly what it was going to become, and it was joined by a good many members of the Left whose views were certainly not those of the Communists of to-day. In 1920 Russia was, as I have indicated, the hope of the world ; not merely had the Russians expropriated kings, priests, and capitalists, and at a terrible price beaten off the attacks of their enemies, their new State was boldly introducing most of the reforms which Socialists had been vainly demanding for generations. Women were, at a stroke, put on a political and economic equality with men ; the new labour laws gave them protection and rest with pay at the time of childbirth, and the child labour code, even if it was not everywhere in force, was on paper the most generous in the world. In the midst of war and civil war the most illiterate country in Europe announced its intention of establishing universal free education organised on "free," co-educational lines, and began a tremendous mass drive to liquidate illiteracy among adults. (The Propaganda Train which drove through Russia in 1920 bringing news, posters, and spelling-books to peasant villages was one of the things which caught everyone's imagination.) The Soviets were setting out to build hospitals and crèches in great numbers ; they had introduced easy and equal divorce laws ; above all, they had reversed the social values of capitalism and were giving the highest rations, the best pay, and the greatest influence to the groups whose work was of the greatest social importance—miners, for example, heavy metal workers, the Red Army—and teachers. Pretty well the whole of the thinking industrial workers, whether or not they became Communists, thought of the Russians as blazing the trail for Socialism, and it was extremely easy to believe that Communism was simply advanced Socialism, and that the best thing a left-wing Socialist could do was to become a Communist as speedily as possible and follow the guidance of Lenin and Trotsky. A good number of "the Movement," including Arnot, William, Ellen Wilkinson, Ray, and Frank Horrabin, did in fact join with the Glasgow Marxists, the extreme left of the I.L.P., and some other groups to form the Communist Party ; the political leaders, however, Henderson, MacDonald, the Webbs, Herbert Morrison, etc., were strongly opposed. They had read the second resolution of the new Party, which began :—

> "The Communist Party repudiates the reformist view that a social revolution can be achieved by the ordinary methods of parliamentary democracy, but regards parliamentary and electoral action generally as providing a means of propaganda and agitation towards the revolution,"

and went on to declare that any Communist elected to Parliament or any other body must regard himself as holding a mandate from the Party only. It was around this fundamental point of divided allegiance that the leaders of the Labour Party all through the 'twenties and 'thirties fought, sometimes against heavy opposition, the affiliation of the Communist Party with Labour. For a long time I thought they were wrong, but subsequent history has shown that if they wanted to preserve their own organisation they were right.

Neither Douglas nor I joined the Communist Party. Douglas, I think, saw from the beginning that it was no place for him; my own case was more accidental. I was not asked to join at the outset; but what prevented me from subsequent application was the fact that the Communist Party was formed, not spontaneously, but as a branch of the newly set-up Third International, the Comintern, whose headquarters were in Moscow, and was to carry out the orders of the governing committee of that body. If it had been the other way round, if the Communist Party had been the first-born, I think I might have joined it. But I did not feel that I could take orders from foreigners, however much I might respect them and their achievements. So I never became a Communist, though I was far from being opposed to them. For some time I worked side by side with Communists in the L.R.D. and the National Guilds League without much difficulty.

It is an easy and a cheap gibe to say that if ex-Communists were laid end to end they would reach from here to Moscow. It is true enough, but it does not explain why they originally got into the Party. Looking back over the history of Communism in Britain for twenty-five years, I would say that those who joined it seem to me to fall into four definite groups. I mean those who *joined* it; I am not thinking of the mass of sympathisers, particularly in the ranks of the industrial workers, who felt, and went on feeling through many years of shock and disappointment that, whatever the Russian leaders did in the particular interests of Russia at any particular time, theirs was still a "workers'" government. These for the most part have never joined the Communists, nor even voted for their admission to the Labour Party; but their feelings towards the U.S.S.R. were clearly shown in, for example, the bursts of factory production which followed June 22nd, 1941. They were far less worried than the intellectuals by the twists and turns of policy or even by the development of the Soviet State into something very different (to put it mildly) from what it seemed in the 'twenties or in the days of the Spanish War; and even now, in 1948, if Russian policy towards the West would give them half a chance, they would love it again.

Of those who joined, the largest group have been, I believe, those who wanted a plan and a direction, who wanted to feel themselves part of a society which was going somewhere and could say where it was going—which Britain between the wars certainly could not—and who also felt, as Catholics feel, the need of some human authority to explain, interpret and guide the individual in his own actions and spur him on if he went slack. Even so strong a mind as Beatrice Webb's felt that need,[1] as can be clearly seen from the high praise which *Soviet Communism* gives to the Russian Communist Party—though she never felt any temptation to join the British version of it. Secondly came all those who were politically impatient and frustrated, who felt that the Labour Party was doing nothing for *them* and getting nowhere, that " the inevitability of gradualness " (the famous phrase first used by Sidney Webb in 1923) meant in practice stagnation or even retrogression, and that the Communist Party intended to get things done. People who felt like this were to be found in all groups, but particularly among the unemployed and the young, with regard to both of whom the official Labour movement has a pretty dim record. When mass-unemployment began, the leaders of the Labour Party had no real idea what to do about it, and tended to look upon the unemployed as tiresome creatures who ought to become Trade Unionists and make suitable representations through their Trade Unions—and who had certainly no business to be organising and demonstrating on their own as though they needed special attention. The National Unemployed Workers' Committee (formed 1921) was officered by Communists—naturally; and if the official leaders disliked this, and resented organisers like Wal Hannington becoming national figures, they had only their own unimaginativeness to thank for it.

Similarly with the young. If there is any more depressing story than that of the official Labour Party's relations with its League of Youth and cognate organisations, as told in its own Annual Reports, I do not know it. The League of Youth mustn't do this, and it mustn't do that; it must not pass resolutions about policy, or embark on any action on its own, until it has Asked Mamma—and passed through a severe qualifying period of addressing envelopes and running errands for its elders in the local Party offices. One

[1] Again and again, during the 'twenties, when Russia was still anathema to her, Beatrice told me that what Britain and the world needed was a new Dedicated Order, something like the Society of Jesus.

is inclined to think that "children should be seen and not heard" has become the Party slogan; and sadly notes the youngest of the political parties behaving as though it consisted of old grey-beards and old crones who can do nothing more helpful than mutter, "I wasn't allowed to act like that when *I* was young." Statistically, of course, it is true that Labour M.P.s have always had a high average age—this is no discredit to a Party which cannot send gilded youth to Parliament. It is also true that the very proper unwillingness to throw an old servant on the streets, even with a pitiably small pension,[1] inevitably resulted in the long retention of elderly persons in important jobs. "*Si vieillesse pouvait*" is, however, equally true.

These were the two most important groups. But there were also two more. The first was that of the "natural insurrectionists," people like my comrades of the war years, who had had fun during the war and thought they would have much better fun, and could continue being insurrectionists, if they joined the Party. To a large extent, in the beginning, they were right. The Communist Party, in its early days, was conspiratorial to the point of being a joke. I remember one comrade being instructed to meet a higher-up comrade in the middle of Blackfriars Bridge; he did so, and received a sign to walk on to the south end of the bridge and then return. After a repetition of this manœuvre, the two, having, I suppose, successfully thrown the police off the scent, sat down together and transacted their business in a convenient Lyons. On another occasion, members of a Party cell were told to rendezvous in an unfashionable part of Bloomsbury at 11 p.m. *in separate taxicabs*, a proceeding which naturally concentrated the attention of the entire neighbourhood on their activities—it may have been then or at another time that the assembled comrades succeeded in setting afire the flat in which they were having their secret meeting, and had to be rescued in a literal blaze of publicity by the London Fire Brigade. Harry Thompson, who was more-or-less honorary solicitor to a good many bunches of crack-pots, used to have a fund of anecdotes of this kind. But in the last resort all this fun-and-games was controlled, and increasingly controlled as time went on, by the fourth group, the dyed-in-the-wool Marxists (or Leninists or Stalinists according to date) who believed in the class-war as expounded from Russia and in all that that implied, who were convinced *without any reservations* that the one thing which

[1] I was once asked by a woman organiser of a big Union if I could find her a Parliamentary seat, "because the X Union doesn't pay pensions." Pathetic, but not really a way to get good M.P.s.

mattered was to establish the Soviet revolution and to make the rest of the world act in accordance with Soviet interests, and who took their own orders, therefore, down to the most trivial points of detail, from the preceptors of revolutionary tactic in Moscow. This group is typified to me by Rajani Palme Dutt, the brilliant secretary of the International Section of the L.R.D., for long editor of the *Labour Monthly*, the tall dark son of an Indian and a Scandinavian, who has more skill in dialectical theory than anyone I know and no mercy for any soft place either in his opponent's heart or in his life. Rajji was the strongest stiffening influence in the early Communist Party ; but there were a good many others, intellectuals and Trade Unionists, together making a formidable group which eventually took tight control.

They took tight control because they were ordered to. In 1923 word went out from the Comintern that the constituent Parties must be "bolshevised," *i.e.* reorganised on proper class-war lines. Every member was to do his whack of the unpleasant and depressing organisational jobs—this in itself squeezed out a number of the more casual revolutionaries—and was to submit to severe discipline and inquisition as to how he spent his time. Furthermore, penetration,[1] and capture, of other organisations was to be taken seriously. The Communists in *any* organisation were to form themselves into a cell, to make and carry out plans for carrying resolutions and for initiating action on lines laid down by the central committee, and for freezing out or otherwise disposing of non-Communists who held inconveniently high positions ; naturally, any and every tactic should be employed to manœuvre the victims into a position of helplessness or false security. This pattern of campaign is *the* Communist pattern ; I have described it in this chapter, because it was in 1923-24 that it first came into my life, but everyone who knows anything of Labour history, or, latterly, of world history, must have seen it in working time and again ; it is the reason why *on their own showing out of their own directives* it is impossible to give full political trust to Communists even when they are working alongside you with apparent whole-heartedness. And one of the main reasons why so many recruits to the Party have left it has been the discovery that they were expected to behave in ways which outraged their own decent instincts. Sometimes they tried for a while before they got out—and then got out, imbued, too often, either with the kind of disappointed hatred which caused

[1] "It is the duty of the lower organs of the Party to penetrate the backward parts of the proletariat," remarked a Comintern instruction which had been rather infelicitously translated. (R. W. Postgate, *How to Make a Revolution*, (1934)).

them to see nothing in the world but Communist infamy, or with a premature cynicism about all things political. This is the bitter part of the legacy which Marx—for it comes from Marx, as can be seen from his correspondence with Engels—bequeathed to modern political discussion.

The Communists played their part in the death of the National Guilds League and the Guild Socialist movement, which had reached its peak in 1920-21. "National Guilds" as an immediately practical proposal could scarcely have survived the slump and the defeat of the wartime Trade Unionism and the shop steward movement which had given it so much support; but in addition the advent of the new orthodoxy of the left split its intellectual protagonists. One group, led by Orage and Maurice Reckitt, fled from the horrors of Sovietism to financial fantasies such as the Douglas Credit Scheme; another, of which Clifford Allen was the main protagonist, hoped for a brief while to yoke together Guild Socialism and the left wing of the I.L.P.; the third "deviation"—though we should not have used the word—was the group which joined the Communist Party at its formation. For some time, it is true, the split was not overt; indeed, there was no split, in the spectacular sense, at all. The N.G.L. survived the collapse of the National Building Guild; I became its secretary, and Douglas and I continued to edit its journal, the *Guild Socialist*, until 1923; various supporters, of whom the most devoted and untiring were Mr and Mrs Bedford of Hampstead,[1] continued to work and to organise for it; but membership and interest gradually dropped away, and it finally ceased to exist, though, as I said on an earlier page, recent events have shown that the idea behind it badly needs restating.

But the Communist Party made very little headway among the organised British workers, less, so far as I can judge, than in the U.S.A.—except among the unemployed. Only one Union joined the Red International of Labour Unions, and only one very minor Union was split. It affected a good many lesser bodies, such as

[1] The Bedfords were, and are, two of the nicest and most selfless people in the world. In their house in the Vale of Health, where Mr Bedford, a retired Indian Government official, delighted us by arranging his library strictly according to colour of binding, the books on each shelf being in their turn arranged in a curve of height, with the shortest in the middle, they have assisted dozens of organisations and organisers of many causes, from politics to clinics, to dancers and musicians—all without a thought of return. They have been our friends now for thirty years; in those days, also, Jane and Anne, at the non-political ages of four and two, knew "Mrs Befford's house" as a place to which one went for tea once a week, had a Boiled Egg with one's tea, scrambled up and down steps to the garden, and returned home clutching a small bag of sweet biscuits. Only the other day, Jane brought her eighteen-months son to scramble up and down the same steps—with no Egg to follow, alas!

Trades Councils, Labour Parties—particularly very small Labour Parties—and Trade Union branches, and kept up a running political feud. And it did capture the L.R.D. by means of a deliberate campaign, of which I was unaware at the time ; I only felt, vaguely, that the atmosphere was getting less and less friendly. The details do not matter now ; but the Communists succeeded in provoking Douglas into resignation in the spring of 1924. I was a paid officer, and not so easy to sack, and I was not feeling inclined to sack myself. In 1925, however, our removal to Oxford settled that question ; I went on doing some work for the L.R.D. for another year and then terminated the connection. " The Movement " was dead anyway.

PART IV

NINETEEN-TWENTIES

Chapter Eight

1.

JANET Elizabeth Margaret Cole was born in a nursing home in February, 1921, while her father was delivering a public lecture somewhere ; Anne Rachel in our Hampstead house, in the middle of the night and without medical assistance, in October, 1922 ; Humphrey John Douglas not until January, 1928—a gap which, as his sisters bitterly pointed out, resulted for many years in their having a brother who was too small for them to discipline and not near enough in age to be anything but a nuisance.

If I had adhered to strict chronological order, my children should have appeared earlier in this narrative. But with the passing of adolescence the pattern of most people's lives begins to be made up of many strands, of which only one can be traced at a time ; and in my own pattern the political strand which was " the Movement " was in existence long before Jane was even contemplated ; and I further think—without being absolutely certain—that it meant more to my *conscious* self, at any rate until 1924-25, than my young daughters. It certainly accounted for more physical time.

This is not because the daughters were in any way unintended. Brought up in a family of children, it was simply unthinkable to me that marriage should not result in babies—several babies. When quite small I had presented my mother with the names of eight children whom I intended to produce,[1] " one a year, but not oftener " ; and I am still convinced that six would have been, abstractly, a better number than three, providing more variety and more people to play with. But quite apart from anybody else's opinions or such economic facts as the cost of education, there was the question of other interests and occupations. I should undoubtedly have been bored and frustrated by a life of pure domesticity, such as a large family would almost certainly have involved ; I wanted " public work "—paid or unpaid. I had a

[1] One, poor creature, was to be christened Nimrod Jonathan. Such was the influence of a Biblical upbringing.

nurse from the beginning[1]; that was part of our standard of living. And before Jane was born and for some time afterwards I gave up working down town; but I very soon found that being mother, and keeper of house and larder, with a full-time nurse and cook on the premises, was a quite inadequate occupation, and before Anne arrived I had returned to a part-time (in practice about three-quarters time) job at the L.R.D., which was only intermitted for two or three months for the baby's birth—Anne, considerate creature, appeared to thrive on a mid-day bottle, and I was only once or twice behind time for my six o'clock engagement with her. As she and her sister grew up I also started them on their first "lessons"—they went to school at five—reading, writing, figures, singing, and "drill." I taught them in much the same way as I had once taught my brothers, and I expect that it was all wrong according to modern educational standards. But in those days young mothers were not terrified by manuals of psychology; our manuals were exclusively physiological, concerned mainly with feeding, weight, and evacuation—though the one I had, compiled by Dr Truby King, was certainly portentous enough to convince me that it would be a miracle if my child survived the perils of life and inexperienced care long enough to reach its first birthday. I am glad that I did not know at the time that I was probably ruining its psychology for life!

From the salary I had from the L.R.D. I made enough, with a few journalistic scraps thrown in,[2] to pay for the nurse's services; but I was never under the illusion that the establishment would have been a financial possibility but for Douglas's steadily-increasing earnings. We were, in fact, a household on the Edwardian pattern, very similar to those in which he and I had been brought up, different, even in the 'twenties, from the household of Ray and his wife Daisy and their two sons, and those of many of my other friends—and staggeringly different from the households of young married professionals of the present day, where domestic assistance is hardly obtainable, or, if obtainable, only at almost prohibitive cost. Jane and Anne, like the daughters of Phyllis and Stella, came into

[1] Lily Middlemist, who stayed with me for five years until her marriage, and many years afterwards returned as Lily Swain to be my cook-housekeeper.

[2] "Scraps," indeed. For most of my life I have had an unerring gift for attaching myself to periodicals which either paid their contributors nothing at all, or if they did pay went out of existence within a year or two. *The Guild Socialist: New Standards: The New Commonwealth: Lansbury's Labour Weekly*—I could make a long list of them, ending with *Fact*, a monthly described in a later chapter. I wrote my best for all of them; but the public did not bite, and no one can teach me anything about the disappointments (and the satisfactions) of unpaid writing for the impecunious Good.

existence, statistically, as part of the "post-war bulge" of births, which, happily for the young mothers, coincided with a return to domestic service of the women dismissed from the war industries and suffering from the unemployment of their males which began in 1921; to-day there is another "post-war bulge"—following, however, not upon a wartime decline but a wartime *increase* of babies—and there is no unemployment or wage decline to force the daughters of miners and agricultural workers "into service." This must deeply affect the circumstances of young married women trained for a job, who cannot hope for the favourable conditions for bringing up children which I had (particularly as the supply of nursery schools is nowhere near equal to the demand nor likely to be for a long time); they must, except in very rare cases, for some years choose absolutely between work and children—this is even truer of that home of progressive liberty, the United States. What the long-term effect of this will be I do not know; I merely note it as one of the components of revolution-in-our-time.

In 1923, however, there were two babies, their parents, and their staff living in a large Hampstead house, with a rectangle of unimaginative garden with flower-beds at the sides, grass sufficient for a badminton court in the middle, at the far end ash trees and aspen poplars which were dismally grey and damp in a typical English summer, and as its sole distinguishing feature a yard of sand for the babies—which I am sure was highly insanitary; there were so many cats in the neighbourhood. On the nurse's half-day, there was the Heath, or the movements of trains to be watched from a vantage-ground near Finchley Road Station (where no fewer than *three* lines cross); during the nurse's holiday there were friends to stay with such as Phyllis and Stella, both now domiciled in country cottages with babies of their own[1]; every year the family went to stay with my parents-in-law in a red villa at Hove, where the children could be aired and bathed on the rather shingly beach. Their father and mother explored Sussex on foot and by bus, or sat on the grass by the bowling screen on the Hove Cricket Ground, watching Tate and Gilligan bowl for the always lively Sussex team, or poked about second-hand shops in Brighton. The routine was established "post-war"—not 1913 again, of course, but moderately stable.

Of the children I do not propose to write very much here, partly because parents have an unfair advantage in talking about

[1] Small families, unless of extremely unsocial type, should, I think, join with other small families for holidays; better games can be played and expeditions made, and the grown-ups can be freer and less fidgeted.

their children—they can remember too many embarrassing facts !—and partly because no mother that I have ever known (including myself) has the capacity to be detached about her own children. The belief that they are exceptionally something or another—beautiful, clever, kind, or original—or, at the very least, worthy of exceptional attention—is far deeper than the reasoning knowledge that they are probably nothing of the kind ; in our early days as mothers, my sister-in-law Daisy and I had a kind of tacit agreement that each was to be allowed an approximately equal measure of time to dilate in turn upon the doings of Jane or John.

So it is with due hesitation that I say that Jane was from her first appearance in the world a pretty child, as witness those who called upon her in her cot in the nursing home, and has never ceased to be pretty, fortunate creature, from that day to this—or to the day when I last saw her as a visitor from New York ; but a child who always had a strong mistrust of the world. The first thing which she regarded with suspicion was her mother's breast ; it used to take a full hour to feed her, and she looked with an equally apprehensive eye upon any new form of food, the sea, a domesticated goat, and almost any strange human being, until she was nearly grown-up. This, when combined with her earnest desire to be good and to do the right thing—she is one of the most honourably conscientious people I know, as her employers, the Chelsea Housing Committee, testified during the London air-raids—and an almost complete lack of confidence that she knew what *was* the right thing, made life difficult for her when she was an adolescent, and also made her seem young for her years ; even now, when she is a happily married mother three thousand miles away, I believe she scarcely begins to think of herself as a matron or realises how many people are ready to like her at first sight. And I know she always anticipates the worst, whether in weather, politics or what not—therein she takes after her father.

Anne—Dr Anne since 1947—does not ; she hopes for the best, and bears up, generally speaking, if the best does not happen. She began life by bouncing into the world while her medical attendant was vainly trying to pick up a taxi in the small hours ; when invited to take a drink she did not screw up a reluctant face like her sister, but opened her mouth and drank, day after day, till the milk overflowed on to her cheeks ; round and absurd, with a head like a boy's and a ridiculously thick crop of brown hair, she was the cheerfullest and best-tempered baby in the world, and always ready for a game. Perhaps that is why, in later life, she seems to have so much success with children, both in hospital wards and outside. She has, as far as I can see, nothing at all of her father in her ; both her faults and her merits are Postgate in origin—which, incidentally, meant that I could do little towards " bringing her up " in the proper sense, for any " talking-to " was so apt to end in a mutual fit of the giggles.

As to Humphrey, the late-comer, no mother is supposed to be even remotely dispassionate about her only son, particularly when that son has lyrical reports throughout his school life, becomes a scholar of Trinity, and distinguishes himself in (to the layman) so completely unintelligible a pursuit as quantum electro-dynamics. I will only say that in build and carriage he is ridiculously like his father, that he has all his father's ability to retain and reproduce quantities of information, all his father's political precocity and his father's charm, together with a great willingness to wash dishes and help with chores—and that all I wish is that he had been twins, so that I could have had a variety of sons as well as of daughters. What hand I have made as a parent to the three of them I am hardly in a position to judge. I do not feel that adolescents who frequently addressed their mother as I.O.G. (abbreviation for Inebriated Old Goat) can claim that they were unduly repressed ; but I cannot say what may have been the psychological effect of having parents who were keenly interested in outside affairs and had some outside reputation. The young Coles must speak for themselves if they want to—even if they say no more than the devastating remark of one of them at the age of twelve, " O Mummy, why didn't you have me in your prime ? "

2.

We went to Oxford in 1925, an experience, as will be seen, not at all to my liking. If I had not felt, as a sort of dull and growing misery, the break-up of " the Movement " and the ending of my " political-undergraduate " life I doubt whether I should have agreed to leave London. But when Douglas, having tried successively the job of organiser to the Labour Party's Advisory Committees, Labour correspondent to the *Manchester Guardian*, and full-time head of adult Tutorial Classes for the University of London—a very hard assignment, involving a great deal of travelling and evening work—felt that he needed something more settled, more quiet, and of a more academic kind, and was opportunely offered a Readership in Economics at University College, Oxford, I was not averse to going to live with the babies in a University town where one's shops and acquaintances would be within walking distance, and one would not have to be away from home and children for hours daily, going long distances by Tube to work that had ceased to satisfy among comrades who had ceased to be comrades. So in the autumn we packed up and took over from Julian Huxley an old house in Holywell Street, opposite New College, bringing with us Mrs Farrant (whose husband had died unlamented two years before), her youngest son Harry, the nurse, and a black and white cat of great intelligence named Joe. At the time, Douglas only meant to stay in Oxford for seven years; and such sorrow as there was in parting from London was softened by the fact that we both intended to take W.E.A. classes, and therefore got ourselves a *pied-à-terre* in the shape of a single room in the flat of a W.E.A. colleague, which we proposed to inhabit one or two nights in the week. For the first year after the move I took two evening classes on two successive nights and spent the intervening day working at the L.R.D.; if it had not been for this let-up I doubt whether I could have endured.

For, as soon as I got to Oxford, I found that I disliked it profoundly—and only wanted to get out of it again. I am quite prepared to admit that this dislike was not fully justified—I would have to be blind to a great deal of literature as well as of contemporary opinion if I denied that it is possible to love Oxford. But it is surely clear that Cambridge is much *nicer*.

I do not think I arrived in Oxford feeling any conscious university patriotism; apart from a token wearing of light blue favours on Boat-Race Day, I had never thought of myself as a Cambridge partisan—I had been much more of a Trinity partisan in my childhood. Nor did I, until I had lived there for some time, really take in the deep-rooted arrogance of Oxford which is best expressed in the epigram that "A Cambridge man thinks he knows everything; an Oxford man knows he doesn't—but he knows that you can always get a Cambridge man to do the sums." My knowledge of Oxford was derived from a long-ago visit to my uncle when I was a child and a few days spent there on honeymoon, in high summer, dining on cold salmon and wine in Douglas's impressive Magdalen rooms, and in the daytime being walked round his favourite Cotswold villages, Bibury, Kelmscott, Chipping Campden, and the other lovely bits of golden-grey stone. I did not know what Oxford—Oxford in a damp winter—was like. (It poured bucketsful all the while we were moving in; when our large settee was finally lugged into position it proved to be so sodden that we lighted the biggest fire we could manage, and went for a raincoated walk while the drawing-room slowly filled with clouds of steam.)

Oxford is no doubt Great, Good, and Important, the premier University of England, the city of dreaming spires, the home of lost causes—and a forcing ground for some good ones; but Cambridge, as I said, is so much pleasanter a place to live in. Talking the other day with a friend who had the good taste to agree with me, I compiled a list of items in which anyone not hopelessly prejudiced would have to admit its patent superiority; and out of a long tally I choose the most important. Cambridge, in the first place, is a real market town with manufacture suitable to a market town; it is the centre of a countryside, not an annex to a minor Detroit, nor an eddy in a monstrous river of traffic going westward. It has a market-day and a real open market, not the closed-in horror, smelling of butchery and slippery with blood and slimy squashed vegetables, that goes by the name of market in Oxford;[1] and in that market-place you can stand and stare and meditate, as you should be able to stand and stare in the centre of any decent town that claims medieval origins. If you stand and stare in Carfax, the centre of Oxford—not that you can, for you will be bumped and crushed by pedestrians and perambulators—your meditation will be cut short by sudden death or a leap for the pavement; and, beautiful as the High Street is in intention, you can hardly see it nowadays for traffic. Secondly, Cambridge, having much the less natural advantage in the way of water, at least makes the most of what it has got. The best of the Cambridge colleges lead the traveller through their precincts to the river's edge and the weeping willows, across the bridges, through the Backs, and almost immediately out of the town altogether. Oxford colleges seem to have forgotten their river entirely, and, with few exceptions, they force the explorer of their precincts to come out by the same gate as in he went. Nor, with all their architectural triumphs—much improved, by the way, since they have replaced the blistered stone which in my time made whole quadrangles look as though they were just recovering from a severe attack of sunstroke—have they made any discoveries in the beauty of brick; there is nothing in Oxford like St John's or the Garden Court of Queens'. Best of all, Cambridge is on the way to nowhere, or hardly anywhere; in particular, it is not on the way to Stratford-on-Avon, which between the wars brought such masses of raucous-voiced transatlantic traffic "doing Oxford" in a couple of hours or so. Blessed be Baedeker, if he really said—I have never verified it—that "the traveller pressed for time may omit Cambridge."

[1] There is, I am told, an open market hidden away behind the Prison, where fruit and vegetables can be obtained by those who know. But it is not "the market," nor in any sense the centre of the town.

Oxford is, of course, beautiful in late spring, with the elms coming out in the broad stretch in front of St John's, and the gardens of North Oxford—at which novels of Oxford life jeer so happily—hanging out great luminous bunches of double white cherry against a blue sky—but so is almost any other town that is not actually hideous. In winter there is not much to choose between the two for temperature. Both are cold ; but the cold of Cambridge is an active, open cold, brought by the icy wind blowing across the Fens, whereas Oxford, lying in a hole, has a dank, soggy, miasmic chill like the bottom of a disused water-tank. If you climb up Magdalen Tower, as I have done who knows how many times, not to sing May morning carols, but to propitiate week-end visitors, you will see below you the damp cloud of Oxford's breath and will understand the atmosphere in which a character in an Oxford novel[1] "continually felt as though he had had too much lunch and would die if it weren't soon tea-time." In spite of our pretty medieval oak-beamed house with its real walled garden—marred by the new and architecturally hideous building of New College which loomed over it on the southern side of the street and cut off most of the winter sun—neither Anne nor I were really well so long as we lived in Oxford. Readers who have got thus far will doubtless conclude that this fact accounts for my jaundiced view of it.

This is partly true—though I maintain that all I have said is perfectly accurate. But it is also true that I was not naturally cut out to be a don's wife. In London, I had had a job as well as a family, and a place in the front row of whatever was going on ; if there was an interesting discussion I was in the middle of it. But in Oxford, it seemed to me, all the really interesting discussions, the occasions when something important was done, took place in colleges where women could not enter ; even if you entertained a distinguished visitor, say R. H. Tawney, in your own home, you were only expected to feed him ; after dinner, if not before, he went off and talked in a male common-room. I did not find the routine occupations of female Oxford—taking lessons in Spanish, for example, going to listen to Magdalen Christmas carols in a high cold loft reserved for Ladies, having children to tea-parties, and escorting one's own to Greek Dancing lessons, dressed in tomato-coloured silk frocks—at all satisfying. I made a number of acquaintances, of course, of varying degrees of intimacy—I should not like to give the impression that there were not many nice people in Oxford ; there were. But I did not make any friends, with the exception of the G. N. Clarks, who hardly counted since " James "

[1] Ivor Brown, *Years of Plenty*.

had been one of Douglas's closest college companions, and the Murrays at Yatscombe up on Boar's Hill—but no one could say that Lady Mary Murray was a typical don's wife, or Gilbert, for that matter, an ordinary don.

To the Murrays I owe an immense debt of gratitude, during these four years and for long afterwards—not least because they lived on a hill up above the miasmic valley, and were always inviting some of us to take the bus into the clear upper air. The first time I was thus spirited away was during our first winter, when our kitchen boiler burst just before Christmas, and Lady Mary, having heard by grapevine of our plight, appeared like a beneficent witch and whisked the lot of us, Mrs Farrant and all, to spend some days in the lodge at Yatscombe—not the first, nor by any means the last, of the homeless refugees to be accommodated there ; the time I remember most vividly was just before Humphrey was born, when I was suffering from a choking catarrh which refused to dissipate itself, and Lady Mary promptly came to the rescue with hospitality. As Humphrey was all but due to appear, and might easily have staged a premature arrival in her house, this was, I think, an act of friendship of the very highest order ; and, as everyone who knows Lady Mary knows very well, it did not by any means stand alone.

Lady Mary, is I believe, the kindest person, at *whatever* cost to herself, that I have ever known. There can hardly be anyone in trouble in Oxford—I had almost written, in England—whom she has known who has not been helped by her at one time or another ; withal, she is nothing of a colourless and stereotyped Lady Bountiful. She is, after all, a Howard, and comes of the eccentric (to say the least of it) Stanleys of Alderley, several of whom are described in Bertrand Russell's *Amberley Papers*. Her mother was that formidable prohibitionist, Rosalind, Countess of Carlisle, who would allow no fermented drink anywhere near her house—her later connection with a well-known brewing family caused some ironic amusement —and is reported to have looked round a meeting and said in a menacing tone, " Does anybody here *dare* say I am not a Liberal ? "—naturally nobody did. Another relative, left widowed by a spouse whose choice of language had made her very unhappy at times, conceived the idea of having the house purified after him. This was done, after some discussion, by the local priest ; but shortly afterwards the house turned out to need structural repair ; and when the workmen came in, it became sadly apparent that it was going to be polluted all over again. In despair, the owner appealed to the foreman, explained the delicate condition of the house, and begged him (since she realised that Men must swear) to ask them if they would be so kind as to go *outside* to do it. With this sort of ancestry, Lady Mary is not likely to lack mild eccentricity or strong opinions on matters other than pacifism and temperance, which seemed to me to be her deepest convictions; and, indeed, her lame ducks have often been helped to the accompaniment of kind and well-deserved lectures on their shortcomings. But the jam in which these pills are embedded has always been of such first-class quality that no one could resent them.

As to Gilbert, he was—and is—an intellectual and spiritual host in himself. He is the original of the Greek Professor in *Major Barbara*—though not therefore to be credited with an interest in armament shares! To this he has added a world-wide reputation as an apostle of internationalism (when there was any internationalism to preach). He and Robert Cecil were the pillars of the League of Nations Union, which once had so great an influence;[1] he was a pioneer of international intellectual co-operation; and while never a politician, he was a power behind the scenes influencing politicians.[2] This meant, *inter alia*, that at Yatscombe, particularly at week-ends, one was liable to meet all manner of people, British and foreign, who were interested in promoting world co-operation—mixed up with undergraduates or friends of the Murray children who were in need of a friendly pat—I remember, among many others, Smuts telling stories of the South African War and Count Coudenhove-Kalergi, the Hungarian, explaining in detail Briand's plan for the United States of Europe, of which he was, I think, the real author. (This must have been in 1928-29, or thereabouts; the plan appealed to Arthur Henderson, and to Gustav Stresemann in Germany; and for a brief while it looked almost like becoming a reality. But Stresemann died; Philip Snowden, at the Hague Conference, decided to quarrel with the French; the slump hit the world and put Henderson out and Hitler in; the dream was over.)

Furthermore, Gilbert, when he was not working, was always ready to talk. Not to hold forth, but to talk—upon politics, philosophy, the classics, Milton, or the values of life. And since, notwithstanding his domed head and the impression of general benevolence which he diffuses from behind his glasses, he is far from being an uncritical lover of his kind, his talk was adequately spiced with mischief and malice; and, he is, like his wife, a democrat in conversation. He does not, like some great men I have known,

[1] So great, indeed, that Baldwin in the 1935 election told, as he afterwards admitted, a calculated lie rather than have the weight of the L.N.U. flung against him.
[2] See *ante*, p. 58.

Student reading party—author on right

PRE-WAR GIRTONIANS

Same students paddling in the North Sea

G. D. H. Cole, May, 1918

lay down the law ; he admits criticism and contradiction, and he can even play. He likes to exhibit the curious gift of telepathy which enables him to tell, by holding the hand of someone sufficiently *en rapport*, what has formed the subject of conversation while he was out of the room ; he can also—sole trace of his Australian birth—throw a boomerang on the fields facing his house, and see it return to his hand. He has always refused honours, except the Order of Merit, which he deserves far more than some to whom it has been given ; and if Oxford were full of Gilbert Murrays, how different would be one's view of it ! Apart from these few, however, I definitely high-hatted Oxford ; and both to the residents and to the London friends who came to spend week-ends with us I adopted the pose of disconsolate exile. I really think I behaved rather badly.

One exception should, however, be made ; there was one part of my Oxford life which seemed to me, on the whole, worth while—and still does. This was work among the undergraduates. As a don's wife I had batches of Douglas's pupils to lunch weekly, which was mildly entertaining ; but as wife of a Socialist, now almost the doyen of Socialism in Oxford, I collected more interesting evening gatherings of the young left-wingers. Douglas then, and for very many years afterwards, regarded it as part of his duty to act as guide and philosopher to successive generations of Socialist undergraduates ; and every Monday night there met for coffee in our house a study group of the keenest among them, who read and discussed papers upon all aspects of Socialist policy. There has never been any senior University member who has performed this service for Cambridge, or for that matter for any of the civic universities ; this fact has contributed largely to the comparatively greater influence of Oxford men among the younger intellectuals of the Labour Party.

It so happened that when we arrived in Oxford we found there a number of undergraduates of exceptional ability, many of whom joined our group. The cycle of ability in the undergraduate population of the older universities makes an interesting study. Douglas's own generation, so many of whom were killed in France, was of outstanding brilliance ; nearly twenty years earlier there was the flowering which included J. L. Hammond, Hilaire Belloc, and John Simon, the lawyer—and of which Belloc wrote the nostalgic " Years ago, when I was at Balliol." There was a rather smaller crop in the years just before the last war—many of them in Parliament now [1] ; another is about due. In 1925-29 those who talked with

[1] The outstanding example is Harold Wilson.

us regularly included—I take names as they come to my mind—Colin Clark, the brilliant statistician, now advising the Government of Queensland, E. A. Radice of the Foreign Office, James Meade, afterwards of the Treasury, and Christopher Saunders of the Board of Trade, John Betjeman, John Parker, long Secretary of the Fabian Society, and the first Parliamentary candidate to win a really populous constituency for Labour, Eugene Forcey of the Canadian C.C.F., W. H. Auden (who once telephoned to enquire whether he had left *two hats* in our house overnight), the late Evan Durbin—Hugh Gaitskell, Lord Listowel, Michael Stewart, and John Dugdale, all now holding Government office, and a good few others. Most of these followed up their efforts in discussion by more practical training, in the 1926 General Strike, in adult education lecturing, and in the work of the New Fabian Research Bureau and the Fabian Society ; and there is no doubt that that Oxford group contributed a great deal to the organisation and policy of the Labour movement of the 'forties. It was certainly worth the time spent on it.

3.

My other worth-while activity of those years—the results of which also I could see in the victory of 1945—was in the adult education movement, or that part of it represented by the Workers' Educational Association and the Tutorial Class tutors who ministered thereto. The W.E.A., the organisation founded by Albert Mansbridge and A. L. Smith of Balliol, with R. H. Tawney as one of its earliest tutors, for the idealistic purpose of bringing cultural education of high standard to those who had never had a chance of it in their youth, came of age in 1924. Douglas had been taking university tutorial classes for many years,[1] and we had regularly entertained his students to tea and badminton at our Hampstead house—occasions on which I made practical discovery of the difference in physique between social classes by having to lend *my* tennis shoes to the men and being unable to fit out the women at all ! In 1925 I myself " commenced tutor " and continued with some intermissions until I had to give it up in 1944.

Taking classes was a very interesting, but a pretty hard job. The University Tutorial Class was, as its name implies, intended to give its students education of university standard for two hours

[1] One, conducted during 1916-17 at the Holborn Hall, was joined by a number of restive and argumentative young Guild Socialists. It must have been a most peculiar class to teach ; Kaye and I, I remember, once spent an entire class session under the table, composing a satire.

a week for twenty-four weeks over three consecutive years, the students, in return for the grant given by the Board of Education towards their tutor's salary, being expected to put in a minimum number of attendances, to read quite stiff books and to write essays. There were and are, of course, shorter courses run by the W.E.A. and by local authorities, which made less exacting demands; but my experience was almost wholly with the tutorial kind, until wartime conditions in London made it impossible to ask students to pledge attendance for three years on end.

This "university standard," admittedly, was in some cases little more than a window-dressing phrase; a good many of one's students had neither the knowledge nor the equipment to do work which was really of university standard—though a surprising number did. The conscientious tutor, who had to certify on the class register which students had come up to standard so far as "written work" was concerned—and who not unnaturally did not wish to lose grant by certifying too few—thus had a perennial problem to cope with, and every tutor squared it with his own conscience in his own way. I imagine that the sort of criterion which most of us applied was, "Has this man, considering what I know of his ability and background, expended as much effort and understanding in the time given to his written essay-work as might be expected of an ordinary undergraduate in a similar amount of time?" and certified accordingly. Even so, it is enormously difficult to appraise the work of, say "A," a man from a supervisory grade, who can really produce a first-class essay when he tries, but again and again puts you off with the explanation that the work he has done does not satisfy him; "B," a real horny-handed who hands in a half-sheet of notepaper which has obviously involved hours of effort; and "C," who writes fluent journalese of the worst type (of which he is very proud), gives up twice or three times as many papers as the other two, most of which are not worth the ink they are written with. It is not merely conscience which has to be squared; there is also the difficulty of both being just and *seeming* to be just, of encouraging "B," discouraging "C," and prodding "A," without giving the impression that you have widely differing standards—as of course you have—for the free and equal members of a democratic gathering of adults. If you fail them, they may walk out on you.

They may walk out also for other reasons, because you are too dull or too dogmatic, because you don't know your stuff, because you talk too much and don't give the class a chance—tutorial class sessions are supposed to be half lecture and half discussion—

or because you don't control the discussion sufficiently and allow the voluble and unsnubbable to waste other people's time unbearably, or because being voluble *and* snubbable they feel that they have been snubbed. One of the reasons why tutorial class teaching is so interesting and extends the teacher so fully is that there is no compulsion and no tangible reward—no diploma or certificate—for the taught ; you have to hold them by your own personality and the satisfaction which they get out of the class. I suppose in this it resembles teaching in a " free " school, which I have never tried. But there are at least two great differences ; first, that you do not have long periods of time at your disposal ; you have to get it all done, for everybody, in two hours, in whatever quarters you can find ; and secondly, that your pupils are of very different standards and experiences, and have somehow to be brought together and drawn out (or shut up), even if that occasionally results in your own discomfiture. For they are adults, and may have specialised knowledge which you do not possess ; and I know of few things more humiliating than to have delivered a textbook disquisition on some industrial process or some detail of local government administration and find when you have finished that a man sitting sucking at a pipe in the back row, who has not uttered a syllable on previous evenings, has worked for years in the Borough Treasurer's office or a textile factory and proceeds in half-a-dozen sentences to expose you as the amateur you are. It is great satisfaction when you do pull it off, but a miserable evening when you fail.

Furthermore, the physical conditions are, or were, fairly tough. I once took, for example, on successive evenings, classes at Dartford and Croydon, which meant going straight from work, with hardly time to snatch a bite to eat, on a crowded suburban train, to teach for two hours in an uncomfortable room with a glaring light and a broken-down gasfire—which on one occasion caused me to pass out, and incidentally to set a rather " sticky " class jabbering like magpies—then hurrying to catch the train back, generally with a bagful of books, and arriving home somewhere between eleven and eleven-thirty at night. We used to say that, whatever tutors did or did not know, they had plenty of practice in going without food, and in charging up station inclines laden with books. Tutors who worked in rural areas had longer and more awkward (and colder !) journeys ; but I think had to cope with less overcrowding and less extraneous noise. I have lectured to the accompaniment of a shunting-yard, a choral class conducted by a distinguished modern musician, and *underneath* the meeting-place of a remarkable religious sect, which registered inspiration by collectively jumping up and down on the floor ; one of Douglas's classes was held in a building in which it was sandwiched, with only glass partitions intervening, between a company rehearsing Gilbert and Sullivan and a bunch of Army recruits learning to play the drum.

Except for the travelling, I believe that conditions for tutors have improved since the 'twenties ; accommodation and lighting and heating are better, and the spread of secondary education must have narrowed the gap between the attainments of students ; the problem of the man of fifty or sixty who left school at twelve exists no longer. But some of the fun may have gone out of the job. For the small numbers, the need for intense individual attention, and the fact that the classes, and the W.E.A. itself, were social as well as educational institutions, meant that one made a number of friends in very differing walks of life. The best of my classes, from that point of view, were two at Croydon, organised by the District Secretary of the National Union of General Workers, my very old friend, Eglon Shepherd, who with his warm-hearted and most eccentric wife[1] mothered all his members, and enrolled a suitable selection in my classes ; I remember they included two teachers who looked exactly alike, a postal official who had read Herbert Spencer and apparently very little else and devoted all his essays to arguing Spencerian evolutionism, a public sewerman, who was frequently late because it was not really desirable that he should come to class in his working clothes, one of the Council's gravediggers and his friend who gardened in the cemetery, a gnarled old person appropriately named Elms. In the case of the last three the question of " written work " arose acutely ; they duly handed in the bare minimum, but I strongly suspected that it was written from dictation in Shepherd's home. I never made tactless enquiries ; the contribution they made out of their experience was good enough.

The teaching which came nearest to " university standard " was that given at University summer schools to individuals or small groups. I wish I had space enough to evaluate the influence of the Summer School, that peculiarly Anglo-Saxon combination of holiday-making, sociability, and more-or-less intellectual effort, on the development of British radical thought. I met it first at Keswick in 1919, when Douglas, C. E. M. Joad and others delivered lectures to a group of " Northern Fabians " in an uncomfortable

[1] " You have no idea," she once cried to the assembled class, " how hideous you look without your clothes to anyone who has seen black men naked ! " A remarkable contribution to discussion—but the class was used to her and only grinned.

hotel whose manager excused the toughness of his joints by explaining that his previous job had been that of a lion-tamer—lions not being fussy about their meat. Two years later, the Guild Socialists invaded the Fabian School at Godalming for a riotous week, during which we clamorously forced the Guild Socialist point of view down the throats of the old stagers, much to the indignation of their leader, a worthy gentleman called Mr Bottle ; and produced a magnificent revue called *The Homeland of Mystery*, all about the U.S.S.R., for which Douglas and Maurice Reckitt wrote most of the songs, Lovat Fraser and Arthur Watts painted the scenery, and we had a beautiful ballet danced to the music of *Prince Igor*. It was followed by L.R.D. schools, W.E.A. schools, and others, all with song and dance as part of the programme. But the intellectual side was important, too ; even in the less serious summer schools, *i.e.*, those not supported out of university and/or public funds, to people coming from cramped unliterary homes the boon of space and time for *leisurely* discussion and the making of contacts and friendships was immense, and enabled many to proceed to Ruskin College or to universities as extra-mural students. Here, again, the harvest was reaped in 1945.

We had a good time in the W.E.A. world, teaching, playing, and organising, working for reforms within the W.E.A. itself, on the committee which ran its classes, and for better conditions of pay for the tutors. Douglas was for some time chairman of the Tutors' Association, and I secretary of its London branch ; and we made new friends among our colleagues there—R. S. Lambert, whom Douglas had known at Oxford, and who later went to the B.B.C., became hero of the famous "Mongoose" libel case, in which he got damages of £7,500 and retreated triumphant to Canada ; Amyas Ross,[1] the most original and wayward of all my friends ; H. L. Beales, now Reader in Economic History to the London School of Economics, and many others. In writing syllabuses, pamphlets, books, and booklists, in discussions at week-end conferences and summer schools, above all at Easton Lodge (of which more hereafter),[2] we managed to cram a great deal of co-operative activity ; what is more, in 1945 a large number (over

[1] I cannot in a footnote describe Amyas, my friend from his schooldays until his death at forty in a motor accident, or chronicle his chameleon career from the most intemperate and (literally) shocking of tutors to an importer of fine art reproductions who made a success of his business in the midst of a slump, and thence to a valuable servant of the Ministry of Supply, and who was more personally unaccountable, honest, disconcerting and entertaining than most people put together. One day I shall write his legend ; in the meantime, this is a brief salutation.

[2] See p. 145.

a hundred to my knowledge) of the Labour M.P.s had been trained as tutors or students in the adult education movement, some of them having received their first trial as organisers in the great industrial battle of 1926.

4.

The General Strike of 1926 was a tragedy ; but it was an exciting and, in retrospect, an important and illuminating experience. It was the last throw of " insurrectionism," of " direct industrial action," belief in which had been for so long part of the cardinal faith of the " Left." Ever since, in 1920, the threat of direct action had stopped the Polish war, the Left had not ceased to believe that the *industrial* movement, if really united and determined, could make its will prevail, and further that some day the opportunity would come, and the shame of Black Friday (when the Unions, except the miners, were neither united nor determined) be avenged ; and this belief was only strengthened in 1924-25, after MacDonald's first government had come to its inglorious end, while at the same time the period of post-war wage-cuts seemed to be over, trade was improving, and many groups of workers were making tentative forward moves. When the strike failed, in spite of the most impressive exhibition of working-class solidarity seen since the days of Chartism, and when, after much post-mortem discussion, it gradually became clear that it could not possibly have succeeded, the long dreams of Syndicalists, Direct-Actionists, and the rest of them withered and died. No Trade Union, since 1926, has seriously proposed to use withdrawal of its labour as a means of coercing Parliament or the Government on a large issue ; nor does any Tory of any intelligence now attack the Trade Unions for presuming to give a lead to the nation. At the beginning of 1948, indeed, the Tories were actually abusing the Trades Union Congress for failing to give a lead—on wage policy, for example. But in 1926 Trade Unionists who tried to help the miners to resist slashing wage-cuts were traitors, striking against the Constitution, according to the present Viscount Simon, and according to Winston Churchill to be crushed at all costs.

I think there can be no doubt that the outbreak of May 1926 was deliberately provoked by the Government. By the summer of 1925, the Trades Union Congress was getting much too uppish, flirting with revolutionary ideas, forming, wicked creatures, an Anglo-Russian Trade Union Committee—and that at a time when the return to the gold standard made it desirable that wages should be lowered, not raised, if the price of British exports was to be kept down. But when the mineowners, always ready to lead on the downward path, proposed large reductions in miners' wages, they were promptly met by the announcement that the miners would strike, which they had expected, and that they would be supported by all the transport workers, which they had not. The other side was not ready for a big strike ; there were no stocks of coal on hand ; so the Government put off the showdown to a more convenient season, buying off the owners with a large temporary subsidy. There was much premature rejoicing in the Labour ranks and talk of "Red Thursday" wiping out "Black Friday"—and the leaders then sat back and did nothing whatever, so as to avoid "provocation." The Government and the employers, however, started to make serious preparations, piling up big stocks of coal in convenient places and creating, through Churchill's Organisation for the Maintenance of Supplies, the first, and only, avowedly strike-breaking force ever seen in this country. (Earlier strikes had been broken by the private recruitment of blacklegs, or, in extreme cases, by the use of soldiers and sailors ; the O.M.S. was a general invitation to middle-class loyalists.)

The subsidy was to end in the spring ; and in the spring the mineowners again presented their programme of lower wages and longer hours. The Miners' Executive, led by the stubby and obstinate Yorkshireman, Herbert Smith,[1] and Arthur Cook, the fiery Communist orator from South Wales, responded with the slogan, *Not a penny, not a minute* ; and called on the other Unions for help. On May Day—Labour Day—there was called a special meeting at the Memorial Hall in Farringdon Street, at which representative after representative went up to the table to hand in his Union's promise to come out with the miners. Over three and a half million workers were put at the disposal of the T.U.C. General Council ; but it was still not certain that they would be called out. The leaders were deeply concerned to prevent the strike ; they "grovelled," as J. H. Thomas said, in the attempt to get any concession at all which they could take to the miners. They got none ; the Government had made up its mind, and when on the night of May 2nd the compositors of the *Daily Mail* refused to set up a leader violently abusing the miners, Baldwin, the Prime Minister, jumped at this convenient chance, called off all negotiations and went to bed while the negotiators were actually sitting in his house. Next morning the "front-line troops" came out—all

[1] The same who in a previous wage dispute had given great pleasure by adjuring the Prime Minister (Lloyd George) with the words, "Ye silly old boogger, are ye daft ?"

rail and road transport workers, power station workers, iron and steel, metal and chemical workers, builders (except those building hospitals and houses) and printing workers. This last was a bad mistake, since it prevented the Unions from getting their case put publicly to anyone outside their own ranks, whereas the Government commanded the radio (B.B.C. employees were not organised and so could not have been called out, even if anyone had thought of it). Eight days later, the strike call came to the second line—engineers and shipyard workers ; on the following morning, after the miners had refused even to discuss a compromise memorandum presented by Sir Herbert (now Lord) Samuel,[1] the T.U.C. announced that the limit of support had been reached, and ordered the solid ranks back to work. The miners stayed out according to their slogan, and fought on until *November*, only one coalfield breaking away ; in November they went back on the owners' terms.

Because the General Strike lasted so short a time and could not be reported in non-existent newspapers, the general public knew very little about it, either at the time or afterwards, except in so far as it affected them individually—*e.g.*, by making them walk to work. After it was over, they heaved a great sigh of relief—though they spared a little sympathy for the miners' wives and children—and promptly forgot all about it. This was unfortunate, because it brought out some facts that were extremely interesting and which students of society ought to have studied for the future.

First, the solidarity of the working-class, which astonished their own leaders as much as anyone else. In town after town, including many—like Oxford—where the Labour movement was generally considered weak and unreliable, reports of nearly 100 per cent. response to the call was reported ; during the whole nine days, even after Sir John Simon, speaking as a Liberal, had threatened all strike leaders with imprisonment, there were scarcely any breakaways ; and, most impressive of all, when the men obeyed the orders to return and found that many of their employers were seizing the opportunity to do a little victimisation on their own, they promptly came out again until that attempt was squelched. A wise man might have guessed from this what account of themselves they might be able to render on other occasions when they had a chance—in 1940, say, or 1945.

Secondly, the extraordinarily peaceable character of the whole

[1] This was not a " peace offer " ; the Government never promised to take it even as a basis for discussion ; if the miners' leaders had accepted, some small face-saving concessions might have been made. We shall never know ; but if they had accepted, their constituents would certainly have turned them down.

brief war. I cannot assert that no blackleg was ever maltreated; but I can say that the report of a local strike committee to its district headquarters to the effect "Found lorries labelled FOOD not carrying food; put in canal; hope correct," was regarded as a case of exceptionally vigorous action, although a safe conduct had been manifestly abused; that there was no bloodshed at all, and that in at least one town the police drafted to keep order played a football match with the strikers. This, I think, could have happened in no other country in the world; it certainly could not have happened in the United States; and the fact that it did happen here, with all the self-restraint and regard for public order that this implies, might have caused one to hope that, given reasonably favourable conditions, a good deal of fundamental change might be carried out in Britain without civil war.

The third fact, and the most important of all, though the least observed, was the quantity of organising ability that was disclosed among the rank-and-file Trade Unionists who manned the local Trades Councils and Strike Committees. They had a great deal of work to do, particularly since the national leaders had made no plans at all; as the orders were that food and health services were not to be interfered with they had the responsibility of issuing permits for the transport of food and where necessary of coal; they had further to organise meetings and pickets, occupation and amusement for those on strike, intelligence services and news services to fill the place of the vanished newspapers.[1] For the most part they did it extremely well, showing plenty of initiative and decision—fully as much as was displayed by local civil defence groupings during the last war; even to-day we have not yet found out how in ordinary times to tap effectively the reserves of ability in ordinary people and use them in the public service.

All this we saw at first-hand in Oxford. We did not run the strike or sit on the Strike Committee; that was the Trade Unionists' business, and we very soon found that we had a job of our own among the undergraduates. For the University did not shut down; the men stayed in residence, and presumably were believed to be working. But of course only very unusual undergraduates would do anything of the kind with a grand strike going on; and it became clear that, unless some worthwhile occupation were quickly found for the Socialists among them, they would be away driving buses and trains for the Government out of sheer boredom. So from

[1] After a day or two, the Government succeeded in bringing out a violent daily, the *British Gazette*, and the printing Unions allowed a *British Worker* to appear in response; but its distribution was naturally not very effective.

our study group and from the members of the Labour Club we formed a University Strike Committee, which set itself three main jobs; to act as liaison between Oxford and Eccleston Square, then the headquarters of the T.U.C. and the Labour Party, to get out strike bulletins and propaganda leaflets for the local committees, and to spread them and knowledge of the issues through the University and the nearby villages. My job was to be liaison officer, and half-a-dozen times during those nine days I was driven up to London by Hugh Gaitskell or John Dugdale to Eccleston Square, to collect supplies of the *British Worker*, any other news or instructions that were going, and while we were there to have a look at the centre of things; and to transport anyone who happened to require transport about the city.

On one occasion, as I was leaving the T.U.C. office, a voice yelled, " Can you give a lift to the House of Commons ? " I shouted back an affirmative and waited with the door of our little Morris open until a slow thumping down the stairs announced the approach of the enormous person of Will Thorne of the General Workers. I looked at him, and at the car, apprehensively comparing their relative sizes; but he said, cheerfully, " Never mind, I'll get in back'ards; but you'll have to get me out wi' a shoehorn." When we had delivered him successfully, we went on eastwards to the offices of *Lansbury's Labour Weekly*, where we helped Aylmer Vallance (then enjoying a nice sinecure as an official of the National Maritime Board) to draft a fierce middle-page article, waited interminable hours in Fleet Street for the bundles of the *British Worker* to come off the press—they were shockingly behind time, and we enlivened the waiting period by listening to stories of the East End and the docks where no car or lorry could go unless it bore the yellow streamer of the T.U.C. permit—and finally made a wild dash through the night to get back to New College before the gates closed at midnight. Hugh could have climbed in, of course; but under all the circumstances, the unorthodox way into New College from Holywell being long and complicated, it was considered undesirable for him to take the risk of being seen and possibly sent down.

It was a strange experience, driving down through those bright May days over roads almost entirely empty, save when approaching towns one might come across a bus driven by a volunteer worker—once at any rate from John Dugdale's own college—lurching and staggering about the road; or seeing near Maidenhead the same trains, day after day, standing in sidings or on the main line where they had been left that first Monday morning. It was exhilarating, too, except when we reached headquarters; for even in brief glimpses one could perceive that there was no exhilaration there, only gloom, muddle, weariness, and a barely-concealed wish to credit the rumours the B.B.C. kept putting out concerning "mass returns to work," which were almost entirely untrue. The difference in feeling between London and Oxford was unmistakeable, and it must have been much wider in the northern industrial towns, which were struck absolutely solid and had no messenger service to give them any idea of the London mood; it is not surprising that when the news of the surrender came some of their Committees announced it as a victory. They could not believe, looking at their unbroken ranks and the accessions of strength they had received, that it could be anything else.

Back in Oxford, we would hand over our cargoes and hear the news. Everyone had been very busy. The final drafting of documents was, I think, mostly done by Douglas; they were duplicated by a squad in charge of one Ivor Thomas, not the present M.P., but a young consumptive undergraduate, who reminded me sharply of Alan Kaye, and who upheld the cause almost alone in the Tory ranks of Merton College; my carpets never recovered from the dollops of thick purple duplicating ink deposited through his efforts. *Everybody* who could put two sentences together went out speaking; and after the Archbishop of Canterbury had been forbidden to make an appeal for compromise over the radio, we arranged to work in collaboration with a group of Churchmen and Liberals who were not prepared to back the strike, but were anxious for a peaceful settlement. Douglas was called in to consult with a committee of leading clerics at Balliol Lodge, where A. D. Lindsay was Master; the entrance hall of the Lodge is very dark, and he nearly sat down on what appeared to be a bundle of rugs. Just in time he noticed that the bundle was emitting Liberal sentiments in a high indignant squeak; as it was unrolled it turned out to contain the ex-Lord Bishop of Liverpool. *Some* headway was, I believe, made by all this effort; *some* people showed a readiness to hear and to understand the workers' case; but it was sweeping the sea to try and dispel ignorance within seven days, with the B.B.C. against one and the Press closed down. If there had been a *Manchester Guardian* or a *News Chronicle* in circulation we could have got some manifestoes into them, as we had done in 1919; as it was, the most vivid, and to my mind the most accurate, account is contained in a satiric revue, *The Striker Stricken*, which Douglas wrote in one hectic week-end for performance by a Summer School at Easton Lodge—*fecit indignatio versum*. It was too libellous, not to say treasonable, ever to appear in print; but it toured with great success in the colliery districts and has been revived by student groups from time to time.

Not that better Press publicity would have made much difference in the end ; for the Government had made up its mind that " direct action " must be scotched once and for all, and, that being so, the Unions had no choice between surrendering and going on to civil war and revolution, which was the last thing they had envisaged or desired. They surrendered, ingloriously, but with the ranks unbroken ; and though the immediate outcome was, naturally, a falling-off of membership, and a good deal of angry recrimination, the absence of any real *revanche*, any sacking of the leaders who had so patently failed to lead, showed that the movement, when it had had time to think things over, realised that it had in effect made a challenge to the basis of British society which it was not prepared to see through and that, therefore, post-mortems on who was most to blame were unprofitable.

The industrial workers forgave their leaders. But they did not so easily forgive their enemies, particularly when the Government, to punish them for their insubordination, rushed through the 1927 Trade Union Act. This was a piece of political folly ; it did not (because it could not) prevent strikes ; what it did was to make it more easy to victimise local strike-leaders and also to put obstacles in the way of the Unions contributing to the funds of their own political Party. It was a mean and petty reprisal ; as such, it was repealed *en bloc* in 1946—the only act of the Labour Government which could rightly be termed class legislation ; resentment at its provisions, combined with fury at niggling attempts to worsen conditions for the unemployed, made itself felt two years later, in the 1929 election.

I well remember that election. Like that of 1945, it was fought in high summer weather—good for a party without cars, many of whose supporters were also without overcoats ; the Labour Party went into it with a programme, *Labour and the Nation*, produced much against the wish of MacDonald, who already disliked being tied to any definite printed statements, and with ammunition largely provided by Lloyd George's Liberal research department. Labour chances in Oxford being minimal,[1] I took little part in electioneering ; on election night I was in London, drifting around, with Francis and Vera Meynell and others, between Trafalgar Square, where the results were announced in moving lights, and various Bloomsbury flats which had radios. We took drinks, and

[1] I have never yet been represented in Parliament, either locally or through the University, by a member of my own party.

listened . . . *Labour Gain* . . . *Labour Gain* . . . *Labour Gain* . . . Two hundred and eighty-seven seats in all. Not quite a majority, but certainly a Labour Government supported by the Liberals. Though *Labour and the Nation* was a muddled temporising document, many of the candidates had fought on a Socialist programme more far-reaching than that of 1945 ; they had made many idealistic speeches—and not without result, for the elected included a strong contingent of members of the I.L.P. and others who really believed in " Socialism in Our Time." This time, George Lansbury would have to be in the Cabinet ; and Henderson, now a convinced internationalist, would almost certainly have the Foreign Office. This was the summer of 1929.

5.

The 'twenties were not, however, all politics and working-class education ; there were other interests. It was then, for example, that I made my first acquaintance with the previously unknown world called " Abroad "—unknown because Postgate pocket-money did not run to crossing the Channel before the war, and for some time afterwards I was otherwise occupied.

I first went Abroad with Ray and Daisy, in the spring of 1923, having callously weaned my younger daughter a month ahead of time ; and I shall never forget the pure excitement of the first approach to Dieppe on a decrepit little cross-channel steamer, the appearance on the boat of blue-clad porters hanging luggage all over themselves and talking French as though they knew what it meant, the long crisp rolls, the cheap wine and *paquets jaunes* at the station estaminet, and the hoisting of oneself up from the unexpectedly low platform on to the Paris train. It was like the tuning up of the orchestra before the symphony begins ; and I think one should always approach foreign countries in this gradual way, if one is to get any savour out of them. Of course, if all you want to do is to arrive quickly, go by air ; but apart from the boringness and stuffiness of air travel there is nothing to touch the imagination in being shot out of a catapult into an airport just like any other airport. (And if you want to appreciate the Pyramids or the Manhattan skyline approach them from eye-level ; don't look down on them from above.)

We were bound for Northern Italy ; and exciting as I found it at the time I do not, to be honest, retain very much memory of the trip except scattered recollections, as that Monte Rosa is more like a picture postcard of itself than one would have believed possible, that spring in the north Italian lakes is very cold, that small "foreign" foothills are much higher than Welsh mountains and delude the tourist into climbing long hours without ever reaching a satisfactory summit—and that the twilight is much too short for the descent. This does not mean that I did not enjoy myself; but I have generally found that places to which I have gone purely for holiday-making have left far less impression than those where I have managed to feel myself part of the community, either because I was doing some work there or because I was living with friends. Russia, Sweden, Egypt, New York, Argyll (let nobody say that the West of Scotland is not a foreign country!), all have become much more part of me, even in their uglier aspects—and there is a good deal that is ugly or boring or both in Russian rail journeys, interminable Swedish forest, the Bulaq slums of Cairo, the southern suburbs of New York or the revolting little towns with which the Scots deface their lovely natural harbours—than the fine sights of Venice, Madeira, Lugano, Bruges, and other places where I sojourned as a tourist. The only exception I can recollect is Athens and the isles of Greece, which I suppose were charged with special meaning for anyone brought up on the classics—I have never been to Rome. (But I used the Greek scene as a setting for a detective novel, so perhaps that is not an exception after all.)

So, though in the following year I went with the same companions south from Clermont-Ferrand and saw Roman France, Vercingetorix's statue, the huge staring white Arènes at Nîmes, and the Pont du Gard black against an angry purple sunset; and proceeded south to Cette, where the white road lying between blue sea and crimson vineyards makes a perfect tricolour (and read the news of MacDonald's fall sitting on the cinema back-cloth ramparts of Carcassonne), what remains most with me is neither of these trips, but the occasions when I stayed with Stella and Ford in Paris, picking up, as a truant matron, something of the poet-painter contacts I had missed since 1918. Ford and Stella had sold their Sussex cottage and lived with their small daughter Julie in a succession of studios in Montparnasse, in the days before the Great Slump, when Anglo-Saxon tourists were swarming over Europe, and the Dôme and the Rotonde and the Closerie des Lilas were all blooming, though, as anyone would tell you, the *Quartier* was not what it had been before the Americans came. No doubt American money did pay for a great deal; but at least the French as well as the Americans got good value out of it—and nobody in those days thought of calling the foreigners "scheming imperialists."

A good many of Stella's and Ford's friends were Americans,

contributors to or backers of a journal called the *transatlantic review*, which Ford edited until it went bankrupt after a year or two ; some were writers, some painters. I remember meeting Gertrude Stein, a stoutish lady whose clothes seemed held up with safety-pins, surrounded by Picassos ; Ernest Hemingway, not yet well known ; the painters Tcherlitchev and Cedric Morris, and a good many others ; going to many cafés and restaurants which Ford, always the most discerning gourmet, picked out as suitable for various occasions and varying conditions of the pocket ; and walking home under a full May moon, over the Seine and through the Ile de la Cité, noticing the shining white feet on which the boards carrying election placards used to stand, looking as though they were going to march away down the street at any moment.

On those visits I did not see much of the Paris which the ordinary tourist sees—Ford and his friends were distinctly high-brow, not to say snobbish, about the Champs Elysées, the Tuileries, the Rue de Rivoli, etc., and it was not until much later that I studied and loved the gracious loveliness of planned, laid-out Paris, and began to wonder how the British can possibly be expected to plan or even envisage decent-looking towns when the great bulk of them have never in their lives set eyes on a beautiful city. Ford's ciceronage confined itself severely to the Rive Gauche, the Montparnasse and the Boul' Mich' ; and at his gatherings, I would add, I was always the philistine from across the water, representative of the smug and commercial civilisation whose unappreciative dust Ford had shaken from his feet, and I listened rather than talked. But I always enjoyed listening, and generally got much pleasure out of Ford, even at his most perverse. I loved those glimpses through the curtain—a curtain of beads, surely, rather than of iron !—which still hung between London and Paris. I think, however, that Paris, for all its beauty, is a merciless city, in which I would not like to be ill, old or penniless ; and I am not sure that this is not true of French civilisation as a whole. If this is so, it may partly explain why—to my sorrow—the British people in general do not like the French ; given the smallest chance, they are much readier to love German sentimentality.

In London of those years, also, on the odd days I stayed up after taking classes, there was a certain amount of fun going on. This was the heyday of the Nonesuch Press, when Francis and Vera Meynell were the glass of fashion and mould of form to their friends. I remember a party given by them for the coloured chorus of the *Blackbirds* revue, at which a guest going to collect his overcoat

THE COLE CHILDREN

Anne, aged 2

Humphrey, aged 2

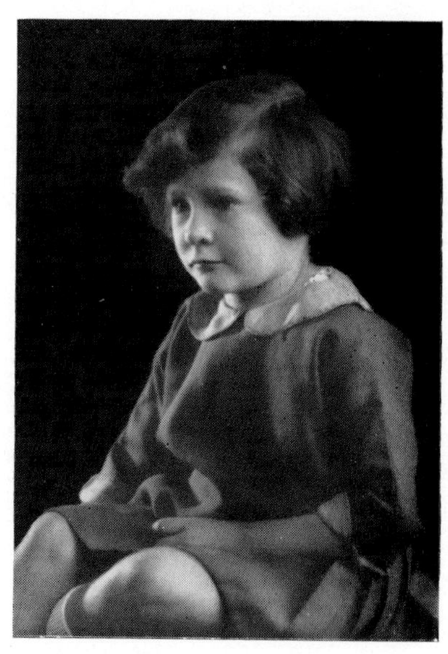

Jane, aged 3½

G. D. H. Cole, 1935

Margaret Cole, 1938

saw a silver shoe lying by it, and on trying to pick up the shoe drew out an entire Blackbird, fast asleep. When the lady's escort was found he explained with a little embarrassment that this was not her normal behaviour at parties but that on reading the invitation she had exclaimed to him, "Oh, boy, look! A party only three blocks off! Whatta channce for a blind!" I made acquaintance with a night-club—an infinitely respectable night-club; but though over thirty I was sufficiently unsophisticated to relish it and its open roof-top from which one could look down on a hot night at the lights of London.

And there were week-ends, or slightly longer periods, when Douglas and I left the children and went walking or bussing with packs on our backs over parts of southern England—the Cotswolds, Mendips, Quantocks, Sedgmoor, Cranborne Chase. It was on one of these journeys, I remember, that we came into Lyme Regis without having decided where to put up; and seeing in front of the Three Cups Hotel an enormous figure sitting in an armchair on the stoep as though it were the presiding genius of the place we said simultaneously, "What's good enough for Chesterton is good enough for us," and went in. G.K.C. entertained us for the whole evening, partly with dissertations on the difficulties he found in assisting those who tried to translate his writing into foreign tongues. "How," he asked, heaving mountainously in his chair, "would *you* put the phrase 'the child she-bear so beloved of hymnologists' into idiomatic and intelligible French?"

* * *

I am conscious that the diversity of my interests—and of my habitation—during the 'twenties has made me draw a somewhat disconnected picture of that decade; it is composed of many spots of different colours, like a *pointilliste* picture. It was, however, itself something of a *pointilliste* picture—though a picture none the less. Looking back from the grim and dolorous 'thirties, it might reasonably be called a Golden Age, although the million unemployed and the continual wrangles about reparations and war-debts made it seem anything but golden to those who could remember 1913. But the war was definitely over—well over; people who talked about it were apt to be thought old bores, and even the ex-officers touting brushes and vacuum-cleaners had ceased to be subjects for novelists.[1] It even looked as though the Peace, and the League of Nations, whatever their defects, might be going to last our time.

[1] *All Quiet on the Western Front* and *Farewell to Arms* were only published in 1929.

There was nothing very alarming on the horizon. The Irish had fought for and won their freedom ; the French had been made to get out of the Ruhr and the Locarno Pact had been signed with enormous acclamation in 1925. The Russians had had a New Economic Policy, which some said was a step back to capitalism and some more correctly that it was nothing of the kind ; but at least Russia-baiting was on the wane, and visitors like George Lansbury spoke of the great increase in production and comforts that the Soviets had achieved in half-a-dozen years. The long-drawn out battle between Trotsky and Stalin which ended in 1927 appeared to be an internal row—interesting only to Communist theologians. Even the Succession States of the Austro-Hungarian Empire seemed less quarrelsome than might have been expected, and the Austrian Socialists were making Red Vienna a model Socialist city. There was of course Mussolini, who appeared to be doing very unpleasant things with castor-oil and had actually arranged the murder of the Socialist leader Matteotti—but did not those who knew their history say that Parliamentary government had always had very weak roots in Italy, so need one bother ? The stolid indifference or detached distaste shown by most Britons even of the Left to the behaviour of the Fascists must have been maddening to the refugees from Italy.

As to Hitler, he had made a brief lunatic appearance and vanished into ignominious oblivion. Most people had never heard of him. The Japanese were still receiving hearty praise from the Webbs. And at home, despite the failure of the first Labour Government and the General Strike, there was a perceptible move to the left, as was amply demonstrated in the 1929 election. The Labour movement, especially the women, was solidly and deeply pacifist ; and the fact that foreign travel was again possible—often to countries with conveniently depreciated currencies—and was beginning to be available to some of the working class—the Workers' Travel Association was founded in 1922—encouraged many optimists to believe that internationalism might grow with intercourse across frontiers.

Socially there was certainly a move forward, towards the loosening of tradition and convention. Women were nominally admitted into all professions and in practice to some ; there were a few women in Parliament and more in local government, and many of the old taboos had vanished, never to return. Smoking, swearing, and playing tennis in shorts became inalienable feminine rights, though equality either of pay or responsibility was still far to seek. The women who came into industry during the war had mostly gone out again, thereby making it fairly easy for their middle-class and professional sisters to get daily help, even if tenpence an hour seemed a great deal to pay. Production, notwithstanding the jeremiads of the Labour Research Department, was rising reasonably fast ; and what was more the things produced—or imported—seemed to be of a more entertaining kind—radio sets, gramophone records, Chaplin's great silent films, cheap and pretty glasses at Woolworth's, and clothes and furnishings of new materials and bright pretty colours. When we went to Oxford, " Oxford bags " were the height of fashion. These were immensely wide and floppy flannel trousers dyed in exquisite pastel shades ; when three young men walked abreast down Holywell, their six legs, two pale green, two lemon-yellow, and two lavender-pink, moved in the breeze like a bed of spring flowers. It was a pity that fashion did not allow the girls to live up to them ; at that time waistlines were low and skirts at their shortest, a peculiarly ugly combination, in view of the unprepossessingness of the average female knee, especially since it applied to evening as well as to daytime outfits, leaving practically no scope for imaginative dressing. My sister was then up at Somerville, and when I went to a dance there my reflection was that the girls looked exactly like a box of fondants ; you could choose a pink or a white or a green one, but they were all more or less the same shape. Fortunately, that particular form of dreary uniformity vanished within a few years.

As every anguished publicist pointed out, there was, once the restrictions of wartime DORA had been removed, a great growth of dancing, jazz, cocktail parties, and night-clubs—the Shimmy, the Blues, the Charleston, the Black Bottom, all belong to the days before " swing " was heard of. There was also much motoring, the long week-end, and a great increase of sport and of skill in sport ; all games became more and more skilled and left less and less scope for the " rabbit "—witness, for example, the transformation of the pat-ball occupation once appropriately named ping-pong into exhibition and championship table-tennis. Greyhound racing began unobtrusively in the mid-decade, to be followed within a few years by the earliest football pools. Alongside all this, there was a general feeling of experimentation in the air ; some of it asinine enough, like the Treasure Hunts and other exploits of Bright Young Things, which got headlines in the London Press. " Free " schools, free love, free verse, companionate marriage, sodomy and lesbianism, Freud, Marie Stopes, Judge Lindsey, all formed the subject of eager discussion ; and though pre-war giants like Bennett, Wells, and Galsworthy—and of course Shaw—were still writing and being read by hundreds of thousands,[1] intellectual youth tended to take them for granted and gave its serious attention to writers like Joyce, Aldous Huxley, and above all D. H. Lawrence—though *The Waste Land* came out in 1922, Eliot was not yet an authority. For light relief they added Daisy Ashford's *Young Visiters* and Amita Loos's *Gentlemen Prefer Blondes*. Political writing was comparatively at a discount until peace was threatened again ; a Left Book Club would not have had a chance ; and science, Wells notwithstanding, was not yet a subject worthy of a literary gent's serious attention.

It was a bit of a cloudcuckooland, altogether—full of odd aspirations and hopeful speculations—in the social as well as the financial sense. Seen in retrospect, some, at any rate, of the speculation recalls irresistibly the hopeful crocodile in Lewis Carroll's *Sylvie and Bruno*, who enquired of the universe, " Why shouldn't I walk on my own forehead ? " and actually, we are told, " walked a teeny way down his nose." Our world, up to 1930, was contemplating walking a teeny way down its nose ; in the following decade the brute facts won, and the crocodile was abruptly recalled to consciousness of his physical limitations.

[1] It is interesting, though, that Galsworthy almost ceased to be *discussed* from the moment he became a best-seller. *Riceyman Steps*, Bennett's last major work, came out in 1923 ; *St Joan* in 1924 ; and though H.G. went on writing to the day of his death, few would claim that he was saying anything much that he had not said before.

PART FIVE

TURN OF THE TIDE

Chapter Nine

1.

As a matter of cold historical fact, the summer of 1929 was probably neither warmer nor sunnier than the ordinary run of English summers ; it is only the knowledge of what came afterwards that has invested it in retrospect with so golden a glow. It was, however, a time of bright hope for many beside the Cole family. The new Labour Government had just taken office ; Briand in France and Stresemann in Germany seemed to be willing to get together with Arthur Henderson and make a durable peace at last ; the problem of Palestine had not yet taken on a dangerous shape (the Wailing Wall riots did not break out until the autumn) ; there was moderate prosperity on this side of the Atlantic, and on the other the Wall Street bubble, though blown out to an incredible size, had not yet burst. Even in mid-1929, there were still economists who explained carefully, with chapter and verse, that a slump in the United States was *impossible*, because her vast internal market made it certain that all she could produce could easily be absorbed at home.[1]

For us personally, also, 1929-30 registered a change in more than one aspect of life. First, we were leaving Oxford ; we had decided in the spring to come out of the mists and back to London, leaving behind us—a small but important matter—a terrible cretinous couple who had endeavoured to run the house for us for the year after Mrs Farrant retired. (We replaced them by a miner and his wife ; in 1929 and for several years afterwards there was no lack of people willing to take on domestic service in order to escape from the pits.) The intention—never realised in fact—was that Douglas would keep on his Oxford job for a few years, travelling to and fro and accumulating Books in his college rooms, and would

[1] An Anthology of Unfulfilled Predictions, were it not so disillusioning, would be an entertaining compilation. In my own life, I have been most in contact with the *gaffes* of economists, who delighted to prophesy the immediate collapse (owing to their economic foolishness) of the U.S.S.R., or of Nazi Germany. But there are other candidates for fame, as for example, those who continually reiterated, "you cannot fight Nazism without becoming a Nazi."

then find something congenial to do in London.[1] We bought a house, an ugly but undeniably convenient house in Hampstead, west of the Finchley Road ; and prepared to settle down, to have regular gatherings of class-students and dinner-parties of friends and fellow-Socialists—cocktail parties were not then the only form of private entertainment—to send the little girls to school, and watch the growth out of babyhood of the little boy. (Humphrey refused to learn to talk for so long that I wondered at times whether he could be tongue-tied. But the reason was economy of effort ; he could get what he wanted by a judicious use of sounds like Aah and Baa. Similarly, though he knew his alphabet when he was two, he rejected any syllabic instruction like " the cat sat on the mat," but learned to read by pure observation—of street names, for example.)

Schools, as a matter of fact, presented some difficulty. North London had not as yet experienced the invasion which made " Plizz ? " the most frequent answer to any request for information and caused Tommy Trinder to describe his peace-time job as " British Consul for Golder's Green " ; but already there were a good many schools which made a point of taking no Jews, and thus posed a very awkward quandary for civilised parents, since the over-representation of the Jewish community in the other schools resulted in the little Jews (who developed early, on the whole) tending to excel and so to stimulate anti-semitism among the little Gentiles. Our own solution was to send Jane and Anne to the school attended by their cousins, John and Oliver Postgate, which was run by a Dutch couple, and counted at least a dozen nationalities among its pupils. Optimists like George Lansbury, who once gave away the prizes, believed that this admixture would turn the English pupils towards international brotherhood ; I am bound to admit that I never saw the slightest sign that this had happened. But it was a reasonably good starting point for education and had a fair social mixture ; I remember that when Jane wanted to ask a child to tea, and I said, " The only L—— I can find in the telephone-book is a butcher's shop, " Jane replied, " That's all right, Mummy ; Jean's mother lives with a butcher."

This physical change of environment coincided in time with the 1929 election to which I have already referred. The importance of the latter fact was the revival of hope in politics—and in Parliament. Douglas, whose belief in Parliamentary institutions was, to say the

[1] Douglas doubts whether this was ever a formulated intention, and I accept the correction. But I certainly thought so at the time ; it must have been a mental wiping out of Oxford !

least of it, never very strong, was sufficiently moved to join MacDonald's Economic Advisory Council, which in the end turned out so futile, and to allow his name to go forward as a Parliamentary candidate. For a brief while in 1930-31, before ill-health put an end both to that venture and to plans for touring the United States, he was Labour candidate for the King's Norton division of Birmingham, and I was candidate's wife, slated to open Labour bazaars and address Labour women's meetings. In fact, I only opened one bazaar—with a speech which was neither good in itself nor appreciated by the audience ; and by the time of the next general election he had ceased to be candidate and I was only driving decrepit voters to the poll—a much pleasanter assignment.

His candidature—which was, I think, no more congenial to him than opening bazaars was to me—was due mainly to the strong pressure of Henderson, and also of the Webbs, with whom we had become much more friendly since the break-up of " the Movement." (The preface of his book, *The Next Ten Years in British Social and Economic Policy*, which was published early in 1929, renders thanks to the Webbs for valuable criticisms made in the course of its preparation.) I cannot now remember exactly the stages by which Beatrice Webb changed for me from the Bogie-woman I have earlier described, first to a human creature and then to a friend and a woman whom I admired and was very proud to have known ; but it was a gradual process. For a long time, even after we had taken to spending week-ends at their house at Passfield Corner, I felt that Douglas was in her eyes the important person and I a kind of umbrella which he had to be allowed to bring with him ;[1] but slowly I attained to a personal existence in my own right, and was able to talk to her, to interrupt or to contradict without nervousness—and so to discover that, whatever the criticisms which might be (and were) legitimately made of her, she was not merely the greatest woman I have ever known, but a *kind* person with human affections and human friendliness, perennially interested in the individuals who were coming after her—and that she loved a good gossip, of her own kind, as much as any other woman. I am not likely to forget Beatrice telling acid anecdotes of her contemporaries, such as Margot Asquith (of whom she had a very poor opinion), or describing, in her high definite tones, So-and-So as " an *odious* sort of person." She liked to speak of Sidney and herself as " benevolent bureaucrats " in contrast to " aristocratic

[1] On one occasion, she asked him to dinner, and me to come in for coffee afterwards. There were valid reasons for making this distinction, but only Beatrice could have done it.

anarchists " such as Bertrand Russell ; but whatever may be thought of the first description, there was a great deal in her make-up that was purely aristocratic, not to say arrogant.

I have described the Webb ménage at Passfield Corner, and paid my tribute to Beatrice, in my own *Life* of her and elsewhere, and do not want to repeat myself here. But I should like to add a word or two about the Webb partnership as a whole, as I knew it. It was, of course, complete, absolute, and equal—the most perfect, I should think, that has ever been known in English public life. What it meant to Beatrice, emotionally, she has written down unforgettably in the opening pages of *Our Partnership* ; Sidney wrote nothing down, but it was always clear, to anyone who knew him at all, that, having Beatrice, he needed no other human companionship. She, as I said, was less single-minded ; she liked to have friends, and had a considerable affection for some (not all !) of her numerous relatives. Nevertheless, she was the more dependent of the two ; it was fortunate that she died first, for I cannot conceive how she would have lived without him.

Because she was the more vocal, the more lively and impressive personality, many people fell into the error of thinking that she was also the more dominant ; in fact his influence over her was both strong and steady, partly because he was so steady in his own views and so immune from emotional reactions. In the matter of literary style, his ascendancy was unmistakeable and I think unfortunate. The extracts which have been published from Beatrice's Diaries show that she had a natural gift for vivid description which in their joint works has completely disappeared, crushed out by Sidney's remorseless cataloguing of occupations, industries, powers of local authorities and what not, which has always reminded me of the passing of an immensely long goods train at a level crossing. In ideas, though there was no serious disagreement, it was he who held her firmly to the strait path of collectivist and later of Stalinist thought. She could feel gusts of half-impatient sympathy towards the Guild Socialists whom she found so irritating, whereas he felt none at all ; she was shocked like the rest of the world by the alliance of Stalin with Hitler, but he drew her back to orthodoxy. How much he was indirectly influenced by the less rational side of her it is difficult to say ; but on her side there is no doubt that this guiding control made her a far happier woman, able to do far more work, than she would otherwise have been, while he always gave the impression of being one of the most contented men in the world.

This enormous happiness gave them a deep and unshakeable security in their life and work. It did not prevent them from being quite wrong upon occasion, from misjudging either personalities or the trend of events or of popular sentiment—the fact that they were both trained as executives, he in the civil service and she in running her father's household and helping him in his business, may have had something to do with this, by discouraging them from giving rein to imagination. It was this lack of sympathy with, or rather resolute ignoring of what lay outside their comprehensive grasp, which maddened H. G. Wells to drawing the bitter picture contained in *The New Machiavelli* ; but it also made for very great practical efficiency. Extraordinarily few, of the many ventures they started, turned out failures ; and they possessed also the extremely rare gift of self-restraint towards the institutions they had created. They made, to take only two examples, both the London School of Economics and the *New Statesman*, but they did not demand that these institutions should submit themselves to the continuing guidance of the Webbs, nor, when the institutions developed in ways which the Webbs had not expected, did they withdraw their patronage in a huff, as other distinguished and public-spirited persons have been known to do. Personally, also, they were the least rancorous people in the world. Like others, they had their likes and dislikes, sometimes quite strong ones ; but they never rushed into print with them, and they bore the kind of abuse which less stabilised personalities hurled at them without reprisal, and even showed genuine interest in their detractors' future. Their public work and its effect on the social shape of twentieth-century England is now a matter of history—and of Westminster Abbey [1] ; I shall remember most their friendly welcome, over many years, to a couple whom they criticised as foolish anarchists in the 'twenties and in the 'thirties as middle-aged reactionaries without ever losing interest in them. When I went to Passfield Corner for the last time, just before it was sold, I could almost see Beatrice standing at the door, among the heaths and the rock-plants, with her eagle nose and a net cap over her straying white hairs, and her arms opened wide to embrace me.

* * *

Visiting Ramsay MacDonald in the country was a very different thing from visiting the Webbs ; I only did it once, in fact, when Douglas and I went over to spend the day at Chequers, in order

[1] Some people strongly criticised the burial with Christian rites of two people who, whatever their beliefs, were not orthodox Christians, and there was certainly an element of incongruity. But on that point it seems likely that Beatrice would have been less perturbed by the incongruity than pleased to be laid in Britain's nearest approach to a Panthéon ; and if it pleased her Sidney would have acquiesced.

that Douglas might discuss with the P.M. the 1930 Coal Bill, to whose terms he had taken strong exception ; but my recollection of it is vivid enough. There had been some Americans of Importance lunching at Chequers on the previous day ; we were therefore regaled with fish-cakes made of most superior salmon and wine which caused Douglas to open his eyes wide. And MacDonald performed in his best style—several parts in the course of one afternoon. He was obviously delighted with Chequers, with its buildings, its plenishings, and its importance, and his first rôle was that of an inheritor of broad acres, deeply sensitive to the traditions of the countryside. But he was also (for a few minutes only) the Son of the People not born to all this glory but called to it by Fate in order that he might create beauty for all the other sons of the people who had not been so called ; later, he was for quite a long time the Lonely Leader grappling with problems which none but he could understand and burdened with inferior colleagues not one of whom really appreciated him or inspired his confidence, or could be trusted to carry out policy. All this with immense play of expression from his dark eyes and brows and his handsome head with its mane of grey hair, and in his magnificent voice with its rolling Scottish r's—I don't *think* he was wearing a kilt, but he certainly acted as though he were—and all for an audience consisting of two MacDonald girls, who looked as though they had heard it all before, and a pair of sceptics. My immediate reflection was that only a natural-born actor could have expended so much effort on such unpromising materials.

And it is true of MacDonald that he was an actor all his life, that his closest associates in the Labour movement—he had very few real friends there—never knew whether or not he was putting on an act. Yet that cannot be the whole truth about that strange and disastrous personality, of whom so much has been written without succeeding in presenting a coherent picture. Those who know what he became can trace far back in his early years the beginnings of characteristics which afterwards developed so fatally ; the pitiful incoherence of his later speeches in Parliament, his ditherings about " going on and on and on and up and up and up," are not so surprising when one has re-read the cloudy phrases in which before 1914 he wrapped his views on Socialism and internationalism. His early fantasies about his birth might have given an indication of the romantic passion for high society which partly dictated the betrayal of 1931 ;[1] even as far back as 1912 he had

[1] " To-morrow," he said to Philip Snowden on the eve of the National Government, " every duchess in London will want to kiss me."

yearnings to amalgamate the shabby little Labour Party with something larger and more showy ; and the way in which he treated Henderson, for example, showed both the secretiveness and the unfraternal contempt which in 1931 shocked his erstwhile colleagues even more deeply than the mere fact of his changing sides in a crisis. But to observe all that, after the event, is not to explain the fact of his almost magical ascendancy, or how it came about that he commanded Henderson's allegiance until almost the last moment, that he induced the Clyde revolutionaries to vote him into the leadership in 1922, and that, having destroyed the first Labour Government by a piece of secretive idiocy (over the Zinoviev letter), which he never even tried to explain, he was so enthusiastically called upon to command the second. The number of life-sized photographs of MacDonald which, in the autumn of 1931, were torn down from the walls of Labour committee-rooms, I.L.P. halls, and Socialist churches, must have run into thousands ; their subject had his brief day as saviour of the nation and—for a few weeks—of the pound sterling, and when his turn was served he was not even pushed out, like Lloyd George in 1922, by a Carlton Club meeting, but shrivelled off almost unnoticed, like the dead calyx of a flower.

Psychologists, maybe, might with long study make something of MacDonald ; I never knew him well enough even to try. I only knew that I regarded him with profound distrust ; but the fact that there were others who felt as I did, coupled with another fact, that, when in 1930 the unemployed percentages began to creep ominously up again, it became increasingly apparent that Labour, which had declared so loudly that it would cure unemployment, had not the slightest idea how to do so—these facts together inspired us to try again to form a group of intelligent workers for Socialism. The year 1930 was signalised by two events, the beginning of our comradeship with the Mitchisons and the foundation of the society called S.S.I.P., which Francis Meynell christened The Loyal Grousers.

2.

We had been acquainted with Dick and Naomi Mitchison—though not with their five highly intelligent children, who all have so remarkable a gift for passing examinations—for quite a while. Douglas, indeed, had been up at Oxford with Dick, and had known Nou in the pre-war years, when as Naomi Haldane, she was the *enfant terrible* of the Dragon School there—an intellectual forcing-house of a prep. school, where the small handful of girls learned to be particularly tough. I had read and enjoyed *The Conquered*, her first book, and some others ; I hardly knew Dick, except as a large and curiously shy object at parties, who managed somehow to give the impression of always standing on one leg. But early one spring they came to one of the dinner-parties we were giving in our new home, and shortly afterwards I found myself from time to time going out to dine and dance with Dick, at places like Quaglino's and the Hotel de Paris up-river, which was a new experience for me. " The Movement " of my youth, with a few exceptions, either did not dance or danced very badly—Douglas, of course, not at all ; certainly, they did not dance at Quaglino's or treat their partners to oysters and champagne ; and I had been mostly out of London during the dancing developments of the 'twenties. It was a nice new pleasure, and was followed in the summer by another, when the Mitchison family invited the Cole family to make part of their house-party at Craignish Castle in Argyll. Thereafter, until the outbreak of war, there were only two summers in which the families were not together for part of the holidays, sometimes in Scotland, sometimes in Spain, Sweden, or Madeira. Just before the last war Dick Mitchison bought Carradale House in Kintyre, which, when foreign travel was no more and London became, to say the least of it, somewhat unattractive as a continuous residence, turned into a haven of rest not for Coles only, but for many others. This, however, is to anticipate.

It is not soulless greed which makes me mention first the oysters-and-champagne element in the new association ; for though I do not suggest that Dick dined habitually on oysters and champagne—which would indeed be very dull—a perceptibly higher standard of living, amusement, and free spending by Mitchisons was one of the things which most immediately impressed me and my children. I am, I think, more quickly alive than many to comparatively small differences in money expenditure, which probably derives from my childhood impecuniosity, when I earned pennies for the strawberry-suckers and regarded a rocking-horse as a symbol of Midas. In an earlier chapter I have mentioned how the number and size of Douglas's possessions impressed me on marriage ; I have not to this day really caught up with him, and feel a distinct, if weak, sense of guilt when I buy a first-class ticket or take a taxi instead of a bus. This is emphatically *not* a question of economy *versus* extravagance ; Douglas is no more spendthrift than I am, probably less. It is a question of the point at which your sub-conscious, with or without reason, begins to mutter " Too dear " ; and it may quite easily lead to being stingy in small things—it is possible that I gave my children too little pocket-money—while spending recklessly on larger issues when the sub-conscious does not protest.

It was perhaps for this reason that I and my children, when we came into contact with a higher level of spending than our own, tended at first simply to stand and admire. Never having ourselves seen the glories of a shootin' and fishin' party in a Highland castle, with ghillies galore and pipers piping the guests to banquet, we were immensely impressed when the Mitchisons hired for the summer—quite cheaply, I learned afterwards—Craignish Castle in Western Argyll, and put therein a house-party of nearly a dozen besides themselves; we believed that the piper with the enormous swirling plaid who played at a dance—and got very drunk—was a hired band instead of merely one of the guests; we contrasted this splendour with my father-in-law's house in Hove, and felt we were living with dukes, no less. When Carradale House was bought we were equally impressed; if the Coles had bought a place in the country it would have been a large cottage with a small patch of ground, not a house built in Scottish baronial style with pepperpots at the corners, accommodating twenty guests or so, with billiard-room, farmland and gardens, outlying dwellings, woodland, a stretch of trout stream, a mile or so of beach-sea, and large rough heathery slopes for shooting; though the place was, I believe, a bargain, and certainly a very great bargain during the war years, it was not the sort of bargain which would have been likely to come within our ken. And in home circumstances it was much the same. We lived in a fair-sized house, but it was not nearly so impressive as their big dwelling on Thames-side, where large parties were gathered to play round a tall Christmas tree in winter or to watch the Boat Race from the roof in spring—when Rivercourt was sold half Bloomsbury cried in despair, "But *how* shall we see the Boat Race?" Nor did our economy include a butler—even though that butler, sharing to some extent the originalities of the household, once helped a dinner-party to portions of a clear mauve liquid which proved to be methylated spirit, economically stored by him in superannuated hock-bottles.

The Mitchisons, I think, must have been surprised and a little amused—if they noticed—at our attitude of awed admiration for a difference which did not seem very large to them. But they owed this attitude in part to their own generosity. What they had they spent freely; unlike some of my wealthier acquaintances—including the richest!—they did not seem to suffer from continual agonised penury and to be unable without pangs to spare half-a-crown or a pound ; they have always been among the most generous people alive in the giving of entertainment or presents or the helping of friends unable to help themselves. Even though, as years went by and the world slipped into war, their standards, like those of others, were reduced, the sense of generous and spacious living remained and was deeply appreciated.

But it was emphatically not only a question of oysters-and-champagne, or of appreciation by the greedy alone ; it was—and is—fully as much the personalities of the owners of Rivercourt and Carradale House that brought their friends around them like bees around a honey-pot. Naomi is one of the most original of the gifted people I have known in my life. When I first came to know her, she was already an established novelist and had " commenced poet "—I think she has developed into one of the best, as also one of the most intelligible, poets of modern Britain—a reviewer for high-brow weeklies, a pet of Bloomsbury of the late 'twenties, an excellent talker on subjects literary, historical, political, and scientific,[1] with a child-like propensity to scandalise those to whom she talked—and the mother of four children, with a fifth on the way—who wore the most unconventional clothes, which were sometimes beautiful, sometimes reminiscent of an old peasant woman subsisting on cast-offs from the gentry. This, I felt, was a considerable variety of achievement for a woman seven or eight years younger than myself ; but I have since known Naomi as, (*a*) a part-time farmer of some very unprepossessing land, (*b*) an occasional assistant on a Carradale herring-boat, (*c*) a poacher, (*d*) a kind of local chatelaine-cum-prophetess to a Scottish fishing village, (*e*) an active County Councillor for Argyll, (*f*) a member of a Government Commission on the Highlands and Islands, and (*g*) a fervent Scottish patriot—I dare not say Scottish Nationalist, having no wish to embroil myself fatally with any of the groups into which Scots oppressed by English sort themselves, but " patriot " is, I hope, a safe word—who derives her ancestry from Scots of centuries back and has used the ancestors effectively in one of the best of her novels.[2] All this she has done a hundred per cent. while she was at it, bringing to bear great energy, considerable muscular strength—you should see her hump a sack of potatoes—originality, a verbal truculence which is as often as not

[1] The scientific bent was hereditary ; it can be seen in her father, J. S. Haldane, and her brother, J. B. S. Haldane ; both brilliant scientists with an experimental cast of mind which, in Naomi, comes out as a readiness to try anything once, in argument or in action.

[2] *The Bull Calves*—a novel of eighteenth century Perthshire, made peculiarly fascinating to historians by a great bunch of historical notes incorporated at the end.

pure innocence, and what cannot be described as anything else than charm. She will never, I think, convert many people to her views at large, partly because the views are so very individual a bundle, and partly because she does not stay long enough to explain to the slow, and is nearly always trying to expound two different unorthodoxies simultaneously—she is often a little like the White Knight; but her intelligence, and her gift for deep emotional sympathy with many different kinds of people, have made her an influence in more lives than, perhaps, she knows.

As to Dick, he is far less articulate than his wife, and he is deceptive, too, because he looks so large and so respectable. He did, when I first knew him, all the things that a gentleman should, except play cricket; and the first time that I met him out-of-doors he was walking along the Strand in a perfect morning coat and top-hat. (He is a barrister, and a K.C.; my eight-year-old Anne, when contemplating the amenities of Craignish Castle, reflected "Dick must make a lot of money by being a *barrier*"—which her hearers delightedly received as a revealing comment on the English legal system.) He always walked on the outside of the pavement, took the tickets, ordered about the porters and the waiters and the gamekeepers, and had wine and brandy and cigars to offer to everyone. It made an amusing superficial contrast to Naomi, but the difference went much less deep than anyone would suppose, and they are, in fact, as matched a couple as I know; he shares to the full her delight in collecting people of different sorts, listening to them, appreciating them, and above all in being kind to them. When I met him first he was politically a dissatisfied Liberal; and, though he soon became a Socialist and member of the Labour Party, he was for a long time highly critical of most Labour organisations. He is now a Labour M.P. of the sturdy kind who does not speak a lot except on what he knows—and is therefore listened to—and who works himself hard over his constituents' troubles in ways which will, I hope, bear fruit at election time. It goes without saying that he has been a constant and most appreciated friend; he, with Ray, would have been the childrens' guardian had Douglas and I both perished during the war; and we all owe the Mitchison household a great deal.

There is only one word of social significance that I should like to add. This gamut of occupations that I have listed, I am sure both he and Naomi would agree, could not have been undertaken or carried on in the way it has been had they not been people of independent unearned income. The state of society which produced these independent incomes is passing away under our eyes; it is our job to secure, if we can, that the society which succeeds it allows both leisured-energy and disinterested generosity to continue.

Meantime, we went to Craignish with them, and I learned a number of things, *e.g.*, that " walking with the guns " is as dull as any occupation undertaken in glorious scenery can be ; and that there are two kinds of fishing on Scottish holidays, one a ritual pursuit of trout and salmon, conducted by experts, in which the craft is more important than the kill and amateurs are discouraged ; and the other (sea-fishing) a communal fiesta in which you sit crowded, half-a-dozen at a time, in a rowboat and either catch nothing at all (or two huge dogfish with revolting faces) because there are no fish there, or are swamped and slimed by dozens of slippery lythe and saithe biting on bare hooks. But I also learned, on expeditions of this type, how lovely the West of Scotland is—the sun going down in a scarlet blaze behind Scarba, a still sea-loch with the weed slowly lifting and dropping under a full moon, and the constant changes of light and clear colour. From a corner of the high terrace at Craignish Castle there was a view which Richmond and I christened " the picture-postcard series," because it was never twice the same—and I have seen equal loveliness elsewhere in Scotland. If only the Scots could build themselves less hideous dwellings ! What visions we might have seen, had the French or the Italians been given the site of Tarbert, or of Campbeltown. As it is, they are both eyesores. But our first Scottish holiday was a real re-creation, and we came back to get on with the founding of our new Socialist Society.

3.

S.S.I.P. (the Society for Socialist Inquiry and Propaganda) was a tiny organisation throughout its short life ; it had, however, a threefold importance. In the first place, it rallied the intellectual left and set it to thinking out a new Socialist policy when the second Labour Government was obviously barren of ideas. Secondly—a negative contribution—its unwise lining up with the rump of the I.L.P. to form the ill-fated Socialist League proved conclusively that there was no practicable place within the Labour Party for a political organisation advocating a rival or alternative policy, even if it were not a wrecking Communist policy. Thirdly, through its younger brother, the New Fabian Research Bureau, it collected a group of people strong, active, and cohesive enough to take over the somnolent Fabian Society at the outbreak of war, to keep Socialist enthusiasm alive and thinking when the wartime electoral truce had effectively hamstrung a large number of the Divisional Labour Parties, and to think out a number of suggestions which were subsequently embodied in the Labour election programme of 1945. That election sent back to Westminster a Parliament largely Fabian in composition, headed by a Cabinet at least half of whom were members of the Fabian Society; it follows that where Labour policy has gone wrong, or appears to have gone wrong, since 1945, Fabians deriving from S.S.I.P. and N.F.R.B. must bear a part—though not necessarily the whole of the blame—for not having been sufficiently prescient.

Douglas and I founded S.S.I.P., with the initial co-operation of a handful of Socialist friends, deriving particularly from the working-class educational movement, with whom we had been in such close contact during the 'twenties. Mostyn Lloyd and H. L. Beales, both of whom I have mentioned earlier, were our first collaborators. Dick Mitchison was our first treasurer, and he and D. N. Pritt—and later Stafford Cripps—our chief financial supporters. Ernest Bevin was the chairman and I the honorary secretary. The original membership was collected by personal canvass, and the Society came into formal being as a result of two or three week-end gatherings held at Easton Lodge by Dunmow in Essex.

Easton Lodge and its owner, Frances Countess of Warwick, had played a considerable part in the Labour life of the 'twenties; it had been used for conferences and summer schools—the General Strike revue was written and first performed there—and the T.U.C. once toyed with the idea of making it a Labour College, of which Douglas would probably have been the head. It was with a real pang that I read in the newspapers of 1948 that it was to be pulled down as ugly, inconvenient, and beyond repair; it was, indeed, all these things, but it held memories of very happy and very busy days.

It was a great lump of a building, with a modern wing attached to one end and at Conference times generally reserved for the use of its owner, set in large and ill-kept gardens in the midst of a huge and very untidy park. Inside and out, it bore all the marks of bygone state and no present-day money to keep it up. It had enormous rooms, several painted in colour throughout; one, the Peacock Room, contained the vast fourposter in which Edward VII used to sleep, another, the library, had shelves full of books bound in scarlet morocco to match the room—which books, on examination, were not great classics but complete sets of minor thriller-writers of late Victorian times; its roof and its plumbing were continually coming to pieces. Outside there was a terrace along which raucous peacocks, in rather shabby trim, marched up and down and interrupted discourses on economics with squawks of " Pigou ! Pigou ! " ; and below it red sanded tennis-courts on which the marking tapes had worked so loose that a dishonest player who saw a return about to fall within the court could with his foot achieve a temporary readjustment of the boundary. There was a "Friendship Garden," first planted by Edward VII and contributed to by great figures of the Victorian and Edwardian eras, where a ridiculously thin stream of water could be shot into the air by a decrepit gardener hiding behind a bush ; and there were two weedy pools, surrounded by semi-tropical vegetation which looked rather as though it had been brought up on Wells's Food of the Gods, where bathers were caught by unexpectedly icy currents passing through the warm stagnant water. All around was the park with its green stretches and its deer, its trees desperately needing a forester and its drives needing a load of gravel ; and in the midst of the park, a short walk from the Lodge, was the pleasant modern Easton Glebe, where H. G. Wells lived with " Jane " Wells and his two sons, and his visitors, like those of Mr Britling, played horribly dangerous mixed hockey in the park and his own original and exhausting ball game in the barn.

It all wanted money spent on it, and Lady Warwick had no money to spend. She was one of my wealthy friends who seemed to be always genuinely short of cash ; she used too much of it on Good Causes—on Conrad Noel, the Red parson of Thaxted Church, who scandalised everybody by flying the Red Flag alongside the Union Jack, and on Socialists, pacifists, internationalists and under-dogs. (Undergraduate raiders from Cambridge used to make expeditions to tear down the flag or put it up, as the case might be. See Conrad Noel's, *The Battle of the Flags*. Noel was a saint of his time.) Lady Warwick was as much of a period piece as her house ; she had been a great society beauty in her day, beloved of King Edward and I don't doubt of many more ; when I first knew her, though she had grown fat, her face had still the fixed pink-and-white attractions which one associates with the Lily Langtry era, and an " electric light " smile which was turned on in a brilliant flash and gone again. She had a gushingly affectionate manner of greeting, with her wonderfully curled head on one side and her smile blazing, which was none the less perfectly sincere " period " ; she trailed about with her a string of revolting Pekinese dogs, and she had quick and sudden gusts of temper—her relations with her tenant Wells were punctuated by occasional violent explosions. Beatrice Webb looked down on her as a silly woman, and no doubt by Beatrice's standards she was ; her heart was considerably bigger than her head. But she was unfailingly generous, full of zest and interest, and loved by many.

As to H.G., my recollection of him in those days, before "Jane" died and Easton Glebe was sold, is of a highly entertaining, comically irascible little man with a small squeaky voice who behaved—as not all great men do—in a very democratic way to his interrogators and critics. He would become as indignant over one unfavourable review in that Marxist parish magazine *Plebs*—and present it with as much free copy in reply—as though it were the *Times* at least ; he would let any ass question and attack him at length before pouring on him a torrent of refutation ; when I tried to boil down his *World History* for a tutorial-class pamphlet-syllabus he hurled abuse at the result—and then apologised for losing his temper. Of course, no group of people was ever right in his eyes, particularly if they were trying to make plans for the Planned Society which he so ardently advocated ; if they were Fabians they had horrid mean insect souls like Sidney Webb ; if the Labour Party, they were hidebound stupid Nonconformists who wouldn't even preach birth-control ; if Communists, blind worshippers of a bearded, disagreeable old dyspeptic called Karl Marx. I doubt whether there is any organisation which H.G. ever joined from which he did not resign in a rage ; the rage *may* always have been well-founded, since organisations are apt to be exasperating, but the result was a trifle anarchical. Nevertheless he, of all the Great Men I ever met, with the sole exception of John Masefield, really gave the humble the impression that he wanted to hear what they had to say and would take notice of it. The only thing about which he was not democratic was playing games ; at Demon Patience, for example, you beat H.G. at your peril. In a scrambled frenzy of packs of cards, with perhaps a dozen players and a great deal of shoving and scrabbling going on, it was not always easy to secure that the not-very-competent host came out on top.

We stayed two or three times with H.G. at Easton Lodge, and of course met and dined with him on many other occasions—the last in a gloomy mansion on a gloomy winter evening in wartime, when he was obviously ill. We did not see so much of him, or know him so well as did many others ; but—possibly because he was my inspiration in my college days—I have always felt to have known him much better than I have known Bernard Shaw, in whose company I have probably spent more physical time. Of Shaw, since first I met him in the dingy rooms at Tothill Street, when I was a clerk in the Fabian Research Department, I have half-a-dozen disparate impressions . . . Of great physical grace, leaning casually against a wall at a summer school, or in rehearsal of its revue showing an amateur performer how to stand for his act or lunge in his dance . . . of a beautiful Irish voice reading so compellingly that *O'Flaherty, V.C.*—which I do *not* think one of his best plays—sent us into helpless laughter . . . of brilliantly witty oratory, such as that which at a Labour Conference in 1918 knocked down like ninepins those unhappy politicians who wanted the Party to stay in the Coalition . . . of a debater always ready to recognise sincerity and expert knowledge in his critics—when I was very young in the movement he covered me with blushing pride by saying to me, at the end of a discussion on education, " you were the only one who talked as though you knew anything about teaching " . . . of a rich man on whom one sometimes called to beg subscriptions for some good cause or other, and more often than not received no subscription,[1] but a volume of discourse which would have been worth twice as much as any amount asked for, if one had but had the shorthand to take it down . . . of a writer of indignant and wonderfully phrased letters about the political misbehaviour of the Fabian Society. But they do not add up to any single clear picture. I have always marvelled at Shaw and have sometimes been very indignant with him. I think he is unquestionably the greatest British writer of our age ; but I have never understood him. The nearest I can get is to think of him as an artist, an artist of immense virtuosity—and to see the same virtuosity in his political work, from his learning public speaking at soap-box corners and scrubby after-dinner gatherings, learning facts as the friend of Webb and the Borough Councillor of St Pancras, to his later defence of dictatorship. He has worked immensely hard at politics and had his fun ; but I feel, however much he may excoriate me for saying so, that it *was* his fun—the fun of a brilliant artist.

* * *

In the atmosphere I have described—the cheerful, informal between-the-wars atmosphere—S.S.I.P. was born, and retained for some time the traces of its birth. As I said, Douglas and I recruited personally its first list, drawing upon comrades from all stages of our political lives, members of " the Movement " not irretrievably

[1] I have been a moderately successful beggar in my time, but not from G.B.S. Success, however, has been achieved by others ; I once received—for what object I cannot now remember—a cheque with attached note, in the unmistakeable handwriting, which read, " Extorted by Beatrice Webb."

pledged to Communism, W.E.A. students and tutors, Trade Union secretaries and Trade Unionists with a left tinge, and younger recruits from the Oxford and other University Labour Clubs.

It was an exciting and a hopeful year. We had scarcely one refusal among all whom we asked to join, and those who joined came along, discussed eagerly, and seemed prepared to work hard ; it looked as though a new " Movement " of comrades was coming into being. (I should add, for the record, that we contemplated for a time the idea of enrolling Oswald Mosley, who had recently come into the open as a left-wing Socialist and had used his money to finance six successful Labour candidates in the City of Birmingham—a highly demoralising gift, as it turned out. He and Lady Cynthia, Lord Curzon's daughter, came to dinner with us, in company with the Laskis, and he talked a great deal ; fortunately he rushed out of the Labour Party in a temper before we had had time to become compromised.)

The group started operations with considerable energy, enrolling members, holding conferences, delivering lectures and publishing pamphlets,[1] all its work being aimed, as it emphasised, not at opposing the Labour Party or the Labour Government nor at drawing up an alternative policy which it would then try to force upon the Party through Conference resolutions, as the I.L.P. did until its disaffiliation in 1932, but at bringing the existing policy up to date and inducing the Party leaders, mainly by means of individual pressure from convinced and conscious Socialists, to carry it out—hence the nickname " Loyal Grousers." Early in 1931 Douglas, with the blessing of Arthur Henderson, the Webbs, and other leading Labour lights, formed another body, called deliberately the " New Fabian Research Bureau," which was supposed to take on the job of research and enquiry—which the official Labour Party's research department had never got around to doing—while the parent body devoted itself to the propagandist and educational sides of the project. At the beginning both societies were very small, with a membership largely overlapping, and functions not at all clearly differentiated ; most of the pamphlets might have been published by either of them. Teddy Radice, who until the autumn of 1932 was secretary to both, frequently asked that they should be amalgamated so as to save confusion ; but Douglas, who alone had a clear conception of their differing functions, always refused to consider it—an intransigeance which had important results when S.S.I.P., against his advice, decided to

[1] Stafford Cripps and Clement Attlee, and, of course, Douglas, were among its early pamphleteers.

go in with half the disaffiliated I.L.P. to form the Socialist League. The most unfortunate result of that decision was the disappearance of Ernest Bevin from our midst, and the deepening in his mind of the conviction, already implanted by the behaviour of Mosley and MacDonald, that intellectuals of the left were people who stabbed you in the back.

I did not take part in the birth-conference of the N.F.R.B. because I was at the time laid low by a sharp attack of pneumonia and was being looked after by a day and a night nurse. The only reason for mentioning this at all is that it is my sole experience of a dangerous illness resolved by a " crisis " of the classic kind—before the discovery of the sulpha class of drugs—followed by a classic convalescence. My temperature fell seven degrees in a single night, and I woke from the dream-world of delirium to a consciousness of being very wet, very weak, perfectly clear-headed, and infinitely wise. And this condition continued. The fever had consumed the flesh off my bones ; I had no calves left, and it was weeks before I could move about ; but my mind worked with extraordinary effectiveness. I saw the World, the people, and the problems in it with the perfect sharp distinction of something seen in a bowl of very clear water ; I solved a number of problems, some of which remained solved when I returned to health ; I planned a long eloquent poem, and actually wrote some parts of it—which are, I think, the best poems that I have ever written. I thoroughly appreciated and used my convalescence, which was as Victorian as you please ; and I wonder whether modern medical science, by checking the course of fever, has perhaps made it impossible henceforth for medical casualties to have the same sensation of having been over the edge of the world and come back to it with new eyes. I can certainly testify that pneumonia relieved by eating four white pills every four hours, and forcing gallons of fluid down one's throat while propped up in bed, may be a much less serious disease and takes much less long to recover from ; but it gives one no sudden insight into the meaning of the world, rather a soured sense of its general unpleasantness.

My convalescence was completed by a charming gift—a month spent with Dr Stella Churchill in that lovely villa above Portofino which Elizabeth von Arnim has immortalised in *The Enchanted April*, the only one of her books in which she allowed herself to eel kindly towards her characters. I too was in Portofino in an enchanted April ; Douglas all but carried me on to the Rome Express, after we had started from Victoria at nine o'clock on a Sunday morning in a " typical English spring " of murk and sleet, when even the Cook's man appeared to be only half-awake. I slept a drugged sleep across the frontier and awoke just before Turin to a warm sun which caused me to peel layer after layer, like a hopeful onion, before we were decanted at Santa Margherita ; I was carried in a litter borne by alarmingly breathless Italian servants up a steep zig-zag path whose every turn disclosed brilliant blue water far below me ; I was tipped out on a terrace full of sun and flowers and lizards.

There I lived, for the first time in my life, in a southern house where the sun shone *constantly* and you did not have to drop all else and rush out-of-doors to make use of its occasional appearances ; the windows of all ground-floor rooms opened straight on to the terraces, and you went indoors if the sun was too hot, or lay out in the minimum of clothing. (Only when Victor Gollancz came to stay, in a city suit, did he and Douglas, much to everyone's astonishment, repair to a very stuffy round room which contained a very old billiard-table, and there spend a sunny afternoon playing *billiards*, with clouds of dust rising from the cushions and dancing in the sun at every stroke.) I was fed on heaps of Italian food cooked and served by Italian servants ; in the evening I talked and talked with Stella and other visitors—Christopher Hawkes the archæologist, a teacher of English who read Chaucer, fascinatingly, with French vowel-sounds—I am sure he was right and that is what the *Canterbury Tales* should sound like—and a lady who told character from handwriting. As the use of my legs gradually returned to me, I walked over the small steep peninsula on which the villa stands, down into tiny Portofino bay, ringed with houses washed with the faint blues, pinks, and apricots which, for whatever reason, English seaside places have never been able or found time to use ; and further to the hills above Santa Margherita and Rapallo, studded with trees as yet leafless, and clumped or scattered cypresses looking like the rolled-up umbrellas of an immense Keswick Convention—coming down, after a reasonably long walk over what a cheerful Italian described as " brutta strada " (it was), to grapple with the language difficulty in a Rapallo café. In a fine international effort I ordered " macarooni mit nuts "—and got what I had intended.

This Easter gift of Stella Churchill's was more important than she could have known, for scarcely had we returned to England when a continuing malaise of Douglas's was diagnosed as diabetes, and for the next six months at least doctors endeavoured to treat him by dietary restrictions without using insulin, reducing him to a skeleton breaking out in sores (like a tramp in a workhouse ward), and filling the house with the horrible stench of a substance made principally, so far as I remember, of seaweed, which was designed to give him the illusion of eating something without the reality. After a time the profession, thank goodness, accepted the struggle as unequal and impossible and put him on to an allowance of insulin which was afterwards increased. With the introduction of insulin, the strain was eased ; but let nobody be deceived by the complacent statements in some medical manuals to the effect that diabetes is a mathematical disease, in which a calculated dose of insulin will neatly replace the non-functioning pancreas. If human beings were really machines, this might be true ; but the insulin dose meets with many different conditions, of exhaustion, excitement, or indigestion, in the body which it enters, and the result may vary enormously according to the physical or mental state of that body. In the course of experience, one learns to be on the look-out for curious symptoms ; but it is impossible to foresee them with any certainty.

The immediate result of this was that a projected lecture-tour to the United States was cancelled, never to be resumed ; and that, when in the following year the New Fabian Research Bureau decided to send its mission of enquiry to Russia, I had to go without him.

4.

Before the Russian expedition was conceived, however, the unfortunate Labour Government had fallen. It is a measure, I think, of the growing disillusionment of its supporters that neither S.S.I.P. nor the N.F.R.B. suffered any loss of membership or lessening of activity as a result of the crash of 1931 ; it was as though we had realised that the Government was not getting anywhere with its own ideals, and that the work of preaching and working out Socialism was equally necessary whether Labour was in office or outside.

It would be too much to claim that we had seen the catastrophe coming in the form in which it actually came ; to have done that would have meant possessing a Delphic knowledge of the convolutions of MacDonald's mind. But we could see that, as far as unemployment was concerned, the Government was driving on the rocks ; and we were not impressed by its most popular performance—Snowden at the Hague Conference turning himself into a tough British Shylock and alienating the whole public opinion of France for the sake of an extra twopence-ha'porth of German reparations, which in the event were never paid at all.[1] It was not, unfortunately, either the first or the last occasion on which Britain's representatives displayed scorn or dislike of France, with the acquiescence or overt delight of the British voter. Napoleon's memory has lingered far too long among those who know no French —and among some of those who do—so that the friends of France in this country carry too little political weight. One of the tragic factors in the present-day political situation is that the Labour Government missed the chance to ally itself with the French Left after the war—and that hardly any British Socialist noticed it.

It is true, of course, that the second Labour Government had very bad luck. In its first year and a half it had carried out, so far as Asquith and his Liberals permitted, a reasonable programme of mild social reform, and its Foreign Secretary had made tremendous efforts, which for a short time almost looked like succeeding, to bring about a lasting peace in Europe. The economic blizzard which blew up first in the American stock market, and then, as frightened American capital pulled out of its European investments, destroyed the bases of the artificial economic structure of Central Europe, was certainly none of its making. But when, in the winter of 1930-31, there began to appear in Britain the likeness of the terrible breadlines which brought Hitler to power (and, paradoxically, Roosevelt in the United States), the Labour Government, a Government which had won the election largely on a proud promise to cure unemployment, found that it had not the slightest idea what to do about unemployment that was world-wide—and lost its nerve. It dithered about ; it asked J. H. Thomas, Oswald Mosley, and George Lansbury to produce a policy if they could, knowing that the odds were a thousand to one against ; by means of the hated Anomalies Act it took some thousands of the unemployed off the funds. What was far worse, it allowed itself to be bullied into setting up the May Committee of experts—largely non-Labour "experts" ; and when this Committee presented a panic report that the country was on the verge of financial ruin and could only be saved if the Government, in order to bring down wickedly high wages, would give a lead by cutting the remuneration of all those paid by it, including the unemployed, the Government published the Report without comment or rejoinder, thereby telling the world at large that it had lost confidence in Great Britain's future. For this weakness the Cabinet as a body must take the blame ; it

[1] The chief actor, however, *was* deeply impressed. *Viscount Snowden's Autobiography* advertises his Hague efforts for page upon page of print, embellished with appreciative cartoons from *Punch*.

swallowed the Committee's vaticinations whole, and was prepared to make large economy cuts. It was only when the Trade Unions refused to be a party to slashing the miserable shillings of unemployment pay that the majority of the Cabinet remembered what they stood for and at long last dug their toes in—and then found that MacDonald, Snowden, and Thomas had walked out on them overnight to positions obviously "previously prepared" in a National Government.

We were in Scotland, at Craignish Castle, when the news broke, and so had heard nothing of the more fantastic stories that preceded it. What exactly happened to this day I do not know, notwithstanding the various accounts which have appeared from time to time—whether American banking interests were really telephoned to in the middle of the night for instructions to cut the unemployment pay of British workers, or whether finance took some slightly less melodramatic way of informing the Labour Prime Minister of the course expected of him. It is clear enough, however, that it *was* "finance" which brought down the Government, by insisting, with whatever threats and arguments it could use, on the *immediate* balancing of the Budget, and that the threats and arguments fell on ears already well-conditioned to receive them. The general pattern is, in fact, that of the fall of Social-Democracy in countries other than Britain—a weak and inexperienced government anxious to keep up the standard of living of its supporters but without any idea how to do so in the face of world slump, an upper class genuinely convinced that *its* standard of living and *its* social position were menaced by improvements in working-class conditions and prepared to go to any lengths to resist, a backstairs intrigue to bring the leaders of the working-class over to the Right Side—and finally an hysterical appeal, backed by lying propaganda about financial ruin,[1] to a frightened population to Save the Country. The broad lines of the pattern were the same as those we saw in Germany and Italy. British political tradition, however, no less than British Trade Union solidarity, ensured that they were not followed in detail; there was no civil war and no enrolling of bands of anti-semitic thugs to defend law and order. The social revolution retreated a step, no more; in actual fact the recovery of British exports after MacDonald had devalued the pound he had been elected to save, coupled with the collapse of prices in the food-

[1] Snowden's accusation that the Labour Government had intended to balance its budget by stealing from Post Office Savings Accounts and MacDonald's waving a valueless million-mark note on election platforms were two of the most spectacular instances.

producing countries, prevented the standard of life from falling seriously, save for some groups—and even the unemployed, by persistent pressure, wrung some modifications of the Means Test from a Government whose consciences were not altogether at ease.

Not that this helped the Labour Party, which had succeeded in presenting itself (*a*) to the Tories and the floating vote as incompetent weaklings in the field of finance and (*b*) to the extreme left as tools in the grip of a wicked anti-social force called City and Wall Street. (The Webbs, now in process of conversion to the U.S.S.R., agreed with both opinions, more or less.) But we of S.S.I.P. did not realise how big the disaster was ; we were so profoundly relieved to be rid of MacDonald at last ; and we observed that the Parliamentary Party, all save a not particularly distinguished handful, was holding together under the leadership of Henderson and Lansbury. Even when MacDonald, who had pledged himself that his new Coalition would under no circumstances go to the country as a Coalition, within two months ignored his pledge and called for a General Election to give him a " doctor's mandate "—*i.e.*, a blank cheque—we prepared in good heart for a back-to-the-wall campaign. Dick took Douglas's place as candidate for King's Norton ; and we even talked about winning the seat. It was not until I began to electioneer in good earnest, and found hostile audiences—a rare phenomenon in British electioneering, where public meetings are apt to consist mainly of the faithful of the Party holding them—and drove from London to Birmingham through towns and villages wearing nothing but " National " colours and posters, that it dawned on me that it was not a back-to-the-wall fight but a thrashing that we were in for ; and in the excitement of committee-room agitation and driving voters to the poll, etc., I did not realise how big a thrashing until the results began to come out.

We King's Norton workers were in the Sargant Florences' house at Selly Oak when the radio began to speak, and the first score or so of results gave us the measure of the rout. Not merely was Minister after Minister recorded " out " ; but the majorities were so huge, and the constituencies which rejected Labour so many, and some so safe-seeming. Henderson out, of course—Henderson never could hold his seat in General Elections—Morrison out, Greenwood, Dalton ; Lansbury alone of the Cabinet just squeezing home in Bow, Cripps the same in East Bristol, and Attlee in Limehouse ; MacDonald himself returned by Seaham in Durham, which had given Webb so huge a majority in 1922 ; Birmingham all gone, London reduced from 36 to 5 members, Glasgow to 5, Liverpool and Manchester to one and none respectively.

Monotonously, in bitter mockery of the summer night of little more than two years past, the voice went on . . . " National Gain from Labour . . . National Liberal Gain from Labour . . . Conservative Gain from Liberal . . . " After some time of listening, we said to one another, " What's the good ? Let the thing alone and get drunk—that's all we can do." Hours afterwards, it seemed, I went back, and there was still the radio, which no one had remembered to turn off, still reciting disasters to an empty room by a dead fire.

Labour had lost two hundred and forty seats or thereabouts. The number of seats lost, of course, exaggerated the defeat. Everyone was at pains to point out that the Labour vote had only dropped by some twenty per cent. from the 1929 peak, and that over six million Labour votes had been cast. But, as a friendly American observer pointed out,[1] " the four-fifths of their followers (who) stood firm . . . voted for the ideal rather than for the shaken remnant of leaders who were only one degree less terrified than those who went over to the other side " ; and millions of the working class (to say nothing of the middle and lower-middle classes) voted definitely against those who called themselves their leaders. As the next election in 1935 clearly showed, before Labour could hope to recover, it must attach to itself more than the idealist stalwarts ; it must somehow recreate confidence in itself and its leadership—and for that it must re-think its policy. In this job our young Socialist organisations, conferring all winter with the surviving leaders, were eager to assist ; our first major step was taken when the N.F.R.B. decided to sponsor a team of inquirers to look at the Russian Soviet system.

5.

It was at the end of July, 1932, that the majority of our party of a dozen, with a number of other persons similarly purposed, left Hays Wharf for Leningrad in the *Alexei Rykov*. We were a day late in starting, because that ship in characteristic fashion had broken some vital piece of her machinery and a little donkey-engine had to toil and puff for twenty-four hours to get it right. She was not a competent ship ; her plumbing, for example, broke down frequently, and a reflection on her cleanliness overheard by the captain so incensed him that he had her washed continuously throughout the voyage. The only places out of reach of the hoses were two lifeboats, in which, accordingly, Ray and Dick and I and anyone else who cared took refuge from time to time, to be instructed

[2] Harold Scarborough of the *New York Herald Tribune*, in *England Muddles Through*.

in the Russian language by Ray from a *Hugo* phrase-book. I confess I got little out of the course but amusement; if you are no linguist, as I am not, it is much more fruitful to go through a foreign country with the minimal equipment of essential words and phrases—as, for example, "Ladies," "Gentlemen," "Too much," "Enough (or Go Away)," "Thank you," and "I don't understand [whatever is the language of the country]"—and to acquire an interpreter, rather than burden your ears with so great an effort to understand that your eyes cannot watch peoples' faces. Russian is a fairly difficult tongue, anyway; still, I did learn that the Russian for "ready" is "gotoff." "These ladies are not yet gotoff" seemed to occur regularly in the phrase-book!

The *Alexei Rykov* ended her career, later in the summer, by coming in half in the middle of the Baltic. But she was a friendly ship; she fed us well—though I could never get used to small, cold, half-boiled eggs for breakfast; and the crew were very comradely. We finished the voyage with a mutual entertainment, in which the Russians put on an excellent performance of songs, and the tourists a shocking one; and were turned out on the quay at Leningrad, to have our papers thumbed over by an earnest Soviet official, who gave several minutes' serious study to some old cyclostyled documents which had been used for packing, and which he held upside down. We were then stowed in large handsome Lincolns—at the time there were very few cars to be seen in the streets of either Moscow or Leningrad—and driven to (I think) the second-best hotel available. All this was very typical of my Russia.

My Russia of 1932. Curiously, I do not remember very clearly the physical details of that four-weeks' stay—much less than those of some countries in which I have spent much less time. I remember the Kremlin, of course, (I was not very greatly impressed by the outward appearance of Leningrad, thinking it an undistinguished sort of a city whose like might have been seen almost anywhere in Europe), the Red Square, still then inscribed with the words, "Religion is the opium of the people," the monstrous onion-domes of St Basil, Lenin in his tomb with the long slow files of worshippers passing him, and the white slabs which showed where John Reed and the other heroes of the second Revolution were buried. On one thunderous evening the Kremlin wall was magnificently lit by lightning flashed from a sky where a scarlet sunset still lingered in the west.

Otherwise, my impressions of Moscow are largely of heat, dust, and large holes in the road, naked little boys leaping in and out of Moscow River, shops with very little in them, fierce bustle in the hotel, and alternatively infinitely long waits while somebody telephoned somebody else in a long crackle of " Da ! da ! da ! " (Russian for " yes ") ; some huge buildings, more very tumbledown ones, and an apartment where Ivy Litvinov, Maxim's English novelist wife, gave us afternoon tea and asked for news of Bloomsbury; the crowds and crowds of different nationalities swarming in the theatre, and a long session over an extremely nasty drink compounded of kvass (fruit-juice) and vodka, at which Walter Duranty held forth with burning enthusiasm on the new régime. There were longish drives out into the country—not, to tell the truth, very interesting country—to see some institution or other ; there were long tramps over factories, co-operative stores, crèches, hospitals, kindergartens, prisons ; and there was one more distinctive occasion, when at the main broadcasting station we sat until well after midnight listening to an " Olympiad " of musical teams from all over the Union. I remember Germans from the Volga singing songs like Germans all over the world, a band from the Ukraine which employed exclusively banjos of different shapes and sizes, and most vividly the Uzbek contingent—Uzbekistan being then about the most backward of the constituent Republics—whose *pièce de résistance* was a small girl aged about eleven, dressed for the occasion in a white cotton frock which I might have worn in my childhood, with tight black ringlets, and Wellington boots, who exhibited no sign of shyness, but out-squalled all the rest of her party on no recognisable note.

Away from Moscow, I remember the long train journey—on a wide-gauge railway which kept the train so steady that one could boil a kettle—over the enormous plain with its trees and tiny villages to Kharkov, then a great mass of unfinished building, where we looked at more prisons, shops, etc., and where Ray found what looked like an attempt at a night club, in a courtyard with a soft sandy floor and a few little coloured lights ; another long and very gritty journey to Kiev, a wild performance of gipsy dancing there, the Lavro monastery and the impressive view, from the first rising ground we had seen for weeks, of the great logs floating down the Dnieper far below us.

As a collection of views it does not seem much, and my Russia was physically very small—I never saw the Volga or the Crimea, or crossed the Urals. I could have seen more, though, and carried more away, if I had had more time to stand and stare. But I had not come to collect picture-postcard views ; I had come to see a society and its institutions, and the recollections I brought back with me were recollections of the spirit of the country, not of its contours or its vegetation.

Its spirit as seen in 1932. World opinion and the world scene have changed so much in sixteen years that it will be difficult for readers to recapture the feelings of that year, although Philips Price in his little book *Russia Red or White* (1948) comes very near it. Of course we went to the U.S.S.R. believing it to be the hope of the world—but it is more important to remember that at that time, unlike the present, few except the extreme Tories really believed it was an immediate danger to the world. The banishment of Trotsky seemed to have brought the " world revolution " phase to an end ; and though of course many were convinced that Russia was a horrible place, others observed that the Western world, stuck in the mire of unemployment, with Hitler just on the verge of attaining power, did not seem such a very nice place either. In Russia, it was said, there was no unemployment at all. Russia had a Plan, the First Five-Year Plan, such as the Socialists of the West had been continually demanding ; and the Plan was going so well that a slogan had just been adopted—*The Five-Year Plan in Four*.

Of course we were prejudiced in favour of the Union of Socialist Soviet Republics ; we never sought to deny it, or that our tours were arranged for us by the State authorities—we knew the men of the G.P.U., the secret police, as kindly souls who came to our rescue and found us seats on crowded trains. Nor, with currency bought at the official rate of exchange, which bore no relation to the internal purchasing power of the rouble, did we have much opportunity of making long unchaperoned expeditions. If we wanted souvenirs, we had to buy them at Torgsin, the Government emporium which accepted foreign currency only. I remember one highly indignant Co-operator who in spite of warnings insisted on going out and buying his own glass of beer in an ordinary café—our drinks came to us as part of an Intourist all-in service—and would never thereafter listen to a word in favour of a country which charged the poor worker 3s. 6d. for his evening pint. We should not have been allowed, even if we had tried, to see forced labour camps or the insides of political prisons or to attend meetings of the central Executive of the Communist Party. (But are visitors to Britain encouraged to sit in on Cabinet meetings or to explore Dartmoor Prison ?) Naturally, our Russian hosts preferred to take us to visit those enterprises of which they were proudest, even if we were not so deeply impressed by them as they could have wished.

But the members of our party were not fools, nor entirely untrained in looking below the surface. I think we put down, as well as I can judge, exactly what we saw, and on re-reading the book which we produced on our return,[1] I am still impressed by its general objectivity, particularly in John Morgan's chapter on Soviet agriculture. Morgan, the farmer, travelled over the Ukraine and the other southern provinces which ought to have been the granary of the Soviet State, was appalled by the cultivation he found there, and said so. What he did not know, what none of us knew, and what the Webbs for many years refused to admit, was that those provinces in that year were not merely suffering from drought but were also being deliberately and officially punished by starvation for their resistance to the collective farming policy. But as a farmer he did know that the state of the land could not be caused by the weather alone, however bad, and he stood by his conviction. What we others saw was a country which was tremendously excited, with an excitement which could not possibly be feigned, over the huge social experiment which it was making and which it believed was the people's own experiment. "This is *our* hospital—*our* factory—*our* workers' rest-home" ran as a recurrent refrain to all that we saw; and the enthusiasm covered the less as well as the more successful of the experiments. It was sometimes a little irritating to be lectured, by the head of a conspicuously ill-equipped nursery school, as though a nursery school had never been heard of in Britain and as though British children were still driven at seven years old to work a ten-hour day in grimy factories. But there was nothing hostile in such ill-informed enthusiasm, and one only needed to remind oneself that Russia was being industrialised as fast as Britain had been over a century before—but not, like Britain, at the expense of the minds and bodies of her children. Whoever went short—and in the summer of 1932, after the first great drive for collective farming had partially failed, a good many people went very short indeed[2]—it was not the young children.

The whole effect, in social services at all events, was of an eager helter-skelter humanitarianism, modelled on the most hallowed Socialist traditions. Paid holidays for workers, paid rest for mothers during and after pregnancy, equal pay and equal opportunity for both sexes,[3] equal marriage laws and easy divorce, abortion officially

[1] *Twelve Studies in Soviet Russia*, 1932 (ed. M. I. Cole).

[2] The total absence of toilet-paper was one of the shortages which most struck the British. When at Kiev, where life was slightly less spare than in Moscow, the hotel provided paper napkins for the tourist, the first down to meals made a rapid clearance of the napkins on his table.

[3] Ten years later, a woman deputy from Uzbekistan gravely rebuked John Parker for the miserable opportunities given to women in the Mother of Parliaments.

performed in State hospitals, free and equal education for all children, disfranchisement for "class enemies" only, no State religion (though persecution of the religious had come to an end), factory and district crèches and State hospitals being provided as fast as resources would allow, prisons such as the model establishment called Bolshevo being planned as centres of rehabilitation for the anti-social—all these, administered and supported by people who looked and behaved very like the best of the social workers and unpaid Socialist agitators of our own country, suggested, irresistibly, a state of things in which the I.L.P., cranks and all, had suddenly come into the control of an entire country.

It suggested this in more ways than one. I was reminded more often than I quite liked of G.L.'s exasperated gibe at the British Communist Party, "*That* lot run a revolution? they couldn't run a decent whelk-stall!" In many ways, the U.S.S.R. was extremely inefficient. There always seemed to be about twice as many people as were needed attendant upon any job; none the less, those one wished to see were either incredibly late for their appointments, or else not in their offices at all, no one knowing either where they had gone or what they would have said to you had they been there; meals arrived at any hour—I have dined as late as 1 a.m., but that was a record; trains came in half *en route*; machines were smashed by untrained peasant labour, like the girl whom David Low portrayed trying to milk a tractor; shower-baths did not work; the doors of new workers' flats came off and large dents appeared in their walls. Nobody seemed to mind this much, and from Philips Price's book I gather that in this respect things did not alter very much in thirteen years, that notwithstanding all the fuss about *Bolshevik tempo*, which was going on when I was there, and the tremendous efforts to tighten up discipline (which did, be it remembered, halt the Nazis in the end), the Russian way of doing things is still almost as far from what we should recognise as efficiency as Peter the Great found it two and a half centuries ago. It is nothing to do with Marxist, Leninist, or Stalinist Communism; it is simply Russian. But it does give Russians who know something about other societies an uneasy feeling of inferiority, and helps, therefore, to keep the frontier closed.

We did not see much of the tightening up, except in newspaper headlines and factory notices, while we were there. But we did see something of the other side of the "Russian way of life," the human and co-operative side in which everyone in the neighbourhood turned to and lent a hand to a neighbour who had got into difficulties—and in which, further, anyone who had sinned against the collective conscience of his group was forgiven and taken back as soon as he said he was sorry and had atoned for his offence. The key-word here is " collective," which has a traditional and emotional meaning for the Russians, derived largely from the ancient Russian village organisation, which it could not have for people brought up in the religious and political tradition of north-western Europe. Anyone who has nonconformity and *habeas corpus*, conscientious objection and the " duties of the Opposition " in his very bones, and who thinks a plea of " guilty " not very sporting, finds it extremely hard to appreciate, except intermittently, the Russian sense of the supreme value of the community, or collectivity, transcending any individual rights. He, the Russian, wants to be at peace and at one with his group, be it family, village, factory, or society ; and as many of the victims of the treason trials proclaimed, if you must die, it is a burning necessity to die having confessed your sins *against the community* and made your peace with it. (This is not at all the same thing as the condemned English criminal being asked to make his lonely and individual peace with God.)

There is no place to discuss at length the treason trials, either their justification, the state of things which they disclosed, or the panic savagery of the procedure. At the time of the murder of Kirov, Douglas and I and some other Socialists went to the Soviet Ambassador, Ivan Maisky, to protest against the reprisals ; our intervention had no result except to cut us off the Embassy's visiting list. (And Maisky was a milder, more " westernised " man than Molotov.) But I must say that on what I saw of Russia, the assumptions of the horrified West that the confessions were secured by torture or the use of strange drugs seems to me unwarranted. While I was there, a similar form of collective purgation, of a less spectacular kind, was going on in factories which had failed to perform to standard ; it was called *chistka* (cleansing), and will be found very well described in Maurice Hindus's novel *Under Moscow Skies*.[1] Factory workers eagerly and passionately confessed how they had sabotaged and betrayed the Revolution or the workers' cause ; it sounded like mass-hysteria to anyone accustomed to the gruff refusal to admit blame which the British worker often regards as an essential part of his ordinary self-respect, but it was not.

The " collective," however, was not merely an instrument of

[1] A very good book to read nowadays ; it tells the story of a young man from the outer world who came eagerly to Russia, found that he could not endure the Communist pace and Communist outlook, and went back to the West, taking with him the Russian girl who loved him—and how she in turn wilted in the alien capitalist air.

punishment ; it was also playing a great part in the humanising of life, in tempering the wind of a rough generalisation (which much law needs must be) to the shorn lamb within its fold. Time and again I was told, when questioning the harsh operation of a rule in a specific case, " But, of course, in such a case it would not be enforced. The collective (an unspecified, not a legally laid-down collective) would know all about the case and would see that it was all right." Even if that was an optimistic assumption, still it *was* the assumption ; and I have myself seen a " collective " spontaneously arise to consider the case of a drunk and incapable lying in the street, and after deliberation collectively remove him to some place outside the reach of the gendarmerie. (This attitude had its other side, undoubtedly. One saw pretty often beggars, tramps, misfits of various sorts, children with horrible sores in the arms of their mothers outside church doors—the kind of sight which in England would have set angry humanitarians and their societies to work writing angry letters to the papers and asking angry questions in Parliament. In Russia the view appeared to be rather " We have not time to be troubled with these tiresome single cases. Here are the social services we have set up with such strain and difficulty ; if these people don't or won't come in, we can't be bothered to make them." In the U.S.S.R. one wrote to the papers about failures in production, not hard luck stories.)

One anecdote may perhaps serve to throw light on all this. One day in Moscow we were being shown around the Park of Culture and Rest—a misnomer, for there was precious little culture in it and no rest at all, but a continuous row made by people playing in side-shows and throwing coconuts at Aunt Sallies labelled Ramsay MacDonald, Austen Chamberlain and the like. As we went through, we observed a commotion created by a loudly weeping woman who was being hustled along by a posse of officials, and enquired its cause. Our guide, rather irritated by the appearance of this blemish on his prize exhibit, said hastily, " Oh, some little trouble. She cannot find her child," and hurried us on.[1] Later, however, being in some doubt as to the impression he had created, he invited us to be present at the *trial* of the noisy woman. We were intrigued by the idea that losing one's child should be an offence against the law, and followed him into a marquee where a G.P.U. man sat at the head of a table, and the indignant and weeping woman was brought before him. According to the evidence, her twelve-year-old

[1] So, a year later, a waiter in an hotel in North Spain, asked to account for a great running to and fro on the sea-shore explained, " *Ah, ce n'est rien. Quelqu'un se noye.*"

son had failed to come home the previous evening because he found the attractions of the Park so great that he had decided to spend the night there. The attendants had discovered him in the early morning, and she was being asked to explain why her parental control was so weak that the boy could casually stay out all night.

There ensued a long argle-bargle, at the end of which the woman, giving a sort of hoot, suddenly sprang forward. I thought she was about to attack her judge ; but I was wrong. She only wanted *to blow her nose*, on a handkerchief promptly provided by the G.P.U. man. Then there was a great handshaking and back-slapping all round ; and when all was over there crawled out from under the table a Soviet citizen of some three years old, who had spent the time unconcernedly practising buttoning and unbuttoning his shoes. That is my most vivid recollection of Soviet Russia.

* * *

I hope I have made it clear that I returned to England immensely excited by my Soviet experiences. Since then, much has happened, and I do not doubt that the U.S.S.R. is a good deal changed from the confusing comradely country that I knew. I have no first-hand information and must discount a good deal of that received at second-hand ; and I do not want to embark upon a long discussion of Russian and other foreign policy, particularly in the war-hysterical atmosphere of 1948. But, leaving out questions of world policy and concentrating only on what one can gather about internal conditions, it seems clear that :—

1. Materially, living conditions have improved, but are still—partly, of course, because of the war—so far below what a western worker would think tolerable that the rulers of Russia do not want their nationals to go abroad and see for themselves.
2. There is a much greater difference than there was in 1932 between the higher and lower incomes.
3. There is a good deal more formality, expressed in uniforms, ranks, decorations, saluting, etc.
4. The freedom of divorce and abortion and much of the experimentalism in education have vanished altogether.
5. The censorship is fiercer and wider, and writers, artists, musicians and scientists are frequently disciplined and sternly forced to produce the kind of thing which the rulers think suitable for the entertainment or instruction of the millions, and in the kind of language of which they approve.

6. Stalin has changed from a leader who had just beaten another leader in mortal combat to a half-veiled Hero and Father of his country, and consequently—
7. The story of the Revolution, in history, play, and film, has been re-written in terms which I can only call "lying."

Others could probably extend this list; but I have only put down the items of which I am sure. For example, I have not included forced labour or secret police, not because I doubt their existence, but because I do not know to what extent they were present in 1932 and it is impossible to establish the facts in the welter of propaganda. Moreover, not having been back to see for myself, I do not feel competent to judge of the real significance of these changes—how far, for example, they were made necessary by the fearful destruction of the second world war, or how far they represent the "national character" of the Russians reaching an accommodation with the terms of the Marxist creed drawn from the west and the survival conditions of civilisation in an industrial age. I do not like the look of them, in sum, and think that they make the "new Russia" less and less attractive to those brought up in western Europe or the U.S.A. (Which do not make up the whole world, though people sometimes talk and write as though they did. I am making no prophecies about Africa or the East.) The one change I am certain that I find fundamentally shocking is the complete and deliberate falsification of history and the denigration of those who fought to make the Union. I have always regarded it as a deep disgrace to England that we dug up Cromwell dead and hanged his corpse on Tyburn Tree; and though I hold no brief for Trotsky or Trotsky's policies I think the crime is essentially the same.[1] I hope some day it will be remedied; meantime, I still feel no doubt that for masses and masses of Russians the Revolution has brought and is still bringing improved conditions, enlightenment, and, above all, hope, enthusiasm, and a chance of life.

And so home—by train to Warsaw, where the Polish hotel, proudly asserting its superiority over the barbarians in the east, offered us a whole piece of toilet-paper each; to Red Vienna, where the Karl Marx Hof and the other working-class flats stood so clean and happy under the sun; and through the Bavarian lands where the black nihilistic tyranny was just on the verge of attaining power.

[1] Since this was written, the Russian re-writing of history, including the history of science and invention, has, of course, gone to much greater lengths.

PART SIX

NINETEEN-THIRTIES

Chapter Ten

I.

THE nineteen-twenties, in memory, make a *pointilliste* picture ; the 'thirties a distortion—something like the experience of sitting in the very front row of a large cinema, where half the screen is out of focus and one blinks at monstrous objects appearing in the mid-foreground while unnaturally elongated shapes are cloudily discerned to left and right. This effect is partly due, no doubt, to the fact that one *is* still too close up ; not sufficient time has elapsed to allow the picture to settle into its true outlines. But even more, I think, it is due to the events themselves—the events of 1939 to 1945—which have given to the centre of the screen, to the Nazis and the approach of war, a domination and a size in retrospect which at the time they did not possess, notwithstanding all the fears, all the propaganda, and all the earnest discussions. One has to make a real mental effort to remember that one was not talking and thinking all the time about Hitler, that, to continue the metaphor, the shadowy shapes on either side of him were much more important and much less shadowy than memory has made them.

This effort is made slightly more difficult by the change in the reception of personal contacts which seems to be inevitable as one grows older and enters new fields of activity, as one's circle of " contacts " widens more and more, and as there is so little time, with all the accumulations of things-to-be-done which seem to encrust life as it goes on, to dig deep as well as wide. No scientists have proved capable of putting into effect the entrancing suggestion which Wells made, in the story called *The New Accelerator*, of a drug which could compress and expand time as needed, allowing an exciting or interesting minute to extend itself for hours while a period of dreary necessity—a formal party, say, or a long and irrelevant speech made by somebody else—could pass in a flash ; they may have annihilated distance, as they say, but it takes no less time to boil an egg or to wrap parcels, and the day remains inexorably twenty-four hours in length. In these latter years, of course, the statistical amount of time expended, particularly by hitherto sheltered middle-class women, on necessary but hardly exciting or creative chores of this kind,[1] has considerably increased ; but the phenomenon was noticeable long before the war.

I have not in the least abated my interest in people—I still think them the most interesting study in the world. And I have met a good many new people since 1932. But I am conscious of having had little time—or attention—to give to exploring even the most interesting as I should have liked ; and that, therefore, they have failed, on the whole, to leave an impression as deep as that left by some of the less agreeable of the figures of my youth. The personality of a horrid girl with whom one has to live day by day at boarding-school fixes itself far more indelibly than that of the most attractive and interesting of shipboard aquaintances—just as the verse one was forced to learn by heart or the Thucydides one had to prepare for examination remains more annoyingly present in the memory than poetry one has read for pleasure or history studied for the same reason. Moreover, the new personality has to compete for place with the old, the friend of one's youth not forgotten but separated often by place, marriage, or occupation, and the erstwhile close comrade in a society or cause long since come to nothing. My picture of people, then, in these latter years, is of a very mixed gathering, something resembling a market-place as it might have been painted by Breughel. With the exception of my very nearest relatives, they come and go. Here is someone who really merits the term " very old friend," unexpectedly found on a bus, in a club or at a party ; there follows an excited duet of remembrance, somewhat on the lines of Noel Coward's song, " I Wonder What Happened to *Him*," a promise—" We *must* get together again soon "—and then no more. Here is a face from some agitational past. " You don't remember me, Mrs. Cole ? "[2]

[1] I do not mean to suggest that there is anything essentially " soul-destroying " about the job of keeping a house going. Nobody but a fool imagines that you can have *any* job which is interesting all through, which has no boring or tiresome aspects, any more than you can climb a mountain or play a hard game without being very uncomfortable at times. But there is a difference between inevitable-chore and *drudgery*, as the public is slowly beginning to discover—see my book on *Marriage*. Part of Beatrice Webb's magnificent output was made possible by the fact that she had an inherited income and no children, so that her burden of chores was reduced to the smallest possible dimensions.

[2] A merciless opening—particularly if its user was a member of a lecture audience of yours, introduced to you afterwards, and so possessing the advantage of staring at *your* face for two hours on end. I have never discovered how to be tactful on such occasions, if I really cannot remember.

" Yes, I do . . . if only I could *see* your perfectly-remembered features against their proper background . . . Was it a Summer School at Easton Lodge ?—a W.E.A. class ?—a Popular Front meeting ?—a party of Stella Bowen's ? . . . No, it was that Tutors' Conference in Yorkshire, of course ! How *are* you, Mr Brown ? " Or it is someone quite new, but someone who after a very few meetings turns out to have extraordinarily sympathetic and interesting ideas, and to want the right sort of world in the right way, to be, in fact, exactly the kind of spirit one would like for a friend. (*Verweile doch, du bist so schön !*) The suggestion is made that it would be nice if he or she could come to dinner ; he or she would be delighted. Any time after the 25th ? Oh, dear ! he or she is going to Edinburgh—or Washington—or Jugoslavia—on the 22nd, and will be away three months at least. Perhaps after that. . . Perhaps ; perhaps not. The contact may be made again, but the odds are against it. So this personality, too, goes to the side of the screen—real enough, if one could see clearly, but, as it is, something of a phantom.

2.

Of course, the distortion of memory is not complete distortion. The seven dismal years which ended in 1939 were dominated, if not so wholly as we tend to think to-day, by the slow approach of war and the slow conversion of the British people, not to war-mindedness, for we were never so war-minded as many vocal Americans seem to be to-day, but to acquiescence in its inevitability as the Nazis plans proceeded, and we gradually came to realise that Hitler meant exactly what he said.

At the beginning of 1933 we did not know. I remember, on a January afternoon, seeing the poster which said, " HITLER CHANCELLOR," rushing into the N.F.R.B. office with the news, and my indignation when the men in the office said, " Well, what of it ? He's no worse than von Schleicher, is he ? " I was not particularly prescient, but I did know better than that. Then came the burning of the Reichstag and Dimitrov's spectacular defence of himself against Goering, the accumulating stories of Jew-baiting and concentration camps on which the *Manchester Guardian* harped so tiresomely—what sensible person wanted to go *on* reading about atrocities ?—the 1934 Night of the Long Knives, when Roehm and the others were murdered, and any hopeful belief that a " left-wing " could get the upper hand in the Nazi Party died a quick death, the German withdrawal from the League of Nations, the Saar vote—an unpleasant surprise for liberal newspapers, which continued to believe, in face of all the evidence, that the Saarlanders must surely declare for our western liberal values—the reoccupation of the Rhineland, the capture of Austria by telephone—a steady progression which the British public received with a kind of paralysed incredulity.

It (the public) in 1933 and 1934 was beginning to read *Mein Kampf*—in translations mostly bowdlerised—with a feeling of astonished disgust, but no idea that Hitler's perfectly clear statements of what he intended to do with France, Britain, and Russia could be seriously meant. Most people who thought about it at all thought that he was a rather madder Mussolini, with perhaps more excuse than Mussolini had for his madness, and that if he were let alone he would get over it. A great deal of the "appeasement" attitude—as distinct from the attitude of those who definitely thought that a taste of Fascism would be good for the British worker—must be put down to simple lack of imagination and inability to comprehend that anyone could be really setting out to dominate the world by force of arms.

We could not believe it ; we had been conditioned not to believe it. Memories of 1914-1918 had left the British people pacific to the core. We had not, of course, become completely "non-resistant" ; we did not propose to abolish armaments altogether, although when the Peace Ballot was taken in the winter of 1934, four million of those who voted their support to the League of Nations refused to vote for giving it military sanctions—a pretty considerable minority. But we regarded existing armaments as a kind of insurance, the cost of which we were hoping would steadily diminish ; and we were certainly convinced that war did not pay in any sense, that it wounded the victors only less cruelly than the vanquished, and that it settled nothing, certainly not the questions about which it had ostensibly been fought. This attitude was strongest of all in the Labour movement, partly because it had been reborn in the disillusioned years of 1918 onwards, partly because its numerous women members, particularly those in the Women's Co-operative Guild, were determinedly pacifist in the strict sense of the word, and to a certain extent because George Lansbury, the leader whom after the 1931 catastrophe it loved and trusted best, was a pacifist too. Almost to the last, the Labour Party in Parliament was expected to follow tradition by voting against the Service Estimates.

We were pacific, but we were also frightened—not of Hitler, but of what might happen if we went to war with him or with anyone else. And here certain earnest publicists with the best intentions did us and the world a grave disservice. Books like *What Would be the Character of a New War?* with their half-correct prophecies, above all the film, *The Shape of Things to Come*, with its scarifying and unforgettable picture of the bombers let loose over London, the buildings crashing in flames and the world delivered over to pestilence and famine, had a tremendous effect, but an effect on the wrong people. They did not move the hearts or divert the purposes of the warmongers; they only shook the nerves and paralysed the will of those who might have checked them. (I did not, myself, give very much credence to Wells's film as a whole; it had too absurd an ending. But the opening sequences convinced me so far that when the Home Counties sirens went off half an hour after Chamberlain's voice had told us we were at war with Germany, I went down to the garden shelter in the firm belief that the Luftwaffe was close upon us.)

Add that we, especially those on the left who were instinctively revolted by all that Hitler stood for, were confused by having bad consciences about the Versailles Treaty and the occupation of the Ruhr. We had learned Maynard Keynes's lesson all too well; we believed that we had tried, deliberately and very incompetently, to ruin Germany and had imposed humiliating conditions on a proud people, and we were therefore disposed to make every excuse for exhibitions of arrogance and aggressiveness, as if they mattered no more than the gangster pranks of a maladjusted child. "New" psychology and "new" penology, fashionably and unthinkingly applied, have had quite a lot to answer for. Add, further, that besides the die-hards who were delighted to see kikes and Communists suitably dealt with, the elder statesmen who observed quite correctly that Hitler was kinder to capitalists than Stalin, and the earnest reformers who rejoiced to hear that the "immorality" of post-war Berlin was being cleaned up, there were others who felt in a confused way that whatever its faults Fascism was to some extent concerning itself with the underdog, the Forgotten Man, and so was in tune with modern times in a way in which governments which acquiesced in a ten to fifteen per cent. level of "normal" unemployment were not. Fascism seemed to be appealing to a man as a man, even if it seemed also to think that he was a very stupid and unenlightened sort of man; it did not affront his human dignity by treating him as a piece of scrap metal or a crop of unsaleable coffee. The Nazi régime was putting him to rearmament at the moment, truly—but that was obviously the most easy thing to do. Surely some day Hitler would see the light and use the Little Man for better purposes. From such thoughts, such hopes, and such wish-fulfilments, we had to be slowly awakened—but the awakening came at different times and in different manner to different groups. The British people as a whole were not, I think, convinced until after the seizure of Prague—some not until the invasion of Poland—that war was inescapable ; the organised Labour movement realised soon after Munich that it might come, and by September 1939 was certain enough to make it impossible for Chamberlain to give in again ; the intellectuals, at least that majority of them which did not go pacifist, were convinced much earlier. Unfortunately, they were convinced for a great variety of reasons and to an equal variety of positive policies, so that the lead they gave was neither clear nor coherent. I seem to remember dozens of conferences and week-end schools with a great babel of voices, each crying up his own immediate plan to the exclusion of all others.

For myself, as I can now see clearly, the process of conversion from the pacifist standpoint began in February 1934, with the crushing of the Austrian Socialists. This had, strictly speaking, nothing to do with Hitler ; as I said earlier, he did not occupy the centre of my stage nearly so much at the time as he now seems to have done. I detested the thuggery and the anti-semitism, of course, but as it were on general principles and from a distance. I had no acquaintances among the early refugees ; German modes of thought have always been unsympathetic to me ; and I was not alone in thinking—somewhat illogically, since I still called myself a pacifist—that the German Social-Democrats, in Prussia and elsewhere, had collapsed before the Nazis in a peculiarly uninspiring manner. But I had seen and loved Red Vienna, and when Chancellor Dolfuss and Fey, the head of the Heimwehr, turned howitzers on the Karl Marx Hof and began trying and killing my Viennese comrades—though comrades of a day or two only—my emotions were roused at once. I well remember reading, on a wet February evening, on my way to attend a lecture on Central European problems, the placards saying SHELLING IN VIENNA, and the choke in the throat it gave me—this was two years before Guernica, remember. And when a very few days later there arrived in our house an emissary from Hugh Gaitskell, Douglas's former pupil, who had a teaching job in Vienna, with a demand that we should try and save the defeated Socialists from the fate of their fellows over the German border, we sprang immediately to attention.

The messenger was admirably chosen, a long lean fair fellow named Hans Mars, an Austrian economist who had nearly burst with rage on finding that the London School of Economics, in accepting him as a post-graduate student, assigned him to the tender care of Dr Hayek, who represented all that he most abominated in economic doctrine. He had incredible energy and vitality, was ready to speak all day and dance all night, and to go out and pour out torrents of passionate eloquence, in excellent English, to anyone whom we judged might be of the slightest use. As he had great charm as well as oratorical ability, he proved a most effective ambassador, and we sent him all over the place. In addition, we enlisted, through that most faithful and kindest of liberal historians, our friend J. L. Hammond, the publicity services of the *Manchester Guardian* ; we collected quickly a modest relief and defence fund, pricked on the slow-moving Council of Labour to release its much larger funds, and sent out an expedition, which included Naomi Mitchison and Elwyn Jones,[1] to find out on the spot what was happening, distribute help, and send reports home. It was a hectic fortnight of work for the Stage Army of the Good. I do not know exactly how much our efforts achieved in the end ; we did not save the Trade Unions from suppression or Koloman Wallisch from hanging. But we certainly brought hope and comfort to many, and I think that the public noise we created at least helped to prevent the Austrian Jews from immediately suffering the same fate as their fellows in Germany ; the great guns—Hitler and Mussolini—were not taking part in this preliminary skirmish.

The Abyssinian issue, the following year, brought me a step further on. As most will remember, it marked the final and painful abandonment of pacifism by the Labour Party, which declared itself in favour of sanctions against Mussolini after the long and bitter debate in which Ernest Bevin accused Lansbury of "taking his conscience round from Conference to Conference, asking to be told what to do with it." I was a spectator in the gallery, sitting with Lansbury's daughter Daisy and Rudolph Messel, the picturesque young founder of *Fact*[2] who afterwards became a sort of bear-leader to G.L. in his Continental pilgrimages for the saving of peace ; but I was not at all happy about the vote. The view that I and

[1] Who afterwards took part in the Nuremberg trials, and is now M.P. for Plaistow.

[2] See p. 183.

some others held at that juncture was one that I now recognise to be impossibilist, however theoretically attractive. We were willing to accept the arming of our country, if it meant saving Europe and ourselves from Fascism ; but we were not willing to give those armaments into the control of Baldwin and Chamberlain and their friends, lest when zero hour arrived the guns should be found to be pointing the wrong way. As there seemed no likelihood that Baldwin and Chamberlain would cease to be the government of the country—the disappointing election of 1935 showed that clearly enough—this policy was no use at all as a policy ; you cannot, as we had good reason to know later, turn a rearmament programme on and off like a tap according as you approve or disapprove of those who are likely to use it. But, looking back upon Munich, upon the shifty dealings of 1939 which Professor Namier has so gloomily collated in *Diplomatic Prelude*, and to the attempts, even after the war had begun, to recruit a British legion for Finland, who will dare say that our fears were without foundation ?

3.

It was the war in Spain which completed my conversion and that of many others. Before that July of 1936, however, we had changed to some extent the routine of our family lives. We had moved to a larger house ; we had invested in a car in which, since Douglas was no longer able to take long walks or go tramping at week-ends, we toured large parts of England, Wales, and Scotland, and we adopted the practice of taking holidays abroad with other families.

Freeland, our new home in the north-east corner of Hendon, is the only æsthetically satisfactory house I have ever inhabited—the oak-beamed dwelling in Holywell was spoiled by the lack of sun and air. It is a long low white (or off-white !) building of varying date. The oldest part is a hundred and twenty years old or thereabouts ; the youngest we built ourselves. It stands in rather over an acre of ground sloping down to the embryo river Brent, all the footbridges over which were suddenly removed by alarmed Authority in the summer of 1940, " for protection against Tanks," I was told. The proximity of the streamlet—which, considering its size, can produce most impressive oily floods upon occasion—means that we are never likely to be hemmed in with buildings ; but means, also, that enterprising youth can easily wade the normal eight-inch depth of water and help itself to the fruit from our garden. It is built, somewhat incongruously, in a road of semi-detached two-storeyed between-the-wars houses which extends to the grounds of Mill Hill barracks ; and I was amused to find, in 1939, that the authorities apparently considered it a survival doomed to perish before long. For when, in order to lighten the postman's job in black-out, they decreed that the houses in Holders Hill Road should bear numbers as well as names, they numbered ours 74, but the next door one 68. It seems we are intended to fall down soon and to be replaced by three neat little redbrickeries.

The garden is big enough to contain tennis and badminton courts as well as fruit, flowers, and some vegetables—before the war nice non-utilitarian vegetables such as asparagus. We were within easy walking distance of the families of Lance Beales and my brother Ray, who made a regular nucleus for garden-games parties on Sundays before the war ; while Humphrey, not yet a tennis-player, found the garden useful for staging treasure-hunts for his school friends. Inside there are lovely large rooms lit by huge windows (all of which crashed in fragments on a morning in August, 1944), and a great deal of space for furniture and books—though not nearly enough to satisfy the book-collector's aspirations of its owner ! It is a *nice* house, praised by all who succeed in finding their way here ; you can stand on the balcony in a leafy summer, looking east, and scarcely see a roof to remind you that you are less than nine miles from Hyde Park Corner. But it is greedy of attention to keep it going and of fuel to keep it warm, and it calls out for life and company that it has not had since children and friends began to be scattered, since rationing made it difficult to ask half-a-dozen to " stay on to supper," and petrol scarcity doubled its effective distance from the centre.

From Freeland we radiated out by car, as I said. I have no space to detail our journeys or even adequately to praise those best of all motoring maps, the folding Michelins with their green streaks indicating " beautiful road " and blue stars for " View "—weather permitting—which I still cherish so hopefully ; but in those half-dozen years I got a knowledge of my own country, insofar as it can be seen by road, at least equal to that of a commercial traveller with a lifetime's experience—and of a rather more interesting kind. There is hardly any cathedral south of the Border which I have not visited (I nearly completed the tale the other day by adding Gloucester) and few stretches of countryside with which I have not at least a nodding acquaintance. In fact, I might reasonably contemplate hiring myself out as driver and cicerone to American tourists—at least, if they wanted really to see something of Britain other than the Tower, Canterbury, Oxford, and Stratford-on-Avon. It is a good thing to have done.

" Foreign parts " are something of another story ; what the tourist gets out of them depends very much on what he brings with him in the way of previous knowledge and/or desire to find out things about the country he is visiting rather than to spend all his time as a sight-seer or basker on warm beaches. Pure holiday-making, naturally, takes you less into the heart of the country of your choice than having some job to do in it ; nevertheless, every one of the places which I visited in the 'thirties has left its own separate and distinguishable mark in my experience.

Basque Spain, for example, in 1933. Though we were mainly tourists in a seaside hotel much like other seaside hotels—except for the extraordinarily late arrival of meals—and though we had come there along the roads of France with their high made crowns and rough unmade sides, into which, when two cars met, each tried to force the other, and rapidly through French towns which said no more to us than they had to other tourists, we knew at once that we had come into a different land. The first Republican Government which succeeded Alfonso XIII had fallen from power, but signs of its work were remaining, of its attempts to divide up the land and educate the children—and even in comparatively prosperous Vizcaya there was enough dirt and rags and misery to show how very far there was to go. We drove up from the green valley to Burgos—soon to become Franco's headquarters—with its innumerable beautiful boot-blacks, into the sun-baked uplands of Castile, dry and brown as one's idea of Bible scenery, where the villages have no shape or cohesion like the villages of France, but each man seems to have planted his garden-less, approach-less house anywhere he pleased, facing north, south, east, or west, without any relation to the houses of his neighbours. (It is tempting to see in this a striking illustration of the " proud individualism of the Spanish character " ; but I suspect that of being the kind of half-baked generalisation the tourist is apt to make.) There were towns, too, of course, tiny ones like Estrella, where the inhabitants appear to subsist mainly on gigantic melons, slightly larger ones like Logroño, scene of a fierce battle in the civil war, and larger ones still like Pamplona, where there were bull-fights and a great noisy meeting of Falangists in the square. And then there was the return through the foothills of the Pyrenees, when a storm, far more spectacular than any we had ever seen at home, stopped the car's engine with its downpour, and sent the Atlantic rolling in huge blue breakers up the beaches, incidentally drowning a couple of tourists as a kind of afterthought—to the little *chacoli* bar where one could buy a glass of thin wine made from the last crushings of the grape-skins for a *halfpenny*, the huge barn-like enclosure of the pelota-players, and the children's fiesta of dances and songs in that extraordinary Basque tongue which makes everyone's name sound like Hitchy-Koo.

Madeira (1935) was also primarily holiday—a vision of hotel sunbathers in enormous straw hats—mine measured four feet across—lying in rows by the sea with little bottles of oil, turning over and basting themselves methodically like so many joints of meat, and returning indoors to drink cocktails and compare their several shades of tan, or riding down to the town in a majestic and incredibly slow bullock-cart to watch the luxury cruisers come in, drink madeiras of many kinds, and pick up bogus bargains. But Madeira does not consist only of Funchal ; it has also an astonishing interior, where the one road that crosses the island climbs some 6,000 ft. in six miles, so that you rise from the heat in which bananas grow, through groves of eucalyptus (ugly things) and other tall trees upwards to Scottish pine and heather and sharp wind—all in a morning's excursion. And in that interior there were little hamlets served by no road at all, not even a path ; to get to them you must walk along the outer edge of irrigation water-courses cut in a precipitous mountain-side, or if your confidence or balance failed paddle ankle-deep in the cold running stream. I could not imagine how building materials and other large necessities were ever brought to the villages, though I did once see a peasant walking along the watercourse edge, balancing on his head an immense sheet of corrugated iron.

Guernsey, home of my ancestors, to which we went in the following year, largely because it sounded cheaper than anywhere in England, is a good example of how little you can tell about a place merely by looking at it on the map. On the map it is a tiny little island, which you would expect to find made up of miniature scenery and dotted with miniature " summer residences," like the Isle of Wight ; but it is not. Though small, it is not in the least miniature. The granite reefs, the reefs of the *Travailleurs de la Mer*,[1]

[1] Victor Hugo's house at St Peter Port was still preserved, flying the tricolour and managing to look exactly like a French police-station—such was the economy of the French authorities responsible for painting and lighting it.

which spread out from its western tip, are more menacing than anything off the Cornish coast; and instead of the mild maiden-lady slopes and chines of Ventnor or Shanklin, its south-western cliffs rise to great heights of rock separated by narrow and sometimes inaccessible bays of deep clear water. Internally, they told me that the real character of the island had been ruined since the fall of the franc drove away the French tourist and replaced him by families from Yorkshire and Lancashire speaking English and demanding steak or fish-and-chips; certainly the menus at Old Government House were unimaginative enough to do credit to any English watering-place. But the essential form of it was unchanged—the form not of a summer resort but of a Greek city-state, with all the curly narrow roads leading from the outlying hamlets or homesteads to St Peter Port only, and served by buses going in the morning and returning in late afternoon, as it might be from Attic farms to market or festival in Athens. In the tiny hinterland, each tiny field was occupied by a calm Guernsey cow, tethered near a glasshouse full of tomatoes where in England there would have been a haystack. When the war came, the Germans overran the tomatoes of Guernsey as the Spartans overran the olives of Attica; fortunately tomatoes take less time than olives to grow up again.

These were just holiday visits; our next—to Sweden—had a more serious purpose, for the New Fabian Research Bureau was preparing a book of studies on *Democratic Sweden*, and I was one of its editors, investigating education in particular. This gave me a job to do, running around with escorts to see schools and colleges, camps and publishing houses, and making contact with public men; and if I had not had the job I doubt whether I should have enjoyed the experience so much. For there is a certain monotony about the beauties of Sweden, at least to the Briton spoiled by his own island's frequent change of scenery, who finds seventy miles of lakeside, bordered by conifers, rather much of a good thing; when you have said Wood and Water, even if you add the bright white sands of Falsterbo and the undeniable loveliness of Stockholm, mercifully shielded from destruction by Swedish neutrality, you have said nearly all there is to say about Sweden in summer.

Not that wood and water are to be despised, by any means; the water, and the power made from it, make Stockholm one of the cleanest cities in the world and must prevent the long winter from being the grimy frowsty fog-ridden horror which it is in Leeds or Manchester. And Sweden is a virtuous, kindly, and democratic country. I shall not soon forget going to interview the Prime Minister, Per Alvin Hansson, who looked like a cheerful farmer of the middling sort, and being asked, as he had an unexpected engagement, to return at six o'clock, " When I will meet you outside [the Chancellery], as the caretaker will have gone home." And so he did, waiting for us on the steps with the Foreign Secretary, propelling us upwards in his own private lift, and himself running nimbly up the stairs to meet us at the top. When, in the course of the interview, Douglas asked a financial question to which he did not know the answer, he then and there rang up the Chancellor of the Exchequer and asked him to go round to Mr Cole's hotel that evening for a chat. Friendly informalism could go no further ; I believe he would have produced the King had he been asked, and I reflected that there was a good deal to be said for living in a country which had disposed of its foreign ambitions, and its ancient dynasty, generations ago, and which had never owned either a White Man's Burden or the financial centre of the world.

During the whole of our stay in Sweden, I only met one unpleasant person, which is saying a good deal. But notwithstanding all its merits I should not really like to live in Sweden, except purely as a shelter from international storm ; it is, alas, *dull*. It has little variety of achievement ; its people are too handsomely alike, too slow in their reactions, and even about its virtues there is a certain faint smugness which would eventually tempt one to make rude noises. To take one example ; their school curriculum had been laid down in detail, subject by subject and period by period, by Parliament in 1919, slightly modified nine years later, and could not be further altered without another Act of Parliament. When I asked whether that did not result in rather inconvenient rigidity, I was told with astonishment that the original provision was so good that there could be no reason for modifying it. Possibly not ; but the attitude seems a trifle complacent, to say the least of it. There was also, truly, *smörgasbord* in lovely quality and variety, and the tiny scarlet crayfish ; but even if supplies are still what they were one cannot spend one's life eating *smörgasbord*. As for politics, democratic and tolerant though Sweden is, I got a greater stirring of the spirit from a chance hour spent at Macon in Burgundy during Whitsun of 1936, when Léon Blum's *Front Populaire* was newly come to power and its local supporters were celebrating and cheering one another on in a large and noisy tent, with small boys in black blouses wriggling under the skirts of the tent in anxiety to miss nothing.

4.

During all these years we were also producing books at a fairly rapid rate. When the state of Douglas's health put a stop to some of his physical activities, he began to write faster and faster, and longer and more complicated books—*British Trade and Industry*, a volume full of the most elaborate tables of figures, was all written during the early stages of his illness, when he was under the severest restrictions of diet. I could not hope to keep such a pace, but I did collaborate on some of the long factual books which we wrote for Gollancz, which are mentioned in the next chapter, and on the detective novels, for which the responsibility was about evenly divided.

Between 1923 and 1942 we published twenty-nine of them, and four volumes of short detective stories, rather to the pain of some of our friends, who thought we were meant for Higher Things. On one occasion one of them, seeing me reading an Agatha Christie, cried out in despair, " Do you really have to *read* the things as well as write them ? " There is no truce between those who are gluttons for detective novels and those who cannot abide them ; but I would plead that they are both a very innocent form of escapism and a quiet satisfactory way of earning a modest competence. (Not a fortune, as many believe ; their public, though insatiable, is not large enough for that, unless you have the fortune to capture the American market.) Considered as a craft, the writing of detective novels is more like a game—a *serious* game, of course, such as cricket or chess—than anything else. It has its rules, and though these are not yet as unquestioned as the laws of cricket—they have not had anything like so long to grow in—they were well enough established for us to take part, along with such distinguished practitioners as Chesterton, Agatha Christie, Austin Freeman, E. C. Bentley, Dorothy Sayers, H. C. Bailey, Milward Kennedy, John Rhode, and Anthony Berkeley, in a Detection Dining Club which required its members to forswear all such illegitimate devices as Death-Rays, undetectable poisons, murderous Chinamen, and the like. The Club continues in existence to this day, though lack of paper has sadly curtailed the interest of intellectual reviewers in the finer points of the craft.

Said craft, has moreover, a definite technique which can be learned point by point. For example, if you intend to write twenty or thirty detective novels and not simply to produce one *tour-de-force*, much the most important element is the detective. (Not the plot, as the uninitiated might imagine ; you can get a plot from anywhere, a chance idea, a press story, a real crime suitably modified ; in the last resort you can steal one and re-dress it so as to disguise the theft.) It is the detective who has to bear the hard labour of the twenty volumes and sell them to the reader ; he ought therefore to be (*a*) a clearly recognisable personality—like Sherlock Holmes, the prototype of all detectives ; (*b*) a *tolerable* personality ; (*c*) able to detect—an elementary qualification which some writers overlook ; (*d*) since he is the representative of Abstract Justice, as immune as possible from human passions. The easiest way to secure this last is to make him a member of the police force, or—such is, or was, British respect for the medical profession—a doctor like Freeman's Dr Thorndyke. But Father Brown was a priest, Rhode's Dr Priestley is a " pure " scientist, and Lord Peter Wimsey had a private income large enough to remove him from ordinary temptation. (When he married, it is worth noting, he soon went out of business.)

It is also necessary to invent a criminal, but a criminal of such a kind that his nature can remain concealed from the reader for about two-thirds of the book—since it is cheating not to bring him on to the stage at an early point. He must, therefore, not be glaringly villainous, or he will stick out a mile ; for the expedient of camouflaging him, on Chestertonian principles, by a forest of potentially villainous characters,[1] is apt to exasperate the reader to the point of feeling that he does not care which of all the unpleasing persons you have depicted for him is hanged, so long as some of them are. There must be a corpse, of course—preferably, for English readers, not the corpse of a child or anyone who might excite too much genuine pity and spoil the essential atmosphere of chase and puzzle combined ; and there must be some other characters, well-devised to play their part properly. That is to say, they must have *verisimilitude* sufficient to hold the reader's attention, while not developing the *realism* which would cause them to tear the carefully-made plot to pieces ; to invent characters so nicely balanced is itself a pleasing exercise for anyone who enjoys stories but lacks the creative gift of your born novelist.

Finally, the working-out of the plot, whencesoever obtained, demands a tidy mind, an attention to fixed details such as time and distance, the speed of trains and cars, the licensing laws, etc., so that the characters, the criminal, and the detective can get to the right places at the right moments without violating conventions

[1] " If a man wished to hide a leaf, where would he hide it ? " " In the forest." (Chesterton, *The Innocence of Father Brown.*)

or probabilities en route. (Note that this condition does not apply to the " thriller yarn "—an essentially different craft, in which you are allowed to make the wildest assumptions if the speed and tension of your narrative is high enough.) It, therefore, assumes of necessity a reasonably settled state of society, in which the forces of law and order are so unquestionably established that the efforts of criminals to escape them can be regarded with as calm and sympathetic interest as the efforts of the losing team in the County Championship. It is for this reason, perhaps, that the detective novel has taken so firm a root in England ; I once read one whose setting was Moscow, but it was a very odd detective novel indeed, though it was actually written by an Englishwoman, Ivy Litvinov.

Chapter Eleven

I.

THE Spanish war finally made up my mind for me on the question of non-resistance. For the majority of the Left, indeed, it bulked much larger during the best part of two years than any threat of universal war. On the rights or wrongs of it, we had not a moment's hesitation. Whatever the propaganda in the Fascist camp, whatever the facts about Red atrocities offered to monks and nuns, we knew on which side the balance rested. We knew that the people of Guernica had not dynamited their own town, as some unblushing Catholic correspondents suggested, in order to discredit the Falangists ; we knew who, with however many mistakes or weaknesses in execution, had tried to bring schools to the children of Spain, to divide up the great estates, and to break the power of the most oppressive Church in Europe ; and we knew the forces which were trying to destroy the Republic from outside. A wave of strong emotional sympathy swept all classes ; a Labour Party Conference cheered Isabel Palencia to the echo ; Douglas, like many others, " adopted " a small exiled Basque boy ; the Spanish Embassy in London was thronged with people yearning to help—I remember Isabel Brown, the Communist orator, promising to collect a million *needles*, I think it was, from public meetings ; its occupants talked to the historically-minded of Moore's retreat to Coruña and of a by-gone Spanish Government which holding Cadiz alone went forward to regain the Peninsula. For the first time in a generation young men volunteered like Rupert Brooke to save the world for a high ideal. Public Opinion polls showed great majorities favouring the Republicans ; and the instructed pointed out that the Fascist Powers were using Spain to stage the dress-rehearsal of a greater war.

The question was simply, What was to be done about it—other than to join the International Brigade, a course open to comparatively few ? One could write, of course ; one could try and tell the facts to the English-speaking world, and a great many did. It was in the 'thirties that Victor Gollancz established himself as the encyclopedic publisher of the Left, beginning with books like Douglas's *Intelligent Man's Guide Through World Chaos* (1932) and the two other Guides which we wrote together, and going on to his great venture, the Left Book Club, which month by month produced a red-bound work of information (as time went on, more and more depressing information) about various parts of the world. Later, Penguin *Specials* took a hand, educating the people in world problems at sixpence a time; and columnists, American and British, weighed in with large books of news and impressions not to be found in the press at large. John Gunther started going Inside one continent after another; Douglas Reed, Hessell Tiltman, Vincent Sheean, and many others brought out descriptions—of Europe mostly—all of which might reasonably have borne the title of one of them, *Insanity Fair*.

The venture of this kind which I remember best—because I played most part in it—was a periodical called FACT, which ran from 1937 to 1939. It was not an ordinary journal, but a monthly pamphlet of twenty-five to thirty thousand words, most of them devoted to one single subject—which thereby got much fuller treatment than it could have done in any ordinary journal. Rudolph Messel was its financier, Ray its editor; I contributed the first issue and a good part of the last; Francis Meynell designed its type and cover, making of it a pleasant and brightly-coloured little book instead of a limp white folio; and it had a number of distinguished associate editors, including writers like Arthur Calder-Marshall, Stephen Spender, and Storm Jameson, scientists like Joseph Needham and (for a little while) Lancelot Hogben, sociologists like Leonard Barnes and others, and George Lansbury, all of whom discussed and worked over contributions with the editor. G.L., I regret to say, thought less of his eminent co-editors than I did; at an afternoon discussion in Ray's home he leaned over to me and said in a loud sibilant undertone, which he presumably believed to be inaudible, "Don't think Ray's going to get much out of *this* lot, do you?"[1] The contributions we got in our twenty-seven issues were mostly of remarkably high quality and rated excellent Press reviews; the establishment, however, had been set up on too lavish a scale, and, after manful efforts to interest publishers in it, it had finally to be abandoned. Not very long afterwards, Ray became the editor of the reorganised *Tribune*.

There was thus a tremendous amount of information available, as much if not more than anyone could reasonably digest—nearly all of it pointing in the same direction and leading to the same conclusion. What was to be done with it all?

[1] G.L., that great and good man, was constitutionally unable to whisper. When Humphrey was a very little boy, G.L. took him with some of his own relations on a tour of the Houses of Parliament; being asked about it on his return Humphrey said, "We went to the House of Lords, and there was a poor Lord trying to talk, but Mr Lansbury whiskered so loud he couldn't."

Clearly, one would suppose, to use it as a basis to mobilise anti-fascist opinion for the stopping of Fascism before it was too late, to follow the example of the French and the Spanish in forming the *Front Populaire* and the *Frente Popolar*, and of the Russians in adhering, despite its capitalistic connections, to the League of Nations and joining in the Franco-Soviet pact. Accordingly, great efforts were made to get a Popular Front in Britain—without, it may be said at once, any success whatever, unless you count the election to Parliament of Vernon Bartlett on a generalised anti-fascist programme ; as, however, Bartlett was at that time the B.B.C.'s most popular political commentator, this did not prove very much. I remember several such attempts, in which Douglas and I foregathered with people like G.L., Victor, Stafford Cripps, Ellen Wilkinson, and "Johnny" Pritt, to formulate Popular Front policies, People's Charters, and what not, all of which roused bright hopes for a few days or weeks, and all of which came to nothing quite soon. The main cause of the futility of all these sorties was that the leaders of no party except the Communists wanted them to succeed ; even the leaders of the Liberals, who could not well have lost anything if they had succeeded and might have gained a good deal, cold-shouldered them. The result was that anyone who broke ranks to join any such grouping found himself sooner or later either in a lonely huddle with one or two of Churchill's supporters and some cross internationalists from the Liberal benches, or on a platform directed and dominated by Communists ; in the end, all returned to their folds or, like Stafford Cripps and Aneurin Bevan, were thrown out of the Labour Party into no man's land. In our inmost hearts, however, I do not believe that we really believed we could succeed ; the experience of 1926, 1931, and the doldrums which followed,[1] had conditioned us to expect defeat at home, and when we looked abroad we saw disaster treading upon disaster and the Russians, rightly or wrongly, sending the heroes of the Revolution to death and exile. The morale of the Stage Army of the Good was at a very low ebb ; it had hardly a dream of coming to real power.

The happiest organisation of those I worked with in the gloomy years was certainly the New Fabian Research Bureau, which did not mix itself up in any political *démarches*, but with John Parker as Secretary, Douglas as Chairman, Dick Mitchison as Treasurer, and myself as Honorary Secretary, gradually accumulated some hundreds of men and women, mostly pretty young, who were

[1] Herbert Morrison's capture of the L.C.C. in 1934 was the *only* sizable success in the whole decade.

anxious to work hard at preparing concrete policies for a possible Labour Government in the future, and getting them criticised, in conference and at week-ends, by sympathetic experts. I remember a good many pleasant and " meaty " discussions at places like the Royal Star Hotel at Maidstone—where more than once we found the irrelevant delights of a small circus, with roundabout, " chairoplane " and all, attached ; in particular, one where I met for the first time that very great and simple Scot, Sir John Boyd Orr. The occasion was a conference either upon world food supplies or home nutrition policy—possibly both combined. I remember very clearly our principal speaker in his nice burred voice expounding the merits of a diet of oatmeal and herrings—which distinctly lowered the spirits of his mainly southron audience—and raising them again when he refused to draw his expenses, on the ground that so small a society could not afford the return fare from Aberdeen. The Bureau was certainly small enough to be very grateful for so characteristic a courtesy.

The subject of that conference is significant. For it was not only in the field of foreign affairs that we were accumulating information and trying to arouse opinion ; the extent and effects of poverty at home were also grist to our mill.[1] Herein we were, I think, a good deal more successful, though we did not feel successful at the time, and the success was not very apparent until war expedients had paved the way for the great social legislation of 1945-48. But the depths were stirred. Walter Greenwood's *Love on the Dole*, as novel, play, and film made a deep impression, the more that it had so simple and low-brow a plot—the heroine saved her stricken family by selling herself into sin. It was accompanied by statistical " revelations," by Boyd Orr and others, about the miserably inadequate food of the poorer strata of the population and the results upon its health, by the findings of the Overcrowding Survey, and by books like *Men Without Work*, which backed up Greenwood with factual details about the long-term unemployed. When outraged propagandists on the other side told Boyd Orr that the fault lay not in the food supply, but in the unthriftiness and cooking incompetence of the working-class wife, they were unexpectedly confronted with a report by a committee of the unimpeachable B.M.A. which had worked out a series of " balanced weekly menus " purchasable with current working-class incomes—and produced a series of suggestions for meals so dull, so tasteless, and so suet-puddingy that no honest person of the middle classes

[1] As in *The Condition of Britain*, by G. D. H. and M. I. Cole (1937).

could decently call them anything but intolerable. All this at a time when men's sense of elementary economy was being outraged by continual reports of food in the world's granaries being destroyed in order to keep the economic system working at all, of railway engines in the Argentine fired with surplus wheat, of Brazilian coffee packed in metal containers, taken out to sea and sunk, of farmers paid for not raising hogs and firms living on the quota of goods which they had *not* produced—it seemed the crassest lunacy.

I do not mean to suggest that the actual condition of the British working class was getting worse and worse ; in fact, the collapse of world primary prices, *i.e.*, the ruin of producers in other countries, had cushioned a good many of them against the fall in their own earnings, and the growth in mass-production of household plenishings and amusements may indeed have made life better for them,[1] if one left out of account the mass of the unemployed and the millions more over whom the fear of unemployment hung like a monstrous shadow. What happened rather was that the public at large became suddenly conscious that, improvements or none, the gulf between the Two Nations yawned only less widely than it did in Disraeli's day, and that this was a disgrace to a nation calling itself civilised. People began to be ashamed of unemployment, as the better sort of American to-day is ashamed of his country's treatment of negroes, and a good many came forward, here and elsewhere, with suggestions, some of the wildest kind, for ending it. The Americans contributed " Technocracy," a scheme for getting rid of currency-domination by evaluating everybody's work in units called *ergs* and *joules*, which swept their country for a brief season ; adherents of the Social Credit proposals of Major Douglas, forgotten since the early 'twenties, put on green shirts and marched about to meetings. They actually won the province of Alberta in a general election, and held it ; they also converted my old adviser, Ezra Pound, who intermitted his literary work to write letters of the most unprintable abuse to all who did not go along with him.

Ezra was a freak ; most of the writers and artists came in on the other side, particularly after Franco's coup and Hitler's burning of the books. Not all, of course ; no one could call T. S. Eliot, who was to the 'thirties what Lawrence was to the 'twenties, a soldier of the Left, and people like Edith Sitwell wrote on unperturbed. But one has only to mention *Modern Times*, *Mr Deeds*

[1] A good deal more food was, undoubtedly, consumed than in Edwardian times ; but the standard had risen so gradually that it had not been noticed.

Goes to Town, and *The Grapes of Wrath*, and the names of Auden, Spender, and Isherwood, and of " social " novelists like A. J. Cronin, to recall the picture of artists told to eschew Ivory Towers and write of machinery, mean streets and the emotions of common men—much of it good enough writing, however depressing for the reader. There was even a rumour that High Places were taking an interest in the sociological problem ; the Prince of Wales had once talked for half an hour to Mrs Sidney Webb, and had certainly expressed strong sympathy for the stricken miners of South Wales. It was the knowledge of this that gave a substratum of reality to the excitement of the Abdication—" that most *enjoyable* crisis," as a friend of mine cynically put it—when it was believed by a number of people that Baldwin and the Archbishops, representing the entrenched and united governing class, had combined to thrust out the King because he sympathised with the People.

Fortunately the Labour Party rejected the appeal of some of its more emotional members to line itself into a party of King's Men ; and the crisis passed with no more than a ripple. All I remember of it now, apart from muzzled and sizzling journalists at cocktail-parties, is the final evening, when the tutorial class which I was conducting in Westminster adjourned in a bunch to listen to the radio, the angry sincerity of the King's voice, with its slight German accent, bidding his last farewell—and the " ancestral voices " of those who connected the event with the burning down of the Crystal Palace a few nights earlier, and gloomily prophesied war and the end of England's glory. (Actually, the number of Londoners who, to the great anxiety of the authorities, swarmed to see the Palace burning was far greater than the number who came to see it unharmed ; the typical reaction of those who did not was the cross complaint of Ray—twenty years a Londoner—" Why, I was just intending to go and *see* the thing, and now it's not there !")

All this social agitation seemed to achieve little more, at the time, than provide the domestic items of Popular Front programmes, though in fact it did do something. It mitigated the harsh treatment of the unemployed ; it produced milk for schoolchildren and paved the way for the wartime subsidies ; it brought into school curricula a great deal more about contemporary life and problems than had been thought necessary or desirable for me to know in my childhood. But the real effect was in the hearts and minds of men ; the public was not merely feeling shame and anger at the conditions disclosed ; it was also digesting possible ways of amending them. There was a great wave of demand piling up for the future and the dams which had held it back were being undermined. Unsuspected, society was on the move, and as Clough said long ago :—

> " Far back, through creeks and inlets making
> Comes silent, flooding in, the main."

2.

But there was a long and dreadful time to wait before we saw it come. Our hopes had been centred on Spain, and through 1937 and 1938 we watched the fortunes of that conflict surging to and fro, but inexorably settling down against the Republic, as her enemies showed that they meant business and her nominal friends that they were running no risks. Before it was over came the crowning disgrace of Munich—the panicky scrambled evacuation of those who could get away and the panic digging of waterlogged trenches, the horrible hysteria at the aerodrome and in Parliament, and worse, the staggering revelation that so many people, even among one's own friends and colleagues, simply rejoiced that war was averted and did not seem to notice the means by which it had been averted and the great step to final defeat that Chamberlain had taken. At that time, surrounded by happy fools, I had no idea that Munich marked the end of the patience of the people—though not of Chamberlain's—I and those who looked with me upon the Skoda works, the mountain defences of Czechoslovakia and the Czech army, packed in a single parcel for Hitler's taking, could do no more than wait to see what he would ask for next. And then, in the New Year, the Republic perished, bare hands and courage battered to death with guns and bombs ; at the news of the fall of Madrid and Barcelona and of the last terrible trek across the Pyrenees to the barbed-wire camps in the snow, people wept who had not shed tears since the Armistice ; the last light seemed to have gone out. It was with a very definite feeling of " now or never " that in February 1939, I went out to Cairo to see my mother and my brother Ormond, head of the English Mission College there, for whom she was keeping house.

I had a job, albeit a small job, of lecturing to perform in Egypt, which according to my theory explains part of the intense pleasure I found in my visit there. But Egypt itself accounts for much more of it. To the historically-minded no country[1] can provide such satisfaction as Egypt, and I would earnestly advise all who can to go there, carrying the essential *Guides*—even if you normally despise

[1] Except possibly Greece, and about Greece too much has been written for me to try and add anything here.

guide-books, you cannot do without them in Egypt; you will miss half the essentials—and stare long and thoughtfully, for as long as you can afford to stay. From the moment I walked across from my brother's house to the Heliopolis obelisk, I remained in a state of bemused fascination. No one had ever told me what to expect; and I had never seen *so much* history at one time and in one country—all preserved together in the dry Egyptian air; I do not believe there is so much in any other place on earth.

Consider just these few facts. Ormond lived in Matarieh, an eastern suburb of Cairo on the edge of an unattractive stony desert—like the foreshore of many English seaside resorts, but with no sea however far you walked, only a débris of discarded date-stones, possibly a scarab or two, bits of metal, stone, and other materials for houses which were projected but never built, and other less attractive deposits of the untidy Cairene. Half-a-mile away stands the great obelisk, set up under the Eleventh Dynasty (more than 2,000 years before Christ). That obelisk is separated by something like a thousand years—longer than the whole of English history since the Conqueror—from the Great Pyramids at Gizeh, which are themselves, as anyone can see from the sculptures found in them, now preserved in the Cairo Museum, the crown of a highly developed society. The early tombs in the Fayyum are many centuries older, and *they* are by no means the work of primitive savages. That is the March of Time in one direction.

In the other, our obelisk was fifteen hundred years (a space of time equal to that between the end of the Roman occupation of Britain and our own day) older than the Pharaoh Ikhnaton, that early religious reformer who seems to have combined with his religious views a streak of Bloomsbury eccentricity, and a little older still than the great megalomaniac, Rameses II, who reigned for seventy years or thereabouts and whose braggings in stone sprawl all over the Nile valley from Luxor to Saqqara which once was Memphis. Having reached Rameses, take a deep breath; for there is nearly a thousand years to pass before Cambyses, the crazy Persian King, stuck a knife into the sacred and immortal bull at Saqqara, just to teach the old priests a lesson. Thereafter, a mere two and a half centuries gives you Alexander the Great, recognised as a god by Ammon in his desert shrine, and his general Ptolemy making Egypt part of the Hellenic world. Wait as long again (as long as from our Glorious Revolution to the accession of George VI), and you will find Caesar and Cleopatra, and Augustus turning Egypt into the private province of the Emperors and the granary of the Roman world. Take another breath now, for you must learn that during all this immensity of time, almost ungraspable by anyone brought up to believe the British Parliament, or at least the Papacy, the oldest institution in the world, no annalist so much as mentions the city of Cairo. For there was no Cairo.

Not until the Roman Empire—itself no Mayfly of a day—had fallen, and Mohammed had come out of the East, was there any Cairo at all—and then it was not our Cairo. The plan of modern Cairo, as any detailed map will show you if you know how to look at it, has been imposed on old Cairo—on *three* old Cairos—almost at right-angles, cutting in half what were once the main highways. But the dead Cairos are not gone ; they are all there at your feet. There is Ibn Tulun's ancient mosque ; close by it is the great open space called Saladin's Riding-School, to remind one of the Crusades ; in a row, on a low bank, are the stumps of the windmills built by Napoleon's soldiers ; on the Citadel, visible twenty miles away in the clear air of the Delta, are the minarets of Mehemet Ali the Albanian, whose son was defeated at Navarino. Descending from the Citadel, you find Coptic churches in Old Cairo, the modern quarter with Shepheard's Hotel reminding you of Robert Hichens and the newspaper *feuilletons* about ladies of Lord Cromer's day having affairs with Sheiks ; and outside in the Western Desert, which blossoms like the rose every spring, the Bedouin tents on the way to Burgh-el-Arab, that astonishing pseudo-medieval town by ancient Mareotis, which was built out of pre-Roman stones by British soldiers marooned there after the Armistice. Out in the Delta are fields under modern cotton cultivation sponsored by the British, and back in the suburbs the archæologists with their perennial and highly technical squabbles. And now the British are nearly gone ; but no more than any other conquerors of Egypt will they be obliterated altogether. Their traces will remain, in that dry air, like the scribblings of the Emperor Hadrian on the base of the statue of Memnon by the Valley of the Kings, or the onion dome of a sheik's resting-place. Nothing dies in Egypt ; nothing rots. Go there if you want to breathe in thousands of years of history—but breathe it gently, lest it choke you.

* * * *

As I came home across the Mediterranean, the ship's radio crackled out the news of the seizure of Prague. Mussolini put Albania in his pocket ; there was announced a sudden and, to us, hollow-sounding guarantee to Poland and to Rumania ; people began to ask one another incredulously, " Are we going to be asked to fight for *Danzig* ?" In high summer we drove north to Carradale, our brains still trying to cope with the shock of the Soviet-German discussions [1] ; the end was very near. In the middle of August we sailed from Glasgow to Dublin—where our respectable hotel was outraged by the suggestion that it should provide us with a morning paper which supported Mr De Valera. From Dublin we drove right across the island, that flat, damp, green saucer surrounded by high hills ; and came to rest at Glengarriff in County Cork, standing at the head of a long quiet sea-lough, just south of the Ring of Kerry and Tim Healey's beautiful road across the pass to Killarney, that horrid parasitic little town which so suitably turns its back on the purple mountains surrounding its lovely Lakes. It was our last family holiday across the water ; and though the water crossed was narrow the place was foreign enough. For there I found the *Irish R.M.* in full burgeoning life.

Until I came to Eire, twenty-five years after I had arrived in Donegal on the eve of another world war, I had believed that delightful book to be an uproarious caricature of a forgotten civilisation ; but as soon as I got there I found that it was all perfectly true. There were Flurry Knoxes around every corner, natives who told your fortune, natives who looked as though they would eat you alive or cast the evil eye over you upon any provocation, and other friendlier natives who were prepared to say anything they thought would please you. "Sure, it'll be a lovely day for ye"—with the rain pouring down out of a leaden sky. The hotel was kindly, dirty—though not as dirty as the only other hotel !—and quite often, it seemed, entirely untenanted. After our arrival, we waited for a long time in an empty bar, gasping for a drink on a hot evening ; when at length a functionary turned up, his surprised comment was, "Sure, what was the matter at all ? Aren't the bottles up there ? Why wouldn't ye be helping yerselves ?"

The weather was fine, for the most part, and the country glorious. We went bathing in rolling blue billows at Barley Cove, went fishing, nine of us in one boat to catch one fish, sought out the tiny grey stone shrine of a hermit poet on a tiny grey inland lake, and drove over mountains scarlet with fuchsia growing as wild and freely over the rock and gravel as gorse grows in the North. For a brief while the "crisis" slipped out of our minds ; but before our stay was ended Hitler began to work up to his climax in Poland.

[1] Of which David Low drew the fierce cartoon called "Shaking Hands With Murder," which showed Hitler and Stalin greeting one another like Stanley and Livingstone in the jungle. The comment was fair enough in itself, but would have come better from a country which had not Britain's record of dealings with the Nazis.

The hotel emptied of visitors as though a plug had been pulled out—and within a day or two began to fill again with others fleeing from the wrath to come. It had no radio—or its radio had broken down. The only working radio was in a shop in the village ; but it had to be plugged in to the only electric light in the place. So, in a small room smelling of stale fish, by the light of a candle in a bottle, which threw long grotesque shadows across the counter, the English visitors huddled together to hear about the last days of the post-war peace.

Then we sailed home from Cork to Fishguard ; as we drove back to London we saw the posters proclaiming EVACUATION TO-MORROW. I tried to lean forward between Humphrey and the placards so that he should not be able to read them.

PART SEVEN

WAR AND POST-WAR AGAIN

Chapter Twelve

I.

At the beginning of September, 1939—as soon as the children had been got away to Buckinghamshire—one's immediate preoccupation, almost driving out thoughts of what war might mean, was BLACK-OUT. Freeland's vast expanses of window and skylight were equipped with what we had always believed to be adequate curtains, which, however, failed entirely to come up to wartime standards, and at one time there were at least six angry air-raid wardens shouting at us from the garden. So for the next few days following our return from Eire, helped by Paul and Milla Rosenthal, the kind and efficient Austrian couple who had taken the place of the pair from the Yorkshire coalfield, I cut and stitched and crawled about fastening what seemed acres of horrible navy and black materials of all kinds to my nice coloured curtains, enlisting Ormond, who had been an Air Raid Warden in Cairo, to march round the house looking out for Chinks. We did get just enough material to veil ourselves adequately ; we were not reduced, like my poor Girton, to daubing the windows with dark blue paint—only with preparations of latex or cellophane, supposed to prevent splintering, whose curiously blurring effect made one feel that one was living in a diving bell under water. However much the discontented may talk of the horrors of peace, not even they can fail to be glad that the black-out is gone, that one need no longer stifle when darkness falls on a summer night or on winter afternoons stumble blindly through black streets, full of hitherto unsuspected kerbs and unevennesses ; and that when benighted in the country one can see once more the lights twinkling from houses in the hills.[1] It was the black-out, I believe, that for five long years sapped morality

[1] It was in a heavy black-out at Victoria Station that five Postgate children saw the sixth (Ormond) leave with their mother for Egypt in a train which, as trains will at such times, remained persistently standing at the platform for a good hour after all possible good-byes had been said ; it was a grim and gloomy parting, for it was so clearly on the cards that we might never see her again—though in fact she returned safe and sound four years later.

even more than queueing or the worst war news ; and the unexpected —and undeserved—beauty of the St Pancras Hotel snow-covered under the moon was not very adequate compensation.

When the immediate job was done, and we had discovered that we were not all going to be wiped out with the coming of war, my first feeling was of shamed apology towards my own children and the children of others—shame because, after all our talk and all our knowledge of the facts about wars and how they broke out, we had in the end done no better than our fathers and mothers, and had let it all happen again. Jane, having won a place at Girton, was due to enter in October upon a three years which ought to have been as carefree and as happy as my own had been ; Anne would be starting medical school in another twelve-month ; both were just about ready for pretty frocks, re-furnished bedrooms, and the fun of being grown-up. (The first—and the only—boy and girl dance which we gave for them happened in the early days of the war.) Humphrey had just demanded long trousers, and might be trying for a scholarship next year. Now, whatever happened to them physically, they were being deprived of those precious years of adolescence—for I could not believe that, unless we were defeated, the war could be short—years which could never be made up. And that was what we had done to them. For myself, I find that my memory tends to treat the war as though it had not happened or had happened in another world or another dimension ; I catch myself saying " when we were in Sweden just recently," when in fact it was more than ten years ago. But in late middle age the loss of six years is a comparatively trifling matter ; it is quite different when you are only eighteen. All over England, now, one sees instances of people who have had no youth and are desperately trying to find one now, or who because of the war have grown up all in one direction—on the intellectual side, for example, or the combat side. Possibly they may turn out the better and the wiser in the end, though I rather doubt this ; but youth is the loss that can never be replaced.

In saying that I think of the war as having happened in another dimension, I do not at all mean that I have forgotten it. I remember its detailed events much more vividly than I do those of its predecessor, partly because I reckoned the former, after the first year or two, as essentially a sordid affair and none of my business, but more because the fortunes and misfortunes of 1939-45 were both so much more dramatic and so much more quickly made known—when they *were* made known—to the public. Thanks to the " triumphs of civilisation " such as radio, news of the disasters of Crete and

Singapore reached us with a speed and completeness which made the news of Gallipoli, for example, seem by comparison as slow as reporting in the Crimean War. Furthermore, the reports, when they came, were singularly little affected by romantic distortions. Even where, as in the case of the airmen who fought the Battle of Britain, the elements of romance were present in full, Churchill's few words said all that needed to be said ; and I can think of no parallel to the cheap sugary love-and-war stories of World War I. The facts were enough ; the British people, at least, was as clear-eyed about war then as it is likely ever to be about anything.

I have no intention of re-telling here the story of the war, which in any event the reader knows as well or better than I do. But there are certain recollections that stand out exceptionally clearly. I remember a long train journey northwards in March, 1940, after long cold months of black-out, phoney war, and absurd demands that we send ski troops to Finland or, more preposterous still, launch an attack on Baku, when I looked out of the window and saw, with a breath of sharp responsive pleasure, the new grass growing and the first new leaves appearing greener, it seemed, than in any spring the townsman's eye had seen—

> " There is one creed—'neath no world-terror's wing
> Apples forget to grow on apple trees,"

wrote Chesterton—who lived before Hiroshima. And a very little while later I was made aware that the long frost had broken, in another and more sinister sense, when at Glasgow Central Station I bought a smudged evening paper and read in a couple of stop-press lines that the Nazis were in Denmark and Norway.

Within a month, the spring had broken into a lovely flowery May, and my suitcase was lying on the luggage-rack of a train that was to take me on a Whitsun visit to Richmond in Exeter, when I read, in another evening paper, the news of the invasion of the Low Countries and the bombing of French airfields—and leaped out and made a dash for home, uncertain whether the Luftwaffe would not be at Hendon or Croydon next morning. That Saturday was a day of blazing sunshine ; and the sun, as all who are old enough will remember, continued to shine for all the early part of the terrible summer. We walked in the evenings down garden paths bordered by sweet and flourishing flowers, absorbing the news that the Germans were in Amiens . . . Abbeville . . . Calais . . .

> " Je n'oublierais jamais les lilas ni les roses,"

says Aragon in the poem which contains the line as simple and as poignant as anything in the Greek Anthology :—

" On nous a dit ce soir que Paris s'est rendu."

Meantime Communists were reiterating their cry that this was an imperialist war and demanding limitation of hours for those trying frantically to replace the war material lost after Dunkirk ; it was difficult to keep one's temper with them.

As the summer went on the signposts disappeared from the cross-roads [1] and the milestones which remained were given coats of bitumen. Paul Rosenthal was swept away to the Isle of Man ; at the end of July the London sirens sounded for the first time for nine months, for the first raid on Croydon. Then in early September came another lovely afternoon. Humphrey and I went walking with a friend in Ashridge Park near Berkhamsted—where we found at the dead end of a road a tiny village which had been equipped, I suppose by some earnest and leisured local strategist, with a series of strong points, barricades, and camouflaged fortifications worthy of a south coast port, at least ; it looked like a creation of Walt Disney's. As we sat on a spur of the Chilterns and looked out across the Vale of Aylesbury, we said to one another, idly, " What should we do if the church bells started ringing *now* ? " When we came home we found the Air Raid notices out on the Watford by-pass road, and later in the evening were called up to the roof of the house to look at a lake of red fire in the south-eastern sky. That was the raid on Silvertown and the Docks ; next evening the Luftwaffe came to the West End. The battle for London had begun.

I remember the feeling of startled incredulity on the first occasion when " Clara " sounded before midnight, and on the first evening when " Mona " did not sound at all—and a night of great fear when, having gone to Bristol to arrange some broadcast talks, I heard the radio talking of a devastating raid on a Midland industrial town. The town was Coventry ; but the name was not given—and Anne was a student in Birmingham. I remember the creeping-disaster of Greece and Crete, Churchill triumphantly proclaiming that " Jugoslavia had found her soul "—how oddly that sounds to-day ; the Nazi attack on Russia and another Churchillian broadcast promptly aligning Britain on the Russian side ; the staggering news of Pearl Harbour, and almost immediately afterwards of the sinking of the unprotected battleships in the China Sea ; and a summer gloomier than the summer of Dunkirk—the

[1] " Can you tell me if this is the road for Bradford ? "
" If Goovermut'd meant thaa to get to Braadford, Goovermut woulden a takken away t'signpoast ! "

summer of 1942, when the desert forces had been thrown back, Tobruk had fallen in a couple of days, El Alamein was months ahead, and the Germans, after their setback in the winter, were driving fast and deep into the Caucasus. This was the nadir; afterwards came Stalingrad—the desert victories—news of the resisters in occupied Europe—naval triumph—the Italian surrender, which gave us so unjustified a hope that the war was all but over—D Day and Mulberry Harbour—and the end. I read and listened to a good deal of war reportage in an attempt to get a picture of conditions wider than that given me by my own correspondents in the Forces; but what remain with me now most vividly are impressions of disaster, not of victory. I am not sure that that is not a national characteristic; the English war poetry that is best-known is found not in victory odes, but in commemoration of those who died with their backs to the wall.[1]

2.

I was in London practically continuously for the whole of the blitz winter, except for Christmas and New Year, which we spent at Carradale, so missing the first great fire-raid. Humphrey was at Winchester, Jane in Cambridge, Anne was in Birmingham, and Douglas, for all the first months, in Oxford. I do not remember being particularly frightened; but that was due less to any courage of mine than to the fact that Hendon was only on the fringe of Goering's operations—in spite of the airfield and the mass of war material at Mill Hill barracks it was not even part of the official "evacuation area." One soon got used to—and bored with!—"tip-and-run" raids on London on cloudy days, and at night endured nothing worse than listening to the angry dronings and bangings overheard. I did not, like so many of my colleagues in the Fabian Society, have to walk streets full of fire and falling metal, or sit still while the bombs screamed down and neighbouring houses crashed to the ground. Freeland had about nine windows blown out by a small bomb falling half-a-mile away—on that occasion Bernice Holt-Smith, one of my wartime lodgers,[2] and I

[1] *E.g., The Burial of Sir John Moore, The Light Brigade*, Housman's *Army of Mercenaries*—and even some of Kipling.

[2] Another was Dick Mitchison—Rivercourt being closed during the war while Naomi farmed her land and received refugees at Carradale—and another Tony Pirie, wife of a biologist and herself an ophthalmological specialist. After the 1945 election, Dick, as an M.P., found Hendon too far from Westminster; and for two and a half years his room was occupied by my brother Richmond, most companionable and charming of cuckoos, newly returned from R.A.F. service in the Far East.

promptly and instinctively dived for cover and after a minute or two crawled out, a couple of dishevelled rats, from behind the drawing-room couches ; later on we received a hatful of incendiaries, which Dick and I stamped out with little difficulty. I was a member of a fire-watching and stirrup-pump party, and practised pumping out a synthetic fire in a local shed ; but we were never required to perform in earnest. (The extent of our comparative security, though we were so little distance from Westminster, may be gathered from a truly democratic discussion at a meeting of our " street group " at which, it having been announced that some houses had failed to provide their quota of fire-watchers, an earnest soul rose from the back of the room to enquire whether it would be in order, " supposing their 'ouses to catch fire, for us not to put 'em out.") The only occasion, in fact, when anything resembling courage might have been called for was when I was asked to organise a W.E.A. class in a place about twenty miles' driving distance away, for the winter of 1941, when, so far as anyone knew, the conditions of 1940 might have been repeated. I accepted, with a mental resolution to keep a thick rug and a flask of coffee in the car as preparation for being stranded ; and felt rather foolish when nothing whatever happened—not even a fog or a puncture !

Freeland escaped serious damage until late in August, 1944, when a buzz-bomb hit a nearby tree and exploded fifty yards from the house, blowing out windows, doors, and half the roof, cracking walls, tearing and smashing equipment, and presenting us with no injuries but a mess of appalling dimensions and a " reconstruction problem " which has not been solved to this day. The ravages which inefficient builders and plasterers can make when let loose must be seen to be believed. We suffered from a peculiarly virulent specimen of the last-named, who *plastered* everything within reach, tearing down irrelevancies such as telephone boxes which got in his way ; and every shower of rain produces fountains to remind us of those who purported to have mended our skylights. It may give one some faint idea of the human meaning of the word " war-destruction in Europe " ; it certainly contributed to the ill-health from which several of us suffered during the last years of the war and the first years of peace.

Most of our holidays were spent at Carradale, which with the coming of war had become the Mitchisons' permanent home and had to some extent changed its character. During the first winter it opened its doors to evacuees—children from the Glasgow slums, bringing with them all the problems so loudly discussed in the press of 1939,[1] other children whose parents were obliged to go on working in dangerous areas, and the Coles at Christmas, as I said. After the fall of France, food production became important. The stretch of warren lying between house and beach was ploughed up—in slightly wavy lines—for oats; cows, sheep, pigs, hens, ducks, and geese appeared by stages; summer visitors intermitted their walking and bathing and billiard-playing to pick fruit, thin turnips, cut trees for firewood, or help bind and carry the corn. In between they were fed and rested, on that faraway coast of Kintyre where there was little more of war to be seen than the explosion of depth-charges far out to sea, a few planes flying over from the Fleet Air Arm twenty miles to the south, a party or two of visitors from the Campbeltown training ships, and an occasional submarine surfacing in the bay;[2] and could feast their eyes on the changing shapes and colours of the place.

Carradale, in its wide shallow bay halfway down the absurd tongue of Kintyre, so barely joined to the mainland of Argyll, is a wonderfully beautiful place, the more beautiful the better you know it. It rains there more often than the southerner likes—to be more accurate, it rains more often and more unexpectedly than he thinks reasonable; but that very wetness keeps it fresh and clear and makes it so lovely, when the sun does come out, that all its past unkindnesses are forthwith forgiven. To Carradale that wickedly misused adjective "colourful" does strictly apply. I have seen it at almost all seasons of the year, and even on the most overcast days of winter the number and differing quality of the browns and greens of heath and larch and bracken, of the greys and yellows of rock and stone and lichen, are almost unbelievable. It was almost a second home, at the least, a very welcome rest and shelter—and supplier of milk and eggs!—to us; and not to us only, but to the evacuee children I have already mentioned, and to young Communist workers and young Labour workers, fighters from the Free French, poets, artists, scientists, and many more, who mixed oddly and with varying success with the very West Highland fishing community—some of the French pilots did best. If the house had kept a visitors' book instead of a utilitarian volume recording only the number of fish, flesh and fowl slain by rule of sport, it would have been a good book of noble deeds.

[1] See *Evacuation Survey* (1940), edited for the Fabian Society by Richard Padley and Margaret Cole.

[2] Campbeltown itself suffered a couple of small raids which caused great alarm; but that was a very different matter from London or Flying Bomb Alley.

3.

I went to Carradale—and sometimes to Devon—for rest and refreshment during the war. But I should not like to suggest that I went because I was acutely miserable. In fact, my own view is that there was far less acute misery between 1939 and 1945 than between 1914 and 1918—partly, of course, although there were more and longer separations (producing, subsequently, some awkward personal problems), there were fewer deaths, far fewer "died of wounds" or maimed or diseased for life, and much more national care for both the soldier and his family. "They were expendable," was a phrase which came into fashion; but "they" were not nearly so expendable as the "cannon-fodder" which was drowned in the mud of Passchendaele; and everyone knew it. There was, of course, a certain amount of nervous strain, even upon the comparatively unbombed; but I can honestly say that, until a series of depressing illnesses affecting myself and my family for over four years had lowered vitality and convinced me that I was growing old, I did not notice myself suffering by rationing, queues, crowding, and all the other nuisances of wartime scarcity. (It is idiotic—and greedy—to call them by any worse name.) As to clothes, few people seem to have noticed sufficiently the good fortune which froze female fashions at the point where, with square shoulders and skirts of middling length, they were unbecoming to as few as possible. Imagine if the first New Look had remained with us for eight long years!

Besides this, there were two other factors which mitigated the "war-weariness" which loomed so largely in the later years of the first world war—work to be done, and a feeling of pride. Of work I write on a later page; but it was significant that from 1939 onwards not only I, but many thousands who had had an upbringing and experience like my own, for the first time for many years felt proud of our country—proud of the R.A.F. fighters, proud of the Londoners under fire, proud of the factory workers, proud of the parachutists dropped into occupied territory, proud of the equalities of our rationing system, proud of the Labour Ministers like Morrison and Bevin, who were given the toughest jobs in the Churchill Cabinet and held them down—and proud, after Stalingrad, of the achievements of our comrades in Russia. This, after the illusions of the 'twenties and the gloomy tale of the 'thirties, was an immense and heartening change; we knew for certain that we had not made the war, that it had been forced upon us, and we believed that whatever the mistakes and inefficiencies—about which we properly made a considerable to-do at times—we were trying our best to kill Nazism without ourselves becoming Nazis. This was an exhilarating feeling—for some time—though I am bound to admit that the first brightness of it tended to fade after the first years, as victory grew nearer and the means to victory clearer. It was easy to be proud of the little boats taking off the men from Dunkirk, of the Desert Rats of the Eighth Army, and of the first R.A.F. raiders; it was not at all easy to be proud of the levelling of Cologne, still less of Hiroshima; and this may be the reason why, although we celebrated VE Day and VJ Day—VE in London; VJ in a small North Devon pub where everyone got very happy on quantities of cider, that kindest of all intoxicants, which affects only the legs, not the stomach or the brain—our real and deepest enthusiasm was called out by the Blackpool Conference of the Labour Party, when, with the German surrender only just announced and the war with Japan going on, as far as any delegate could guess, for a year or more, the Conference decided unequivocally to come out of its wartime shackles and fight an election all by itself on its own programme, against all the prestige of the Man Who Won the War. People forget, nowadays, the risks which the Party ran at that time—the risk that the war-prestige of the Prime Minister, holding up Professor Laski as a turnip-ghost of the Gestapo, would run away with the electors; but it was just that risk which filled the Blackpool Conference with fervour, with the passionate joy of being "together again," free of the hamstringing coalition with the Tories, which made the delegates vie with one another to give Ellen Wilkinson, newly recovered from illness, an easy time in the chair, to pass the election programme with shouts of acclamation and roar impartial welcome for all future Ministers and their future critics—and caused Philip Noel-Baker, clad in what *looked* like correct morning dress, to be seen dancing a fandango down the middle aisle of Blackpool's Winter Gardens.

The Blackpool Conference, the campaign which followed it, and that morning of the twenty-sixth of July when the B.B.C. began to read out the election results—Cabinet Ministers falling "in swathes," as the *Times* put it—was the high-water mark of our excitement, before the post-war problems had risen above the horizon. To this day, as is clear from Parliamentary debates, correspondence in the *Times*, and passages in *The Gathering Storm*, neither the Conservative Party nor its leader has yet understood what hit it in that summer, or why Mr Churchill, so indisputably the father of his country during five years of a war so much more patently dangerous than that of 1914-18, so spectacularly failed to bring off the election *coup* brought off by Lloyd George—Lloyd George who never, throughout his war, enjoyed anything like the whole-hearted support given to his successor.

The explanation is not wholly simple. One-half of it is almost anthropological : in time of great danger to a society the great majority of its members, even of the most intelligent, find themselves needing a single leader, a person upon whose broad shoulders they can lay their troubles and their fears, confident of guidance and protection. No one can deny that Mr Churchill's wartime broadcasts served this purpose well. But once the danger is past an adult community needs this support no longer ; and in Britain of 1945 the people—particularly, be it noted, the people in the armed forces—shook off this tribal feeling and remembered, very quickly, that it was not The Man who had won the war, but they themselves—those who had worked and fought and stood up to bombing and coped with scarcity. " *Your* Courage, *Your* Cheerfulness, *Your* Resolution will bring us victory," said a half-forgotten poster of 1939 ; in the hour of victory it was remembered.

The second explanation is that 1945 was not 1918. A great change had passed over Britain—part of the change which I call " revolution " ; and whatever people's gratitude and affection for their leader, they felt neither gratitude nor affection for the political allies he had chosen. Lloyd George in 1918 had two powerful slogans, " Homes for Heroes " and " Make Germany Pay." Of these, the second was not usable by any party in 1945 ; and, as to the first, the short answer was, " We bought that one once—but not again." The electorate which, during the Victory tour, threw its caps in the air and shouted greetings to the Prime Minister, had grown up ; even if he had not gratuitously thrown away half his prestige by his antics on the air, it would still have been able to distinguish quite clearly between The Man and his party. So it sent back to the House of Commons a very different collection of faces, very shocking to the Forsyte type of mind and to a number of middle-class writers for the press and foreign correspondents. " Why," said John Parker's wife, visiting the new House, " it looks almost like a Fabian Summer School ! " So it did, and that was no accident. The Fabian Society had worked its way into the political forefront.

4.

Much the largest part of my wartime energy was given to the revived and revised Fabian Society. In the last chapter I referred to the steady growth of the New Fabian Research Bureau, which in the late 'thirties was coming to be recognised as the best place for young intellectuals to serve an apprenticeship for work in the Labour movement. Its scope grew ; it acquired an assistant secretary, Billy Hughes ;[1] Christopher Mayhew, now Under-Secretary to the Foreign Office, and Charles Smith, M.P. for Colchester, were two of the young men employed by it on temporary research jobs. Many others came in as volunteers, and its various offices—it moved from time to time as it got bigger—came to be centres of enthusiastic Labour gossip, something not unlike the L.R.D. of the first world war. By 1938 we had only eight hundred or so members, but it was a membership which pulled its full weight, and people were beginning to come to us for advice and information.

As N.F.R.B. grew, however, the confusion between its name and that of the old-established but somnolent Fabian Society began to cause inconvenience. F. W. Galton, General Secretary of the latter, was about to retire on pension ; and Emil Davies of the L.C.C., its treasurer, had by immense efforts succeeded in wiping off a debt that had hung about it for years. So an amalgamation was arranged, under which Douglas and John Parker and I became officers, with Davies as treasurer, an Executive drawn from the Executives of both bodies ; and Beatrice Webb, in order to bless the amalgamation accepted the post of President. (Almost, if not quite, the last of Beatrice's public utterances was her Presidential address to the Fabian Conference of 1941.) The new body was to keep the older name and to continue the affiliation to the Labour Party, which dated from its foundation as the Labour Representation Committee in 1900. But in order to make sure that the Fabian Society should not repeat the experiences of the I.L.P. and the Socialist League and get pushed by a few persistent politicians into endeavouring to force a policy upon—or in opposition to—the Party leaders, we introduced into the new rules a proviso, known as "the self-denying ordinance," which forbade the Society as such to pass or move any resolution on political subjects, and proclaimed that any pamphlet or article must be put out under the signature of its author or authors and must not commit the Society as a whole. The "self-denying ordinance" has been the object of much irritated criticism from those who believe that a resolution passed by a handful of persons whom everyone knows to be a handful has some miraculous power to change the course of history ; but I remain quite convinced that the only way for a small society, consisting mainly of intellectuals, to influence a much larger grouping which contains all

[1] H. D. Hughes, M.P. for West Wolverhampton and P.P.S. to Ellen Wilkinson when she was Minister of Education.

sorts and conditions of men, is for the individual members of that society to gain trust and confidence by the merits of their individual work and not to brandish toy pistols in the shape of resolutions on any and every subject under the sun. One additional advantage is that the Fabian Society, unlike some other bodies, is now a poor hunting-ground for organised Communists ; for if you cannot make it pass political resolutions, what advantage is there in going to the trouble of capturing it ?

The amalgamation was completed by July 1939, just as the war clouds were gathering—war was declared before our first " new " Fabian Summer School was over. During the phoney war, however, my work as its Honorary Secretary was not very heavy ; the increase came during the summer, after the Labour Party had joined the Government and France had fallen. It happened rather indirectly. Douglas had been called to assist Sir William Beveridge at the Ministry of Labour in a rapid enquiry into manpower and war material production which meant collecting information, in a very short space of time, from correspondents distributed all over the country. Billy Hughes and I undertook the enquiry for London, using the Fabian Society's offices and drawing on members of the Society for assistance ; Billy went about interviewing the working-class organisations, and I divided my immense area into a score or so of districts, with a reporter to report on each. It was the only time in my life when I have been even an (unpaid) temporary sub-sub-civil-servant, and certainly I am never likely again to be able to distribute, at my own sole discretion and on the authority of Ernest Bevin, passes admitting their holders to officially secret centres of production ! For about a month we worked extremely hard and in great excitement, pushing into the Ministry urgent reports and memoranda as fast as we could get them typed. I never saw the full report for Great Britain as a whole ; our own, which was finally finished on Bank Holiday Saturday, was pretty comprehensive and I think accurate, but bore some of the distinguishing marks of amateurishness. We seized on everything that had gone wrong—all the waste, all the muddle, and all the stark foolishness, of which there was a great deal to be found ; and anyone reading our report, without any other corrective, must have come to the conclusion that the country was too incompetent to produce any war material at all—this only two months after Dunkirk! I suspect that to be the normal reaction of the intellectual professional, accustomed to a solid working day of fairly even pressure, who is staggered by the uneven rhythm, the delays and confusions, of all but the most streamlined industrial establishments, and hastily concludes that nothing can come out of such chaos ; subsequent accounts, by emissaries to Washington, of the far more chaotic impression presented by the American war machine, have only confirmed me in that impression.

However that may be, our London report could not in any event have been of any lasting service, for within a month the whole situation in London had altered with the opening of the air war. For Douglas, the Manpower Enquiry had far-reaching results, for it led to his becoming Chairman of the Nuffield College Social Reconstruction Survey, which for the next three years did so much work in bringing together representatives of the Universities, the local governing authorities and the administrators, to discuss and report upon all manner of post-war problems ; it ramified out in all directions, bringing us into touch, incidentally, with Leonard Elmhirst's Dartington Trust, and with Richmond's friend, Christopher Martin, the charming and acidly intelligent head of the Dartington Arts Department. Chris Martin was the perfect example of the kind of person whom one so rarely finds, and would so like to find, in middle life ; I recognised him at first sight as someone I would gladly stay with, talk with, and plan with for years after the war was over. He was full of ideas, and always ready to hear of others ; he was kind without being in the least woolly, and his constant ill-health never abated seriously his eagerness and enthusiasm. His death in 1944 was a real loss to his country as well as a personal blow.

The full story of Nuffield, with its many Oxford conferences, some of which I attended as a visitor, sleeping in Douglas's rooms at University College—a wartime innovation and almost a wartime scandal ! [1]—ought to be told one day. On the Fabian Society, the main effect of the Manpower Survey was to cause those who had worked on it to clamour for more assignments of the same kind, and to suggest to its officers that they might organise local enquiries by their membership. The first of these produced the book *Evacuation Survey*, the only work on its subject which drew its information from the country as a whole. (The Government's Shakespeare Committee on evacuation never published its evidence.) But the suggestion took time to develop fully.

We had been busy reorganising the Society, which took a little doing. When we took it over, it was really magnificently elderly ;

[1] " I wonder," one undergraduate was overheard to observe to another, " whether they'd let us have *our* women in College." When, however, Douglas became a Professor and moved house to All Souls, these irregularities came to an end.

it seemed peculiarly appropriate that of its occasional Tracts, the last, published just before the amalgamation, was entitled *Our Ageing Population*. There were the Fabian lectures, which annually drew a large crowd to listen to Bernard Shaw ; there were Annual Reports, parts of which appeared year by year in identical phrasing, as though they had been kept in standing type ; there was *Fabian News*, a small parish magazine with title-piece drawn by Walter Crane. There was also the Fabian Summer School, which dated back to 1907 ; but when in 1938 I went with Billy Hughes to visit it I rubbed my eyes, because it seemed to be peopled with exactly the same faces as I had seen there on my last previous visit—in 1921. After that experience we were not surprised to find that a good deal of the nominal membership of the Society had to be written off for non-payment of subscription—one had last paid 2s. 6d. *nine years before* ! We did not, however, strike off any member who was over eighty in 1939 ; this preserved quite a few ; the others who were not struck off appeared, after some blinking, quite to like the idea of being bustled into a great deal of new activity.

Not all the old Fabians, of course, were moribund or inactive ; this could not be said of Davies, for example, or of Arthur Skeffington, now Chairman of the Local Societies Committee of the Society. But N.F.R.B. had already enrolled the majority of the active ones among them, such as Harold Laski, W. A. Robson of the London School of Economics, Chairman for years of the Political Section, Mrs Webb's niece Barbara Drake, an old "comrade" from L.R.D. days, writer on women's Trade Union problems, educationist and perpetual thorn in the side of reactionaries and slow-coaches on the L.C.C. Education Committee—and Susan Lawrence.

Someone should write the life of that tough and in her later years at least genial old fighter Susan, and trace her development as the lady-with-an-independent-income sprung from a distinguished family, as the intransigeant Modern member of the L.C.C.—how she did detest Sidney Webb's methods on the Council !—as whipping-boy for Mary Macarthur in the National Federation of Women Workers, where Mary bullied her on principle, to larn her to be an aristocrat, and she meekly submitted ; then as fierce Under-Secretary in MacDonald's Government, member of many of the left-wing groupings of the 'thirties, and finally as the happiest and most appreciated visitor at Fabian Summer Schools. When I directed the School, I would always turn on Susan, if she were there, to give a talk on the past personalities of the Labour movement, when her racy anecdotes of the Great Ones of her own day were always immensely popular ; and with equal confidence ask her to be kind to any shy young thing—or shy old thing—present there for the first time. But I remember Susan best by a couple of " snapshot " recollections.

First, one of the most pleasing epigrams I have ever heard. " My dear," she said to me one day, " there are three stages in the life of any woman with a public life. In the first, she is ' that charming and intelligent girl ' ; in the second, she becomes ' that rather frightful woman ' ; and in the third she is ' that very interesting old lady.' *I* am in the third stage now ; "*you*—with a hoarse happy chuckle—" are just in the second."

The second snapshot dates from mid-1945. I was lunching with her at Westminster ; she was full of beans, and rubbing her hands she said, " My dear, isn't it delightful ?—the war's *over*. I have been good for *years*, but I've got a flat in London now "—she had been evacuated to the country—" I'm going to have a party every week, and I'm going to grumble and grumble and *grumble* ! Won't it be *fun* ? " Alas, she only enjoyed her well-deserved fun for a few months, before she had the stroke which finally killed her.

The Fabian Society *redivivus* got a good deal of help from the electoral truce. For most of the local and divisional Labour Parties had had as their main *raison d'être* the organising of election fights, and when there were no elections to fight, their committees packed up or went to sleep for the duration—some hastily turning themselves over *en bloc* to organise civil defence—and there was no place left for Socialists to work and discuss among themselves without getting into political rivalry with the Labour Party, as did the Communists, the I.L.P., or Common Wealth at a later date, until the Fabian Society came along. Stimulated by these conditions and by an eloquent appeal made by Victor Gollancz to the 1941 Summer School, after the U.S.S.R. had been brought into the war, we went ahead with the founding and re-founding of local Fabian Societies in close connection with the local Labour movements, enrolling as members, as well as the local workers themselves, people such as solicitors, civil servants, and local government officers, who for professional reasons might not be able to advertise themselves as members of the Labour Party, but might suffer no harm from joining a body with so fortunately non-committal a name as Fabian Society. The local Fabian Societies seem still to be fulfilling a real need ; at the time of writing there are over 130 of them, and the number could easily be increased if the standard were lowered.

The story of the growth of Fabian activities, the Colonial Bureau, the International Bureau, the dozens of research groups—and the perennial struggle for money to carry on—belongs to the history of the Fabian Society rather than to my own. Here suffice it to say that for six or seven years it claimed a great deal of my time and energy and that this effort was its own reward, in the work itself, in the increasing prestige of the Society and in the grand sight of over 200 Fabians elected as Labour M.P.s. For younger Socialists, I believe, it has been to some degree what " the Movement " of my youth was to me—fun-and-games in politics. It cannot be quite the same—I do not believe it is only the passage of time which makes me feel this, for with Labour close to power and even more with Labour in power the days of joyful irresponsibility can never come again. Even the youngest politicians to-day—even my own son, chairman before he was twenty of the National Association of Labour Student Organisations—have to comport themselves to some extent as grave and reverend seigniors. But it is a good movement none the less.

5.

Wartime found me a job and half lost me a daughter. Jane, having taken her degree at Girton as the first " great-grand-daughter " of the College, since her mother and her grandmother had both been students, trained as a house-property manager, and got a post in the housing department of Chelsea Borough Council ; she lived with a succession of friends in a little old house off the Kings Road, and spent some of her leisure time in the society at Student Movement House in Bloomsbury. During the same period, I was taking a W.E.A. class at Morley College, to which there turned up one evening a young American soldier, asking if he might sit in to my discourse. He came twice ; I talked to him afterwards over a coffee and discovered that in civil life he was an economist and statistician from the University of Chicago, and knew acquaintances of ours there. A little later he also went to Student Movement House and there met a girl who attracted him enormously. Dancing with her, and exchanging personal information, he mentioned his previous occupation, and she suggested that he might have heard of her father, G. D. H. Cole ; to which he replied in astonishment, " Was that your *mother*, then, lecturing at Morley ? "

So I met my son-in-law, though only casually, before ever his wife did ; when I next saw him they were engaged ; and, to cut a domestic story very short indeed, they were married on a brief leave from Germany with a honeymoon of twenty-four hours' duration, and in the spring of 1946 Jane sailed for New York as a G.I. bride on a converted troop-ship, to settle on Long Island in an apartment house inhabited by employees of the United Nations, and to produce for me my first grandchild three thousand miles away.

I must emphasise the miles, because whether or not we are One World now, three thousand of them is a great and sundering distance. Jane's husband may be as nice a fellow, as good a husband, as friendly to his relations-in-law as you please ; Stephen Benjamin Abraham at eighteen months old may be the most intelligent, lively, and purposeful little boy in the world ; Jane may think of her family with as much affection as ever she had, write to them regularly, and even visit them when cost-of-living in the United States allows her and Will to save up money enough for the journey—they are still three thousand miles away, and the casual and frequent intercourse with the younger generation which is the natural and prescriptive right of a mother and grandmother is hopelessly frustrated. One cannot ring up to ask, " How is your cold ? What news of Stephen's double tooth ? Would you like me to take him to the Zoo to-morrow ? Can you spare an afternoon next week to help me choose a hat ? What about lunch on Sunday ? " One cannot write a postcard and get an answer by return. And though I have been lucky enough to see my grandson in the flesh twice in his short life he was a different baby the second time, requiring a fresh cautious approach by his grandmother ; when next I see him he will be a different person again, and *I* shall meet him as a stranger. Any reasonable person will agree that this is not fair ; ageing grandmothers ought to be able to enjoy their grandchildren freely and frequently, knowing that on others falls the main burden of feeding and clothing and bringing them up ; they should be able to offer unsolicited advice, interfere with discipline—and take charge of the small creature while the parents have a rest. But none of this is possible—no family-continuity is really possible—with the Atlantic in between. Perhaps, if I had had six children, like my mother, or the eight that fifty years ago I decided to have, I might feel less sharply the departure of one of them—but perhaps not.

I ought not, however, to complain too much over my loss and America's gain, since but for it I should not have made my last journey overseas or dispelled the feeling of claustrophobia, which came to so many of us as the long passportless years went on, by visiting the United States. On a hot October afternoon I landed at La Guardia airport—a foolish way to arrive in New York for the first time, unless you have no choice, for you miss entirely the view of the Manhattan skyline from the steamer's deck and have only the sensation, as the plane descends towards the tall buildings, of falling into the mouth of an immense mastodon with a great many uneven teeth. But I found an un-Americanised Jane waiting outside the Customs barrier to convey me to the park-like suburb of Great Neck on Long Island Sound, and into an apartment on the ground floor of a three-storey building set among trees—an apartment whose living-room had no door.

I would not say that the absence of the door was quite the first or the most important thing I observed in America, though I did very soon register mild surprise that only the bedroom and the bathroom had shuttable doors, with the result, among others, that there was practically no limit to the movements of the fast-crawling Stephen, and the trademark of his small fingertips could be traced on all the furniture, between outer door and farthest window, that was within his reach when reared to his full twenty-six inch height ; but I mention it because it strikes me as a typical instance of the small but characteristic things which the books of important travellers and philosophers never stoop to tell their readers. I would not, in any event, be presumptuous enough to write generalisations about "America," having only lived in suburban New York, and lectured in Manhattan, Massachussetts, and Washington. Even though I had read, as a preliminary to invasion, most of the enormous and fascinating mass of information which John Gunther collected at a breathless handgallop and published as *Inside U.S.A.*—and which, in spite of its irritatingly unlicked style, reminds me of nothing so much as a prose version of Walt Whitman's poems about his States ; even though I found that I had absorbed from it a good few historical and topographical facts which educated New Yorkers did not seem to know themselves—even so I would not venture. I feel less capable of making generalisations about the United States than about any other country I have ever known. But I was, in the first fortnight or so, impressed continually by small points of difference in daily life which the books I had read had never mentioned, possibly because they were so much concerned with the enormous impact of American civilisation on the world since the first war, and of our dependence upon it.

Some few details of everyday life have been made fairly well known, such as the ice-cream, the *cold* water and the good coffee served automatically with all meals, the immense newspapers, the commercial radio, the shops on Fifth Avenue selling nothing but nylons, the lights of Broadway—though Great White Way is a very bad name for what is now Great Red-and-Green-and-Purple Way—the crush and discomfort of the subway, and the obvious ways in which the American language differs from English. But no one had ever told me about the living-room doors—nor that New York does not consist entirely or even mainly of very tall buildings. You can walk or ride a long distance anywhere except in Manhattan and not see one, but streets and streets of " walk-ups "; I should not be at all surprised to find that, on a statistical average, citizens of New York live nearer to the ground than those of any European capital save London alone. Nor that American telephones, if they fail to make your connection, return your nickel when the receiver is replaced, without any of the nonsensical fiddling with Button A and Button B ; nor that, as a contrast, the Western Union telegraph service is very expensive and the ordinary mail, especially for parcels, amazingly inefficient, reminding one more of Paris than of London.

Nor that in New York, except at the airport, women's lavatories are free, relieving my sex from the iniquitous burden of searching for pennies, nor that the newspapers start all their important items on the front page and continue them on any later page they choose, which means that in order to follow a couple of news stories you have to cover yourself with scattered sheets of newsprint till you feel as if you were in an untidily made bed—fortunately Sunday's colossi are at least divided into chunks before they reach you. Nor that the beautiful washing machines in the basement of the apartment, which for two dimes swirl around a great armful of clothes, use a detergent which has a devastating effect on dyes, so that if you have not taken precautions you find your handkerchiefs and linen and your husband's underpants all blushing an unexpected pink; nor that shops will deliver on your doorstep without advance payment goods which you can refuse to accept if your husband feels you have been extravagant or you have seen something much nicer somewhere else. (Only a rich country, however, could afford to indulge in this form of window-shopping *de luxe*.) Or take smoking ; most English people are under the impression that American men spend their days with cigars or cigarettes permanently in their mouths ; actually, the number of places where smoking is forbidden—the subway, all food stores (obviously an excellent regulation), many other big stores, theatres and cinemas, public buildings like the Lincoln Memorial and *the entire grounds of Washington's home in Virginia*—is so great that I found myself smoking much less than in England and feeling no deprivation, as no one else was smoking either ; one result is a noticeable and pleasing absence of smokers' *débris*.

This list, which could easily be prolonged, is admittedly a list of small and unimportant facts. Yet are they so unimportant, after all? It is things like these, unexpected small differences affecting life every day, which make Americans in Britain go half-crazy about our chilly houses and warm beer, and Britons complain bitterly that they can get no nine o'clock news from the U.S. radio, only a stream of commentators each with his own angle and interested only in his own peculiar items, and which help to exacerbate any political differences between peoples who half-speak each other's language.

For the rest, I found America, as others have found it, a country of violent contrasts. It is a commonplace that in America things never happen by halves—blizzards, floods, mining disasters seem to do much more destruction than they do here. But the contrasts I saw, even in a couple of months, were so great that they simply will not fit into any reasonable picture. While I was there the Committee on Un-American Activities was making a hysterical fool of itself over Communist activities in Hollywood—but only a few months earlier Marshall's speech at Harvard had shown a calm statesmanship which could have been an example to most Europeans. While this book was journeying through the press, we were staggered by the amazing electoral victory of the Democrats—and little less startled to find that a handful of recalcitrant Senators could apparently talk negro rights out of the picture, with nothing to be done about it. In New York State I admired beautiful parkways, entirely clear of rubbish, traffic-blocks, ribbon-building or advertising hoardings—and only a mile or two off the parkways saw as hideous and squalid a collection of winking advertisement on fun-fairs, garages, and hot-dog stands as I have ever seen in my life. In New York there is the finest apparatus of child guidance and child psychiatry in the world; and in Washington, within shouting distance of the Capitol and the magnificent vista which culminates in the Lincoln Memorial, there are disgusting and disgraceful negro shanties about which, my Washington hosts told me, nothing can be done save to knock them down without any provision for re-housing their present inhabitants.

Perhaps the greatest contrast of which one is conscious, however, is in the people. Almost every American whom I have met, and talked to, either in England or in America, I have liked and got on with—and this does not by any means apply only to people like Harry Laidler and his League for Industrial Democracy, who are of my way of thinking; on the other hand, I continually hear of, and read the utterances of, persons in Hollywood, in Chicago, and in Congress who seem to be consumed with an ape-like, gibbering hatred, not merely of Great Britain, which would not be unintelligible, but of every liberal and civilised value in the world. It just does not make sense at all. So I think that, as I now have blood ties there and hope to go back again some day, rather than brooding on the idiocies of the *Chicago Tribune*, the clamour for war of some American generals, politician columnists, and the " sinister influence of American capitalism," I would remember the kindness and the friendliness of the Americans I know, the real desire of people not in high places to be generous to hungry Europeans, and the grave restrained beauty of the great Lincoln Memorial—finer than any modern British monument I have ever seen—standing tall and white under a bright blue windy sky against the waters of the Potomac and the woods of Virginia.

6.

All that remains is postscript—an uncertain postscript, since under present conditions books must be sent to printers many months before they reach the eyes of readers, and no one knows what the world scene, or even his personal bit of it, will look like a few months hence. It is far too soon, in October 1948, to attempt to evaluate the achievements and disappointments of the post-war world after the brief duration of what some have called " the phoney peace." I have watched my friends in the Labour Parliament, in face of the greatest difficulties, surely, which have ever confronted any " peace-time " government in this country, making tremendous efforts to bring into being universal social security and a better division of material goods in the nation ; I have seen us painfully trying to find out what is Britain's real world position in the mid-twentieth century, and what in political or economic organisation she can learn or discover for the future. I have seen the external situation growing rapidly from bad to worse, the freeing of India and Burma and genuine attempts to raise living standards in Africa and elsewhere being partially offset by the diehard stupidity of some colonial officials and terrible blunderings in the Near East ; and, bitterest of all, our wartime hopes of co-operation with the U.S.S.R. and the Socialists of Eastern Europe attenuating until at the moment of writing they seem to have vanished altogether. I have seen, among those who led comfortable lives under earlier dispensations—and who suffer no more than a slight reduction of comfort under the present one—the most shameless and shocking denigration of their country and the efforts of their fellow-countrymen; as good an example as any was the Englishwoman whom in 1947 I heard in an hotel near Dublin proclaiming to the rest of the visitors that she had abandoned England because the Government was deliberately starving her, and intended to eat as much as she could of the Irish food to punish De Valera for his disgraceful behaviour during the war; in contrast, I have found many from all classes working themselves night and day trying to bring into effective existence the changes promised in the legislation of three years.

Changes that affect the whole of society take a long time to implement. This obvious platitude would, one would think, meet with universal if bored acceptance; but it is astonishing how many even of the historically-minded, of those who have read again and again of the years of patient struggle by individuals which were needed before the social adjustments "implicit," as they say, in the 1832 Reform Act could be brought into being yet expect in their own day miracles to be worked for forty million people without hitch, delay, or gross error. I myself have had some small insight, during the last four years, of the labour involved in a single field, the implementation of the 1944 Education Act. As a member of the Labour majority on the Education Committee of the London County Council I have had to take a part in the making of plans for universal and worth-while secondary education for all the children of London and for "further" education—the phrase has hardly yet attained concrete meaning—for its adolescents and for the adults who need it, while at the same time trying to repair the destruction which Goering's men made, and—an even worse problem—to get rid of the accumulated educational slumdom which we have inherited from the days when everyone, including philanthropists, thought that anything was good enough for the poor. The result is that as an educational committee-woman one is always a "split personality," of which one half delineates a vision of county colleges and community halls and buildings as they might be—and as they *ought* to be, whatever the Comptroller's Department says about it[1]—while the other, gloomily contemplating a list of "priority" projects not all of which can even be begun "in the present situation with regard to labour and materials," tries to make a choice between such items as:—

[1] Our County Plan, for schools alone, was estimated to cost £200 million at 1946 prices—and nobody suggested that it was extravagant in itself. But, said Finance, what about houses?—and all the rest of it?

"Conversion of the trough closets at X Road Schools."

"Provision of proper fire prevention for the crippled school evacuated to N."

"Installation of some form of heating on the floor containing the staff bedrooms in St D——'s."

"A new building for S—— Street Day Continuation School"—which is at present sandwiched between an educationally sub-normal unit above its head and a crowded civic restaurant in the basement.

"Rebuilding of the laboratory at B—— Polytechnic"—which is so out of date that, if something is not done quickly, the University of London will refuse to recognise the work done therein.

In a useful phrase, "What would *you* do, chum?"

It would be very easy to give the whole of one's time to public education in the County of London alone. I have not been in a position to do so; I have contributed less than many of my colleagues and I claim no particular credit for my educational services. What I do claim is that trying even in the most inadequate way to get a public service into tolerable order gives one an insight into the problems, into the nature and the thoughts of those who are working in it, and into *their* problems, in a way which no reading of books or Parliamentary debates or sitting in a chair and thinking about it can possibly do. As G. K. Chesterton says in his rich study of Browning, "there are some things which a sixth-rate organist knows which a first-rate judge of music does not know." In politics, I would urge, there are some things which a humble administrator or committee member knows which the greatest philosophers do not know. It is exactly those things which traditional schools of politics at universities have tended to ignore; but they are among the things which the modern world must learn, or perish.

For I end this book as I began it, with the word "revolution." I have grown up into a revolution which since my childhood has changed immensely the whole face and thought of England, and is changing it still, at an increasingly rapid pace. When I was a child, fifty years ago, motor transport was barely in existence; the very top layer may have travelled about, but the great middle layer moved from its home only for an annual holiday, and a great many of the working class, even of the town working-class, never moved at all; now holidays with pay move millions yearly, and the prospect of holidays abroad, even with present currency restrictions, sends rocketing up the numbers studying French in evening classes. When I was a child, you could tell class from class half-a-mile away, by its clothes and general appearance ; now you must get quite close, and have a sharp eye for cut and material, before you can be at all sure of the income-group of any individual. When I was a child, there was no sort of social security whatsoever—I was at school when the first Old Age Pensions Act became law—and those who fell sick or out of work had nothing but private charity (disciplined by the Charity Organisation Society) or the cruel mercy of the Poor Law to fall back on ; for a labourer to have a large family was still regarded, except by Catholics, as a case of illiterate improvidence. To-day the social security system is complete ; the Poor Law is dead, and the enlightened persons are busy discussing how they can stimulate their poorer brethren to breed. When I was a child, private dinner-parties, even of the middling classes, had six to seven courses, and at some City dinners a *cold chair* was provided, as it were at half-time, so that the sodden and sleepy diners could get a second wind and be enabled to absorb the remaining viands ; to-day only black marketeers feast in private rooms—and not nearly so heavily. When I was a child, twelve was the school-leaving age, public secondary education was barely in its infancy, and Oxford and Cambridge were still supposed to be places for gilded youth (with a handful of scholars thrown in), who drank and ragged and gave parties,[1] and got Firsts from time to time, by frenzied and secret studying in the small hours with wet cloths around their temples. (E. F. Benson's forgotten novel, *The Babe B.A.*, gives an excellent picture of the common idea of Cambridge before 1914.) To-day secondary education is growing as fast as it possibly can ; the majority of those who reach universities get there because their brains have earned them a place and financial assistance ; and only recently a distinguished publicist moaned that it was no longer possible to live like a gentleman in Oxford. (But the "public" schools still have long waiting lists ; there is much that is not yet democratised.)

When I was a child, the Empire, the White Man's Burden, and the superiority of British arms, were almost unquestioned, in spite of the Boer War. We still shouted the lines of that doggerel song which stated flatly that :—

"When we say—we've *always* won,
And when they ask us—*how* it's done,
We proudly point to *every* one
Of England's Soldiers of the Queen !"

[1] This was never true, or even supposed to be true, of the women, of course. See Virginia Woolf's biting and charming *A Room of One's Own*.

or on more serious occasions chanted to Elgar's music :—

> " Wider still and wider
> Shall thy bounds be set.
> God that made thee mighty
> Make thee mightier yet ! "

which is surely the simplest statement of pure expansionism ever made in prose or rhyme. But the single thing which to my mind most sharply points the change is the verse which Henry Newbolt wrote for Clifton Chapel :—

> " *Qui procul hinc*," the legend's writ—
> The frontier-grave is far away—
> *Qui ante diem periit :*
> *Sed miles, sed pro patria.*"

The Latin of the epitaph, the assumptions that the ex-public-schoolboy died a soldier, and on the farflung edges of the Empire,[1] combine to depict a society and an attitude of mind that has completely passed away.

This revolution is in progress ; its end is not yet in sight, and no one can tell what the end will be. The essence of it is to be found in Henry Wallace's phrase, " the century of the common man," though it was not Wallace who made the revolution. It was made by the growth of large-scale production, complicated production, which in order to run it increasingly needed trained people who understood what they were at instead of herded slave or near-slave labour, kept poor and ignorant and fed with the consolations of religion or revivalism. This has combined with the spread of the ideas of humanitarianism, equality and democracy to make it impossible for our society ever to return to the calm disregard of the conditions and the desires of four-fifths of its members which was believed to be compatible with " democracy " as little as a century ago. We have moved, and are moving, very fast ; but even now most of us have little clear idea what we really mean by either " equality " or " democracy," as a working proposition. How much inequality, and of what kinds, could a society contain, and yet be fundamentally equalitarian ? how much authority, how much leadership should be found in a society justly calling itself democratic ? We have barely begun to look for answers to these questions in anything but a theoretic and philosophic manner ; we have certainly not

[1] A sociological essay might be written on the meaning which the word " frontier " has conveyed to (*a*) an Englishman—the mountains of Northern India, (*b*) an American—the Western spaces, and (*c*) a Frenchman—the menace of Germany. It would be worth doing.

formulated them in terms acceptable to the Common Man, who is not merely knocking at the door, but entering, in the consciousness that come war, come peace, modern industrial society needs him as an active collaborator in production, as a market for its wares, and as an informed voter, or follower of its leaders. We are just beginning to see that these answers, though not easy to find, must be found, for history will not stay still while we scratch our heads, and, if a democratic technique for running society cannot be evolved, society will either disintegrate, destroy itself in war, or—as I still think is more probable—resort to armed and dreadful tyranny or to crawling and exasperating bureaucracy to do the job for it. Either of these—or a combination of both—is a perfectly possible immediate result of this revolution ; and both will in all probability call themselves Socialist, even though they will have crushed out the values which we who have grown up as Socialists believe to be part of the Socialist faith as surely as past kingdoms which called themselves " Most Christian " rejected and crushed out the values of Christianity. Such a result—which, even if it were not a lasting result, would yet last long enough to destroy most of us now adult—can only be prevented by our own strength, by a strength of heart to hold on to the values—traditional, literary, or simply human—in which we know we believe, a strength of brain and of common-sense to do the hard thinking, both in broad outline and in detail, and a strength of will to carry out what we think to be the right course without either giving way at the first set-back or holding so obstinately and egotistically to every detail of our plans as to ensure their failure.

To live in an age when history is being made at a great pace is not in all ways pleasant, but it is exciting, and can be exhilarating whenever one can get one's mental head far enough above the distractions and inconveniences of daily life. However thick the anxieties and clouds under which we labour at present, I still hope that, before I die, I may see this revolution working itself to rest, and the cause which I have believed in all my life triumphing over the difficulties and disasters which so few of its ardent proto-martyrs foresaw.

INDEX

Index